UNDERSTANDING
AND APPLYING
ASSESSMENT
IN EDUCATION

WITHDRAWN

UNDERSTANDING AND APPLYING ASSESSMENT IN EDUCATION

DAMIAN MURCHAN AND GERRY SHIEL

Los Angeles | London | New Delhi
Singapore | Washington DC | Melbourne

Los Angeles | London | New Delhi
Singapore | Washington DC | Melbourne

SAGE Publications Ltd
1 Oliver's Yard
55 City Road
London EC1Y 1SP

SAGE Publications Inc.
2455 Teller Road
Thousand Oaks, California 91320

SAGE Publications India Pvt Ltd
B 1/I 1 Mohan Cooperative Industrial Area
Mathura Road
New Delhi 110 044

SAGE Publications Asia-Pacific Pte Ltd
3 Church Street
#10-04 Samsung Hub
Singapore 049483

Editor: James Clark
Assistant editor: Robert Patterson
Production editor: Tom Bedford
Project manager: Jeanette Graham
Copyeditor: Sharon Cawood
Proofreader: Rosemary Campbell
Indexer: Anne Solamito
Marketing manager: Lorna Patkai
Cover design: Sheila Tong
Typeset by: C&M Digitals (P) Ltd, Chennai, India
Printed and bound by
CPI Group (UK) Ltd, Croydon, CR0 4YY

Library of Congress Control Number: 2016954133

British Library Cataloguing in Publication data

A catalogue record for this book is available from the British Library

ISBN 978-1-4739-1328-8
ISBN 978-1-4739-1329-5 (pbk)

At SAGE we take sustainability seriously. Most of our products are printed in the UK using FSC papers and boards. When we print overseas we ensure sustainable papers are used as measured by the PREPS grading system. We undertake an annual audit to monitor our sustainability.

Contents

About the authors

Damian Murchan is Assistant Professor in the School of Education at Trinity College Dublin, the University of Dublin, Ireland. With former roles as Director of both undergraduate and postgraduate teaching and learning in the School of Education, he has been involved in initial and continuing teacher education programmes for primary and secondary teachers for many years. Recent research interests include: school-based assessment reform; incorporation of key skills into the curriculum; diagnostic testing in mathematics; e-learning and assessment; and teacher professional development. A former teacher and school principal, Damian has emphasised practical application in his research through a range of school-based projects. He has held a number of advisory roles in relation to development of assessment policy and practice in Ireland and internationally.

Gerry Shiel is Research Fellow at the Educational Research Centre, Dublin, Ireland where he directs a range of national and international assessment projects. His responsibilities include the development of standardised tests of reading (English and Irish), mathematics and science for primary and lower secondary students, and implementation of and reporting on the Programme for International Student Assessment (PISA) in Ireland. He teaches on a number of modules at the Institute of Education, Dublin City University. He has delivered courses on assessment for the World Bank in a number of developing countries. A former teacher, he has worked with children with special education needs and children experiencing difficulties with literacy and numeracy.

Acknowledgements

We are grateful to many people who, in a variety of ways, informed the development of our ideas for this book. Through our work on a range of national and international assessment projects we realised the extent to which teachers and policy-makers sometimes look at assessment through different lenses. Closing that gap so that teachers and policy-makers understand assessment more fully from each other's perspective became one of our aims. Discussions with colleagues and students in Trinity College and the Educational Research Centre in Dublin provided rich stimulus to undertake and sustain our writing. Our various involvements with schools in Ireland and internationally brought us into direct contact with many teachers and students whose dedication and commitment to professional development and learning provided inspiration for us to write an account of assessment that was even-handed and provided ample practical illustration. Through our work with government officials, policy-makers, local educational administrators, NGO personnel and educational publishers, we recognise and cherish the passionate interest amongst this broad constituency in making education systems work more effectively for students. We have sought to represent this inclusive optimistic perspective and commitment to learning in the book. The support and advice of the editorial team in SAGE was much appreciated throughout the conceptualisation and development of the book, with particular thanks to James Clark and Robert Patterson for their helpful conversations over an extended period. The book is richer for the addition of a number of practical illustrations. For permission to use copyrighted materials we owe thanks to a number of agencies identified in the text. We reserve final thanks to the close family members who have watched, waited and supported us patiently as the writing project moved from dream to draft to reality: Mary, Jonathan, Eleanor and Sarah Murchan; and Mairéad, Eoin and Caoimhe Shiel.

SAGE would like to thank the following reviewers whose comments have helped shape this book:

Mhairi Beaton, University of Aberdeen

Marie Clarke, University College Dublin

Sally Hawkins, University of Chichester

Stephen O'Brien, University College Cork

Marnie Seymour, University of Winchester

Companion website

Understanding and Applying Assessment in Education is enhanced by the availability of selected online tools designed to scaffold your engagement with concepts and activities introduced in the book. The website material is fully integrated with each chapter offering readers supplementary material to help them understand and apply concepts explored in the book. Within each website chapter, you will find a number of sections. These typically include:

- **Key points**. Contains a brief overview of main issues introduced in the chapter.
- **Activities and resources**. Throughout the book we have included a range of activities that encourage readers to reflect on concepts individually or in groups and try out assessment ideas in their own work or study environments. For many of these activities you will find a number of prompt sheets online that will help scaffold your engagement with the tasks. Suggestions to check the website are provided in the text whenever website support is available for any activities.

Visit the companion website at: https://study.sagepub.com/murchanshiel

Preface

Understanding and Applying Assessment in Education aims to provide pre-service teachers and practising teachers at different stages in their development with a comprehensive overview of current practices and trends in assessment and suggestions for enhancing assessment in their classrooms. The book, which may also be of interest to teachers acting as trainers and mentors in schools, seeks to provide a sound theoretical basis for understanding and reflecting on assessment practices through a detailed treatment of issues like validity, reliability and fairness, while highlighting the tensions and pressures that teachers need to deal with on a daily basis. This includes tensions in relation to:

- assessment for learning/formative assessment, and assessment of learning/summative assessment
- assessment of basic skills and assessment of higher-order thinking and 21st-century competencies
- assessment that foregrounds the needs of learners, and assessment that is required by local or national authorities for monitoring, system improvement or accountability purposes
- traditional paper-based assessments and assessments that capitalise on the affordances of digital technology.

One of our hopes is that readers will relate the ideas for enhancing assessment described in this volume to their own classroom practices. We hope also that readers will accommodate and implement approaches to assessment that will provide evidence to help them gauge whether teaching and learning are effective.

The volume is divided into twelve chapters. Chapter 1 considers the purposes of assessment and outlines eight key principles of assessment, including the ethical responsibilities of assessors. In Chapter 2, we address three key features of assessment – validity, reliability and fairness – that, like the principles of assessment, are relevant to understanding the different forms of assessment described in later chapters. Chapters 3 and 4, respectively, define and describe assessment of learning and assessment for learning. In subsequent chapters, we review assessment for learning techniques linked to these over-arching purposes, including effective questioning and peer- and self-assessment (Chapter 5), describe the development and scoring of summative written assessments for classroom use, including essays questions (Chapter 6) and oral presentations, e-portfolios and practical experiments (Chapter 7), and examine the interpretation of standardised test scores and examination grades (Chapter 8). Chapter 9 discusses the provision of feedback arising from assessment to a range of stakeholders, including parents, teachers and students themselves. Chapter 10 addresses ways in which assessment can be differentiated to meet the needs of students with varying learning needs more effectively, including learners with special educational needs. The focus in Chapter 11 shifts to assessment planning and policy at class, school and system levels, and considers the role of school-based assessment in student certification. Finally, in Chapter 12, we reflect on some current and emerging themes in assessment including the expanding role of digital technologies, while arguing that a clear emphasis on addressing the individual needs of pupils should continue to underpin approaches to assessment.

Understanding and Applying Assessment in Education incorporates a number of features designed to assist readers to gain maximum benefit from the text:

- **Chapter introductions and summaries**. Each chapter begins with a brief introduction followed by a list of questions that will help you to engage successfully with the chapter. Key concepts are summarised at the end of each chapter.
- **Case studies**. Illustrations of assessment techniques, practices and experiences are provided that assist readers develop a more concrete understanding of the reality of assessment both in classrooms and at the broader system level.
- **Structured formative practice**. *Try this out* activities offer resources and prompts to help readers to apply their learning in practice, for example in daily work or on school placement. Individual and group reflection on practice is facilitated using additional resources downloadable from the companion website.
- **Join-the-debate**. Reflective activities are included that alert readers to the contested nature of some topical issues in assessment. Contrasting perspectives on specific assessment policies or practices are presented and readers are encouraged to form their own views individually or in groups.
- **Personalities in educational assessment**. Brief biographical profiles of selected individuals associated with key developments in assessment over the years.
- **Questions for discussion**. Two or three questions that may be discussed individually or in groups.
- **Further reading**. Chapters conclude with a number of selected annotated references (print and web-based) offering further details about key concepts.

While the content of this volume was up-to-date at the time of writing, we urge readers to bear in mind that assessment is continually evolving in response to policy changes. Consequently, new ideas and approaches are introduced on an almost-daily basis. We invite readers to check official and other sources, including websites, for information on new developments, as well as changes to existing approaches.

Assessment in education
Learning contexts and professional standards

What you will learn in this chapter

This chapter sets the context for the work of teachers in class and links that work with student learning and with professional, legislative and societal expectations on schools and teachers. Schools are amongst the most complex organisations in society, tasked with ever-expanding expectations and obligations by parents, administrators and policy-makers. One key competency expected of teachers relates to student assessment. Teachers who do not grasp clearly the many purposes to which assessment is put and the array of approaches used in modern education systems are less prepared to contribute effectively to the collaborative education ventures that are designed to serve both individual students and broader society.

In this chapter, you will learn about the purposes of assessment, purposes for teachers and students and other purposes that are legitimately expected by stakeholders who are outside school but who are central to the education process. The chapter, and indeed the book overall, emphasise the diversity of assessment purposes. There are many stakeholders at different levels of remove from your work in class. Students, parents, colleagues and school management are in close proximity to your work. Teachers in schools where your students might transfer have an interest also, as do policy-makers who develop curriculum, assessments and codes of practice for teachers. Governments, representing taxpayers and responsible for anticipating future national needs, require information and assurance about the effectiveness of the system. Your work needs to be set and understood not only in the context of your class but also within broader systems and professional contexts. We conceptualise this plurality of information, needs and actions within two key themes that are reinforced throughout the book: (i) using information from assessments to evaluate and plan learning at student, class, school and system levels; and (ii) engaging with assessment as a collaborative process. We identify eight key principles that should inform educators' thinking and practice in relation to assessment.

When you finish the chapter, you should be able to answer these questions:

* For what purposes are assessments used?
* Which individuals and agencies have an interest in information about student learning?
* What are teachers expected to know and be able to do in relation to student assessment?
* How should assessment inform your educational practice?

Role of assessment in teaching and learning

A comprehensive review of current assessment policies and practices across 21 national education systems (Sargent et al., 2013) highlights the following overarching trends:

* centralised or statutory curriculum frameworks, sometimes including specific attainment targets to be reached at specific levels/grades of education
* emphasis on both key subject areas (language, mathematics, science) and cross-curricular skills
* promotion of continuous, teacher-led and diagnostic/formative assessment
* national standardised assessment of students during compulsory education, either of all students in a cohort or of samples of students
* formal certification at the end of lower- and upper-secondary phases, frequently by national or designated agencies.

We can add a few other trends and implications. The policy drive aimed at embedding strategies in curricula to enhance students' cross-curricular skills, such as creativity, collaboration and problem solving, is quite a bit ahead of large-scale practical means to assess such traits. At secondary level, the move towards teacher involvement in formal certification is seen as one solution. There is likely to be an even greater use of assessment information as one of many sources of data in judging educational quality and justifying policies and expenditure. Finally, as assessment systems become more complex we are likely to see further ceding of responsibility for administrative and technical aspects of assessment by education ministries to specialised agencies and the commercial or non-profit sectors. These trends suggest a corresponding complexity for teachers in understanding and working within such systems.

There is no one role for assessment in education. Rather, assessment provides information that can be used by different people for different purposes. Many people have an interest in the work of schools and all may require information that suits their purpose. Teachers strive to promote student learning. This requires careful planning and implementation, often in relation to statutory curricular guidance. The use of assessment is an intrinsic part of this teaching and learning environment. A fundamental role for assessment, therefore, lies right within the classroom, close to teaching and learning. Teachers need to monitor how well students are learning, the successes they are experiencing and the difficulties being encountered by them. Only when teachers are aware of the learning profile and trajectory of students, can they really help them succeed.

Traditional concepts of assessment emphasised periodic 'checking' of how students were doing, commonly understood as assessment *of* learning. One practical problem with this is that students may struggle for some time and have difficulty in catching up on any concepts missed. Contemporary approaches to assessment stress more frequent assessments embedded in normal classroom practice, allowing teachers and students to monitor learning in real time and take corrective action as part of normal daily classroom routines. This assessment *for* learning assumes a central place for teachers in planning for, and using, assessments as a comprehensive and continuing component of sound teaching.

It is not only teachers who need to know how students are doing. Students themselves need accurate information about their progress so that they can understand and adjust their learning. Theories of motivation, self-regulation and attribution, discussed later in Chapter 4, highlight the centrality of learners to their own learning. Students who are highly motivated and who are aware of how they learn are more likely to succeed (Wiliam, 2011). Therefore, equipping students with the skills to monitor and adjust their own learning is a worthy educational goal. Providing students with such self-awareness can place the potential and responsibility for learning on students and encourage them to make the necessary effort. This is a potentially powerful role for assessment in education and one that is best managed and mediated through the teacher in class.

Whereas teachers traditionally enjoyed considerable autonomy in relation to the content and skills taught in class, recent curriculum development internationally has led to greater emphasis on more tightly prescribed statutory curricula. In England and Wales, for example, teachers and schools were relatively free to develop their own teaching programmes until the introduction of the national curriculum arising from the Education Reform Act of 1988. That move towards centrally developed statutory curricula and guidance is mirrored by developments in other systems worldwide, for example in Switzerland, a country with a long tradition of political and educational autonomy at the individual canton level (Sargent et al., 2013). Associated with centralised curricula is a greater specification of how students' work and learning should be monitored and evaluated. This focus has evolved over time, more recently emphasising the formative use of assessment to help both teachers and students continually reshape and improve learning.

Paul Newton (2007) identified at least 18 purposes to which assessment might be put. Of these, perhaps only four or five involve the teacher directly in a day-to-day capacity. Although a small proportion of assessment functions, teacher purposes are nonetheless critically important: identifying learning needs, diagnosing learning difficulties, monitoring progress over time, and aiding the transfer and placement of students in classes and schools. The next section reviews in more depth the increasingly diverse needs for information on student learning.

Wider stakeholder needs for information on student learning

Teachers and students themselves are the most immediate and direct recipients of information about student learning. Parents also have an obvious need for information and thus schools and teachers frequently share data with parents, as discussed later in Chapters 8 and 9. Yet there are many other stakeholders who have an interest in information about the learning and progress of individual students and cohorts of students in schools. It is important that teachers recognise other stakeholders' needs and ensure that these needs are met where appropriate. Table 1.1 highlights four broad categories of assessment purpose, identifying a range of stakeholders within and across categories.

Table 1.1   Stakeholders with an interest in assessment outcomes

Support Learning	Quality Assurance	Policy Development	Selection and Other
Teachers	School management	Policy-makers	College admissions
Students	Local authorities	Public representatives	Employers
Parents	Inspectorate	Researchers	Assessment and test developers
Peers	Policy-makers		
Support services (psychological, speech and language)	Public		Publishers
	Taxpayers		Media

Source: adapted from Newton (2007)

Many of these needs are obvious, as with those directly associated with supporting learning at class and school level. Other needs exist at levels more removed from the classroom: aggregate-level data might be used, for example, by local authorities to consider resource allocation across schools; or inspectors might wish to consider trends over time in the same school. Similarly, policy-makers such as ministry officials frequently require data to justify existing budgets, argue for more funding or evaluate curricula. Admissions officers use students' results in secondary education to help select and allocate students to third-level courses. Similarly, employers draw on students' assessment outcomes as part of recruitment processes. Although teachers individually in class may sometimes not fully see their part in the overall educational endeavour, the scale of educational expenditure means that politicians, the media and the wider public have considerable interest in outcomes also. This is not surprising given estimates of annual contributions to economies by educational activity: US$2 trillion worldwide, £28 billion in the UK and €900 million in Ireland (Lynch et al., 2012). Spending on education institutions averaged 5.3% of Gross Domestic Product across OECD countries (OECD, 2015a), over 6% in the UK and 5.6% in the Republic of Ireland. This suggests a very significant investment by government, other agencies and individual students and families in education. Little wonder then that there is interest in how well the system and the schools within it are performing. Some of this interest, especially from the perspective of policy-makers, has given rise to the establishment of accountability mechanisms in many countries; some in the form of league tables of schools, despite criticisms of such approaches.

Assessment purposes for different contexts

Notwithstanding the diversity of stakeholders interested in information about student progress, the most common uses to which assessment is put can be narrowed down to just two: promoting learning and finding out what students have learned. As a teacher, you will routinely monitor how students are doing in class and adjust your goals, instructional approach, resources or expectations accordingly. Traditionally, three purposes for assessment are identified in classroom and school settings: formative, diagnostic and summative. Assessments that serve formative purposes are implemented while teaching is under way, during lessons or during particular units of work. The key consideration is that the assessment takes place during instruction or an instructional phase and that the information yielded is used to help students learn. (Further detail is provided in Chapters 4 and 5.) Sometimes, teachers encounter student responses to formative assessments that do not immediately suggest how best to proceed. In such cases, the use of diagnostic assessment may be appropriate. Diagnostic assessment can help identify specific difficulties that students encounter, often in relation to language and mathematics. Diagnostic tests are generally developed by commercial or research agencies and frequently administered by specialist support teachers.

Assessments can also have a summative purpose in summing up students' achievement at a particular point in time, for example at the end of a unit of work or of a term, or at the conclusion of a point in schooling such as the end of compulsory education. Summative assessments can be designed by teachers or by external agencies and usually focus on summarising students' achievement across a wide range of learning. Examples of externally developed summative assessments in Britain and Ireland include assessments for GCSE, A Levels, Scottish National Qualifications and the Irish Leaving Certificate. In your teaching, you will need to become confident and proficient in developing, selecting and using assessments for summative purposes.

As highlighted in the previous section, educational planners and policy-makers require information about the progress of students in school. Patterns of grades from public examinations and qualifications such as GCSE (England, Wales, Northern Ireland) and Junior Certificate (Republic of Ireland) offer some limited information, focused on very particular points in schooling. Student achievement data are sometimes gathered at system level throughout the school years on a census basis, whereby all students are assessed. Examples are the SATs in reading, grammar and mathematics at KS2 in England and the Foundation Skills Assessment of students in Grades 4 and 7 in British Columbia. These approaches are not without their critics, many of whom highlight a tendency amongst some teachers to 'teach to the test', focusing significant amounts of class time on the type of content and skills that are contained in the tests. Alternative approaches to system monitoring involve sampling surveys such as the National Assessments of English Reading and Mathematics in Ireland (2nd and 6th Class) and the National Monitoring Study of Student Achievement in New Zealand (Years 4 and 8). It is likely that at some stage in your career, you will be asked to cooperate with such a national sampling survey.

Finally, an extension of national system monitoring is international surveys or studies of student achievement, typically administered in first language, mathematics and science. The Programme of International Student Assessment (PISA) aimed at 15-year-old students and now involving over 70 education systems is discussed in detail, along with other international studies, in Chapter 3. Most international surveys go beyond the mere testing of students and also gather survey/observational data from policy-makers, curriculum developers, school principals, teachers, students and parents to form a more holistic picture of the educational inputs and processes that might shape outputs such as student achievement. Results are used to inform policy development in individual countries. PISA results in 2009, for example, prompted significant proposed policy change in the assessment of students at the end of the Junior Cycle in Ireland. In Wales, students performed below the OECD and UK average in all three areas tested in 2012, prompting the education secretary to declare that 'PISA results were not good enough. The 2012 results confirm my view and that of my predecessor that standards in Wales are not high enough and must improve' (Lewis, 2012: n.p.), comments more or less echoed in relation to results in Northern Ireland (Northern Ireland Executive, 2013). As with national surveys, it is likely that both you and the students in your classes will be asked to participate in such surveys by completing tests, questionnaires or other inputs.

Join the debate: What is the main purpose of assessment in education?

Use your library's online journal service to access the article by Paul Newton (2007) listed in the further reading at the end of this chapter. Review Table 1 in Newton's article. With a colleague, identify those categories of educational assessment purposes that relate most centrally to the role you expect to play as a teacher. From the remaining uses, identify two or three that also seem to be very important in the context of education generally outside of your own teaching.

Legislation and professional codes of practice

The latter part of the 20th century saw increased state regulation and control over all aspects of education. In many education systems, national or regional legislation regulates curriculum development and implementation, teacher education, access to education and the activities of the teaching profession itself. In the Republic of Ireland between 1998 and 2005, eight legislative instruments were enacted that had significant relevance to educational assessment. Some of these have, in effect, codified in law what was implicit in custom and practice anyway. For example, section 22[b] of the 1998 Education Act requires teachers to 'evaluate students and periodically report the results to students and parents', classroom assessment that was already common practice, though not without its shortcomings (O'Leary, 2006). The Education Reform Act of 1988 in England and Wales brought perhaps more observable change to the system in the UK and has been followed by a raft of additional legislation. For example, the School Information (England) (Amendment) Regulations 2012 (DfE, 2012) prescribes specific assessment information to be provided on the websites of maintained schools in England. Further regulation by education ministries or allied agencies draws on legislative provision. Examples in Ireland include the guidelines for *Assessment in the primary school curriculum* (NCCA, 2007a) and the requirement that all primary schools must report students' progress to parents at least twice a year (DES, 2011a).

As seen above, legal obligations provide one context for teachers' engagement with assessment. Another influential factor is standards established by statutory and other professional organisations that regulate teachers and their work. An analysis of teacher professional standards in five education systems reveals a common core of standards evident to a greater or lesser degree across all systems, as summarised in Table 1.2. The Irish, English and Scottish standards apply to all or the majority of teachers in the education system. The Australian and US standards, though not binding on all states or teachers, represent professional codes that have considerable support and influence nationally. All codes include criteria relevant to teachers' knowledge and expertise in relation to assessment.

Table 1.2   Common elements of expected professional standards for teachers: general

Personal integrity	Planning for teaching
Professional integrity	Management of learning
Care and respect for students	Knowledge and use of assessment
Ethical practice	Inclusion and differentiation
Awareness of system needs	Working collegially with others
Content knowledge	Engaging with CPD
Pedagogical knowledge and skills	Being a reflective practitioner

Sources: Ireland, Teaching Council (2016); England, DfE (2011a); Scotland, GTC for Scotland (2012); Australia, AITSL (2014); USA, National Board for Professional Teaching Standards (1989)

In some of the general professional standards, the specific nature of assessment-related knowledge and skills to be demonstrated by teachers is clearly identified. For example, seven general standards are highlighted in Australia. Standard 5, *Assess, provide feedback and report on student learning*, consists of five separate focus areas: assess student learning; provide feedback; make consistent and comparable judgements; interpret student data; and report on student achievement. In Scotland, two detailed sections within the General Teaching Council standards for registration focus on assessment.

A number of agencies within and across countries have published standards for educational assessment. These standards are generally understood and accepted by professional organisations and professionals as important and relevant. The *Standards for teacher competence in educational assessment of students* (AFT et al., 1990) focus especially on teachers' needs and responsibilities in relation to assessment (see Table 1.3). A revision suggested by Brookhart (2011) added further emphasis on incorporating formative assessment into teachers' practice and working effectively within the accountability and standards-based reform culture prevalent in the USA. Amongst the eight *Teachers' Standards* (Teaching) in England, Standard 6 identifies four specific assessment competencies expected of teachers (see Table 1.3), while, in Ireland, specific guidelines for schools in relation to assessment in primary education assume a number of key teacher competencies.

Although the standards in Table 1.3 are directed mainly at teachers, other more generic standards have been developed which are designed to guide overall practice by education ministries, test publishers and users of assessment. The *European*

Table 1.3 Expected professional standards for teachers: assessment

USA: Teacher competency[1]	England: Teachers' standards[2]	Ireland: School guidelines[3]
Teachers should:	**Teachers should:**	**Teachers should:**
• Choose assessment methods • Develop assessment methods • Administer, score and interpret the results of externally and internally produced assessments • Use assessment results to make decisions about students, teaching, curriculum and school improvement • Develop sound grading procedures • Communicate assessment results to students and others • Recognise unethical and inappropriate uses of assessment	• Know how to assess in curriculum areas, including statutory assessment requirements • Make use of formative and summative assessment • Use data to monitor progress, set targets and plan lessons • Give pupils regular feedback and encourage them to respond to the feedback	• Gather, record, interpret, use and report assessment information in relation to both formative and summative purposes • Engage with assessment review and development at school level

Sources: 1. AFT et al. (1990); 2. DfE (2011a); 3. NCCA (2007a)

framework of standards for educational assessment 1.0 (AEA–Europe, 2012) is designed to ensure that practices in educational assessment are transparent across European education systems and that practices can be judged against agreed quality criteria. Core elements of assessment included in the framework include:

1. Assessment goals, use of results and target population
2. Bases of evidence to indicate student attainment of assessment goals
3. Processes and practicalities of conducting assessments
4. Processes and accuracy of scoring/rating
5. Taking decisions on the basis of scores
6. Reporting results to relevant stakeholders
7. Reviewing assessment quality and its fit with intended purpose

In the USA, the *Standards for educational and psychological testing* (AERA et al., 2014) is the latest edition in a series of standards published jointly by the three influential professional organisations since 1966. Like the European Framework, the US Standards aim to establish expected norms of good practice in assessment and provide criteria for evaluating the quality of practice. The standards are aimed primarily at test developers and users of assessment.

Assessment themes and principles

As suggested in the sections above, understanding and embracing the diverse role of the teacher requires sophisticated knowledge, skills, competencies and personal professional attributes. Assessment systems, and teachers' capacity to engage with them, need to be framed around some coherent themes. As one important dimension of professional practice, teachers need to use information from assessments to evaluate and plan learning experiences for students. Whether the assessment is at the micro level of in-class informal monitoring of student progress or at the macro level of national tests, the dual intent is fundamentally the same: evaluate and plan. When we consider the overall professional standards expected of teachers, the need for teachers to work collaboratively becomes apparent. Teachers can usefully collaborate with other teachers and other stakeholders in planning, teaching, assessing and reviewing their own and school and system performance.

Given the array of assessment instruments, approaches and advice available to teachers, it is easy to get caught up in issues of administration, recording and reporting without quite understanding the place of assessment in teaching and learning. Having a clear set of assessment principles to guide planning and practice helps bring coherence to teachers'- and systems-level practice. Over a number of years, the authors have been involved in supporting system-wide change in assessment in a number of countries. This involved providing support to policy-makers, school leaders, teachers and teacher educators, in addition to our sustained involvement in teacher education in Ireland, especially focused on assessment. The assessment principles highlighted below draw from that broad experience at the system and classroom levels to articulate principles that should inform the conceptualisation, development and enactment of assessment in practice.

Our assessment vision emphasises eight principles:

1. Society's conceptualisation of learning broadens as each generation develops deeper insight into the world around and within us. Assessment must strive to reflect, support and promote the plurality and inter-relatedness of learning. Central foci for assessment yesterday may not be as relevant for today's students who will work, learn and live tomorrow.
2. There are different purposes for assessment. Some purposes serve the direct information and decision-making needs of students and teachers. Additional purposes help other stakeholders to understand the learning of individual students and groups of students and the functioning of education at system levels.
3. Assessment cannot be detached from its primary function to support the growth and development of citizens and society. Whether for in-class formative purposes or for system-monitoring-improvement, assessment policies, procedures and practices must be framed ethically and implemented fairly.
4. The human mind, outlook, behaviour and condition represent a complex mosaic. Increasingly, education systems build and enact curricula designed to help learners develop and flourish across a range of attributes and dimensions. It is unrealistic to expect that one or even a small number of assessment approaches can adequately capture and reflect such complexity. Assessment approaches constantly evolve and will continue to change. Such diversity and change should be reflected in the multiple and different ways we assess learners.
5. One of the most obvious recent evolutions in teaching and learning concerns the use of digital technologies. The digital transformation evident in society and many classrooms should be reflected in a greater use of digital technology in assessment.
6. Most education systems cherish broad learning but also prioritise specific areas. Areas of special emphasis include literacy, numeracy and science. For policy-makers, school leaders, teachers and the public, there is a need to find appropriate balance in what and how we assess.

7. Assessment involves the use of continually evolving approaches and tools. This requires informed, competent use so that assessment can provide information that is accurate, interpreted carefully and communicated appropriately.
8. Teaching, learning and education more broadly should be guided by evidence: evidence of what is happening, what is working, what is not working and how processes and experiences can be improved. Assessment offers information that can be interpreted and used in evidence-led practice and policy.

These eight principles underpin the successful use of assessment within education systems, schools and classrooms. There is a particular onus on the teacher to reach an appropriate standard of knowledge and competency so that assessment can be used judiciously. What the principles emphasise also, however, is that technical competency is not sufficient. Professionalism involves careful judgement and the fair, ethical use of approaches that serve the intended purpose, while retaining a focus on the needs and rights of the parties involved, most notably learners.

Situating these principles within broader educational structures and processes is summarised in Figure 1.1. The model highlights the associations between selected curriculum and assessment inputs and regulations, teacher standards and competencies, assessment principles and stakeholder needs.

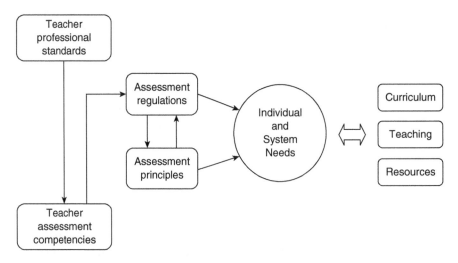

Figure 1.1   Systemic overview of teacher professional and assessment standards in context

Curriculum and assessment frameworks and regulations represent the essential requirement for teachers who use their professional judgement to structure appropriate opportunities for learners. In doing so, teachers draw on and demonstrate professional standards and competencies, responding to assessment regulations and expectations mediated by their understanding of assessment principles. Depending on the system or school within which you work, the curriculum and/or assessment policies and practice will be prescribed to varying degrees, sometimes very tightly, sometimes with greater latitude left to the teacher. Regardless of this, it is up to teachers to use professional judgement in 'bringing' the curriculum to students and in how to monitor student learning. Assessment principles help ensure that system and teacher practices work coherently to serve agreed, fair purposes, with the teacher as mediator, exercising professional judgement.

Chapter summary

What will schools be like in 50 years' time? What will the experiences of teachers and students be like? Given the pace of change in the last two decades, it is difficult to offer reliable predictions. What we can probably say is that information will remain central, particularly information to facilitate learning and inform others about what is happening in schools. This chapter emphasised the central place of information and of stakeholders' needs in relation to education and assessment in particular. Later in the book, we will explore different interpretations of assessment: *for* learning, *of* learning and even *as* learning. Teachers need to acquire the appropriate competency in assessment in light of legislative and regulatory requirements and as part of their wider professional role and identity. Various people and agencies have a legitimate right to information yielded by assessments. If used appropriately and subject to sound principles of use, students, teachers, parents and wider society are all the better for the availability of this information. Teachers, with parents, are positioned closest to students throughout their education. But the important work under way in classrooms resonates in the local and wider environment. Little surprise, then, that many people have an interest in schools' work and seek information about the outcomes of that work. This book is predicated on the concept of multiple, complementary functions for assessment. The challenge for teachers is to acknowledge this and to shape and work with educational processes and structures for individual and societal good.

Questions for discussion

1   Identify any aspects of your assessment practice that are formally required of you as part of school or other regulations. Discuss with a colleague who it is that requires such action/information and why.

2   Access the most relevant set of professional standards governing your role/future role as a teacher. Which specific standards or elements of them relate to assessment? How do you rate yourself in relation to any assessment-related standards? Which aspects do you need to work on?

3   The psychologist Robert Ebel (1980) posed the question 'what are the consequences of not testing?' Identify a range of possible positive and negative impacts of not assessing students in the educational setting with which you are most directly involved.

Further reading

McCormack, O., Lynch, R., & Hennessy, J. (2015). Plastic people in pinstripe suits: an exploration of the views of Irish parents on the publication of school league tables. *Educational Studies*, *41* (5), 513–33.

One use of assessment results in a number of countries is the compilation of school performance or league tables, based on aggregated student test data. In Ireland, such practice is prohibited by legislation, though proxy estimates are used by some media organisations. McCormack and colleagues provide interesting and perhaps surprising insights into the views of Irish parents on the possible publication of school league tables.

Newton, P.E. (2007). Clarifying the purposes of educational assessment. *Assessment in Education: Principles, Policy and Practice*, *14* (2), 149–70.

This article grapples with ambiguities in assessment terminology and meaning. Newton identifies three levels at which assessment purposes can be characterised: judgement level, decision level and impact level.

2

Validity, Reliability and Fairness

What you will learn in this chapter

Assessment outcomes or results, whether at the level of an individual student, a school, a regional education authority, or a country, can have implications for everyone concerned. A score on a standardised test of reading can determine if a student receives the additional support they may need or the accommodations they seek; the grades a student achieves on externally scored examinations, such as the A levels in England, Wales and Northern Ireland, the Nationals in Scotland or the Leaving Certificate in the Republic of Ireland, can determine whether or not they gain access to the post-secondary course of their choice. Aggregated exam results in the form of league tables may determine if parents enrol their child in a particular school. Performance of a country's students on a national or an international assessment may lead to important changes in curriculum and assessment. Since assessment outcomes can have significant consequences for everyone concerned, it is important that assessments are of the highest quality.

This chapter identifies key aspects of assessment quality including validity, reliability and fairness. This is important because an understanding of these aspects can inform the inferences you make about the meanings you attribute to the scores achieved by your students on tests and other assessments, and the decisions you make based on them. After explaining these terms and considering a range of factors that can impact on them, there are suggestions for further reading that will allow you to explore interpretations of validity, reliability (a necessary but not sufficient precondition for validity) and fairness in relation to assessments that are used for different purposes.

When you finish the chapter, you should be able to answer these questions:

* What are the key technical quality elements in relation to assessments?
* What are the relationships between validity, reliability and fairness?

- How is evidence used to ensure quality in assessment?
- How can you avoid misinterpreting the results of assessments?

Validity

At the outset, it is fair to say that validity is one of the most contested concepts in educational assessment (Newton and Shaw, 2014, 2016; Geisinger, 2016). Definitions of validity, and descriptions of the test validation process, have changed in significant ways over the past century, and will continue to evolve in the future.

The *Standards for educational and psychological testing* (AERA et al., 2014), mentioned in Chapter 1, define validity as 'the degree to which evidence and theory support the interpretation of test scores for proposed uses of tests' (p. 11). This definition highlights the view that it is the proposed uses of a test (or other assessment) that are validated, rather than the test itself. It implies that evidence may need to be gathered from a range of sources to justify what a score (or grade) means and how it is interpreted in a particular situation.

The Standards make it clear that validation is a joint responsibility of the test developer (often an organisation charged with developing tests) and the test user (a teacher or counsellor who administers the test, interprets the outcomes and uses the results to make decisions). The test developer is responsible for providing a rationale and evidence to support users in interpreting test scores in particular ways. For example, the developer of a test of reading comprehension might provide evidence to support use of the test to identify students with high and low levels of reading comprehension. The test user (teacher) is responsible for evaluating the validity evidence as it relates to the particular setting in which the test is to be used. The test user must decide if use of the test in his/her school or classroom can be justified on the basis of information provided by the test developer and experience with using the test. While subject teachers in secondary school may not have a say in relation to whether their students take or do not take examinations such as A levels, they will have a keen interest in the content of such tests and how they are scored.

Experts in test development have identified a number of types of validity evidence, including evidence based on test content (sometimes referred to as content validity), the internal structure of the test (construct validity), the predictive power of the test (predictive validity) and the consequences of test use (consequential validity). Validity is often regarded as a unitary concept and so we refer to different types of evidence for the validity of test interpretations, rather than different types of validity. It is not necessary to provide all these types of validity evidence for a particular test interpretation. For example, the developers of an examination covering a two-year course of work may only be interested in the extent to which performance on the test represents how well students have mastered the course content, and may not be concerned with predicting future performance or tracking the progress of cohorts of students from year to year.

Test content validity evidence

If a test score interpretation involves making inferences about performance related to a curriculum or syllabus (for example, how well the student has mastered the content or processes in the curriculum), it is necessary to consider evidence related to test content (that is, the themes, wording and format of the tasks or questions, as well as procedures for scoring answers). Such evidence typically comprises a statement by the test developers about how test items based on a curriculum or syllabus were developed. Often, the test developer will provide a table of specifications (the 'content specifications') showing the content areas and processes that were drawn from the curriculum and included in the test. Table 2.1 provides a test specification table that shows the different content areas and processes assessed by a mathematics test.

Table 2.1 Table of specifications for mathematics test

	Mathematics content areas		
Mathematics processes	**Number and algebra**	**Geometry and measures**	**Data**
Understanding and recalling	10%	5%	5%
Implementing procedures	15%	15%	10%
Reasoning and problem solving	20%	15%	5%

In developing specifications such as this, the test developer will need to justify the emphasis or weighting placed on each mathematical content area and process so that the weighting given to each cell matches its weighting in the curriculum. Otherwise, there is a risk that test users may misinterpret the meaning of test scores. For example, if a teacher administers a test that includes number and algebra items only, and another test user assumes that all the content areas are represented, the test user may misinterpret what a high (or low) score on the test means.

Assessments developed by teachers for use in their own classrooms typically have good content validity. Teachers are familiar with what has been taught and may be in a better position than an external test developer to ensure a direct match between the content of the curriculum (as it has been taught) and the content of the assessment. However, many curricula and syllabi specify standards or learning outcomes and these will need to be translated into test questions and scoring schemes especially for tests assessing national standards.

An important element of test content is the stimulus that accompanies a test question. In a test of reading comprehension, the stimulus might be a narrative or informational text that is deemed suitable for the class level or age group being assessed. Alternatively, it might include web pages and multiple texts (two or more texts around a common theme or topic) associated with a computer-based test. In a science test, the stimulus might be a diagram of the solar system or a chemical formula. The test user will need to satisfy themselves that the stimuli that appear on a test are appropriate for and fair to the students concerned. Similarly, the test user will need to ensure that the content of the scoring key (marking scheme) that is used to score student responses is appropriate and reasonable, and consistent with the curriculum that students have been taught.

Traditionally, curricula and syllabi have described the knowledge and skills that students should learn in school. A curriculum may be described for a particular grade level, key stage or course of study. Curricula may also include learning standards or outcomes (also known as attainment targets) that students are expected to achieve. In England, for example, the curriculum document for state-supported primary schools (DfE, 2014a) includes attainment targets for different key stages (grade bands). The attainment targets for Number–Fractions (a component of mathematics) for Year 2 (the second year of Key Stage 1) are as follows:

Pupils should be taught to:

- recognise, find, name and write fractions ¼, ⅓, ¾ and ¾ of a length, shape, set of objects or quantity
- write simple fractions, for example, ½ of 6 = 3 and recognise the equivalence of ¾ and ½.

An assessment based on Key Stage 1 mathematics, whether developed by a teacher or by a test development agency, will need to ensure that there is an alignment between attainment targets like these and test questions. The test will need to include questions designed to assess whether or not students have achieved these attainment targets. By implication, the test should not include more complex items (such as asking students to find ⅝ of 80) since these cannot be linked in a systematic way to attainment targets for Year 2 and would be unfair to the students concerned.

Construct validity evidence

Construct validity evidence is concerned with whether an assessment reflects the constructs underlying a curriculum or programme of study. A test might claim to assess a construct such as mathematical problem solving, reading comprehension, scientific reasoning or creativity. Evidence should be provided to confirm that the scores or grades achieved by students do indeed reflect the intended construct(s).

One possible source of evidence for construct validity is the extent to which a test correlates with another test that has been shown to assess the intended construct (this is sometimes referred to as concurrent validity evidence). Thus, in generating construct validity evidence, a test developer might administer the new test and an established test to the same group of students, at around the same time. If there is a strong correlation (association) between scores on the two tests (that is, students who perform well on one test usually perform well on the other, and vice versa), the inference can be drawn that the new test assesses the same underlying construct as the established test. The need to administer the two tests at around the same time arises because growth or development may impact on performance if one of the tests is administered at a later time than the other.

A correlation coefficient is a measure that determines the degree to which two variables (such as scores on two tests, or scores on two sections of the same test) are associated. Figure 2.1 presents the scores for the same group of students on two tests administered at around the same time.

The data and accompanying scatter plot show that, in general, as scores increase on Test 1, they also increase on Test 2 (though the scores for Student C deviate slightly from this). The correlation between the two tests is 0.90, which can be considered very strong. The line (of best fit) running through the scatter plot is that which best describes the association between the two tests. It is steep so there is a

Student	Test 1	Test 2
A	88	98
B	88	93
C	105	103
D	119	140
E	95	90

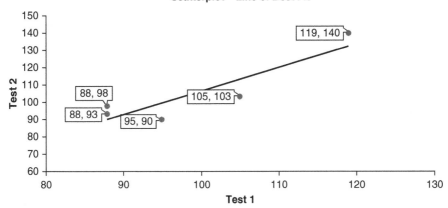

Scatterplot – Line of Best Fit

Figure 2.1 Understanding correlation coefficients

strong association. The number of subjects represented here (five students) is small. Sometimes the test scores of thousands of students may be correlated in this way.

Correlation coefficients range from −1.0 to 1.0. If a negative correlation (e.g. −0.6) occurs, it means that, as performance on one test increases, it decreases on the other. When the value of the correlation coefficient is 0, it means that scores on the two tests are not related. Isaacs et al. (2013) provide the following guidelines for interpreting positive correlation coefficients: 0.0 to 0.2: no relationship or very weak correlation; 0.2 to 0.4: weak correlation; 0.4 to 0.7: moderate correlation; 0.7 to 0.9: strong correlation; and 0.9 to 1.0: very strong correlation. Negative correlations can be interpreted using the same criteria. For example, a correlation of −0.5 can be interpreted as a moderately strong negative correlation.

A difficulty can arise if a test (for example, a test of mathematics achievement) assesses a narrow range of processes, or a restricted set of content skills, when it claims to assess the full range. If a published test claims to assess a mathematics curriculum that includes problem solving, but instead includes questions based on lower-order skills only, and this is not made clear in the test manual, test users (teachers) may misinterpret what test scores mean and may make incorrect decisions based on test scores. They might assume that students with high scores on the test are proficient in all aspects of the curriculum, including problem solving. When test scores reflect a reduced range of skills (relative to what is expected), we have what is described as construct under-representation.

Another difficulty can arise if students taking a test are required to demonstrate knowledge or processes that can impact on performance in a manner that is not intended. For example, students taking a mathematics test may be required to read mathematical word problems embedded in complex vocabulary and sentence structures before they can demonstrate their problem-solving skills. Teachers may assume that the resulting scores reflect performance on mathematical problem solving, when in fact they also reflect reading proficiency. Since differences in higher-level language proficiency are not relevant to the construct being assessed (i.e. mathematical problem solving), and may disadvantage certain subgroups (such as students with low language proficiency), the reading element of the problems can be described as *construct-irrelevant variance*. This doesn't mean that it is inappropriate (invalid) to assess students' ability to solve word problems by asking them to read problems embedded in text. Instead, test developers and test users (including teachers) should ensure that grade-appropriate vocabulary and sentence structures are used in the assessment tasks that are set for students, and hence that test scores reflect the primary construct being assessed. Construct-irrelevant variance also arises when assessing students whose first language differs from the language of teaching in class. For many education systems, this is increasingly relevant given the multi-cultural profile of students, where many arrive in school speaking a different language to that of their teacher and classmates. Further discussion on this is contained in Chapter 10, in the context of inclusive assessment.

Another area where construct-irrelevant variance could be an issue is e-assessment. If access to the construct (for example, scientific reasoning) first requires a strong level of computer skills, the scores achieved by students may reflect more than scientific reasoning, and hence proficiency in computer skills could be described as construct-irrelevant variance. A way to address this is to ensure that the computer-specific skills students require to access the test and respond to questions are kept to a minimum, and that, where relevant, students are provided with practice and feedback on their use before testing begins (for example, through completion of practice items that highlight those skills).

Predictive validity evidence

Some assessments or tests are assembled with the main purpose of predicting student performance or behaviour at some future point in time. For example, an aptitude test that assesses verbal reasoning or numerical ability might be administered to students in Year 9, with a view to predicting how they will perform on a different assessment in Year 11. Evidence of predictive validity can be generated by correlating students' performance on the aptitude test in Year 9 with their examination performance in Year 11. If the correlation between the two sets of scores is strong, performance on the aptitude test administered in Grade 9 can be said to be strongly predictive of examination performance in Grade 11. Scores on the aptitude test administered in Grade 9 can then be used as a basis for advising future cohorts of students on how they can expect to do on the examination in Grade 11. This could result in advice to students to study or avoid certain language or mathematics courses.

It is not always possible to obtain unbiased estimates of predictive validity. If some students (those achieving low scores on an ability test) leave school before Grade 11, it will not be possible to obtain their scores on an examination in Grade 11. Hence, the correlation between the predictor measure (the aptitude test) and the outcome measure (exam results) may not fully capture the relationship between the two measures, since it may be based solely on those students who stay on at school.

Consequential validity evidence

In the past, validity evidence has mainly centred on content validity, construct validity and predictive validity. More recently, the concept of validity has been broadened to include evidence of consequential validity. This concerns the effect of the assessment on participants that results from the assessment process, interpretations and decisions (Isaacs et al., 2013). Common criticisms of high-stakes tests and testing programmes (such as National Curriculum Assessment in England or, as some teachers may believe, the requirement in Ireland for primary schools to submit standardised test results to the Department of Education and Skills) include the charge that they lead to a narrowing of the curriculum. Teachers may place a strong focus only on those subjects like reading, mathematics and science that are externally assessed. They may also teach to the test, by teachers intentionally or inadvertently emphasising specific test content in their teaching (e.g. House of Commons Children, Schools and Families Committee, 2008; The Sunday Times, 6 November 2016). It might be noted that consequential validity is not a property of a test per se, but a consequence of how a test is used (see below). Proponents of consequential validity (e.g. Messick, 1989) argue that there is an onus on test developers to justify the purpose for which tests are to be used, and that there is an onus on test users to justify why they might use a test for other purposes. For example, if a test designed to assess students' proficiency in mathematics is also used to evaluate school or teacher effectiveness, a rationale for this usage should be developed by the agency or individual using it for that alternative purpose.

A range of uses can be made of assessment outcomes such as grades, marks or scores, whether at the individual student level or at a group or cohort level. As indicated in Chapter 1, these roles can be classified as mainly relating to assessment *for* learning (AfL) and assessment *of* learning (AoL). They include:

- using information in student portfolios (collections of work) to identify aspects on which students might need more instruction (AfL)
- using end-of-term marks or grades to provide feedback to parents on how a student has performed (AoL)
- predicting a student's future performance in mathematics (AoL)
- providing students with feedback on their own learning progress (AfL)
- certifying students at the end of a course of study or at the end of a key stage (AoL)
- asking students to reflect on their own work to identify strengths and areas for improvement (AfL)
- mapping the progress of a student or a cohort from year to year (AoL)
- evaluating school or teacher effectiveness (AoL).

In addition to the different sources of evidence considered here, the validity of test score interpretations can be undermined by, for example, difficulties with the administration of tests or with the scoring of test responses.

From time to time, stories in the media point to instances in which the validity of test score interpretations could be challenged or where a programme is cancelled to avoid misinterpretation of what scores mean. Examples include the following:

- *English language tests inquiry declares thousands of results invalid* – invigilators were accused of supplying answers to whole exam rooms; impostors were suspected of stepping into exam candidates' places to sit the test (*The Guardian*, 24 June 2014).
- *Pupil evaluation test scrapped over scoring blunders* – the administration of computer-based literacy and numeracy tests to primary pupils was suspended because of technical problems and scoring errors (*Belfast Telegraph*, 5 January 2012).
- *The year Leaving Certificate cheating stopped being a secret* – a whistle-blowing student used social media to accuse fellow students of having phones on their laps for an entire paper and reading saved messages (*Irish Times*, 19 June 2010).
- *Ofqual: 340,000 GCSE and A level exams 'marked up'* – it was reported that scores had been marked up after students had submitted 'excuses' to justify relatively poor performance, with 94% of requests for higher marks granted (*The Telegraph*, 31 October 2012).
- *Should the exam have been cancelled?* A BBC News investigation discovered that up to 80 people may have bought copies of their maths A level paper, for as much as £400 each, yet the examination authorities decided to go ahead with the exam (BBC News website, 19 June 2001).
- *Take it from an examiner, your students' exam results could easily be wrong* – a former examiner claimed that examining is a 'ruthless' business, with unqualified markers often rushing through papers to reach quotas (*The Guardian*, 20 August 2015).

The focus of these concerns is not on content or on the constructs underlying the tests (which journalists are generally not qualified to interrogate). Rather, it is on issues such as test security, test administration and scoring or marking. Problems in these areas can undermine the validity of test score interpretations and could lead to incorrect conclusions about the meaning of test scores. For example, employers, parents or other users of test scores might assume that an assessment has been administered correctly and fairly, or that a script was scored carefully and accurately, and accept the scores or grades achieved by candidates at face value.

In your teaching, you will regularly develop assessments and use methods and tools made by others. In all of this, validity issues are relevant. In this book, we provide an overview and practical application of some of the dominant views on validity, a complex and contested concept even amongst assessment experts. The further reading at the end of the chapter includes a special issue of one educational journal, *Assessment in Education: Principles, Policy and Practice* (volume 23, 2016), edited by Paul Newton and Jo-Anne Baird. Interested readers can explore divergent viewpoints on validity in this fascinating professional joust.

Reliability

Reliability refers to the consistency of scores derived from an assessment (whether a test, an examination or a task designed by a teacher). Reliability is a necessary condition for validity, but a test that is reliable may not be valid (that is, while scores may be accurate and replicable, they may not measure what they are intended to measure). In considering the reliability of an assessment, we may ask questions such as:

- Are the results (scores, grades) consistent over time? Would the same results have arisen if the assessment had been administered at a different time? Could the student's scores be replicated?
- Is there consistency across assessment tasks? Would the same results have arisen if a different set of tasks had been administered?
- Is there consistency across markers? Would the results have been the same if a different marker had scored the assessment?

In general, where there are high levels of consistency, we can say that scores or grades are reliable. However, no scores are completely reliable, as there is some random error associated with all grades or scores. The goal should be to reduce sources of error over which we have control, such as error arising from differences between markers, or error arising from a particular set of items within the test.

Clearly, it is important for scores and grades to be reliable. Students taking high-stakes examinations such as GCSEs, A levels, Scottish Nationals or the Irish Leaving Certificate will want to be reassured that the grades they receive are a fair representation of their work and that their grades can be compared with those achieved by other students taking the exam. Similarly, parents will want to be reassured that the scores achieved by their children on achievement or ability tests are accurate, and reflect knowledge and skills. Others, including the general public, will want to be reassured that grades on high-stakes assessments are comparable from year to year and that standards are not 'dumbed down' over time.

Reliability of assessments with fixed marking schemes

Historically, the evaluation of reliability has involved the statistical analysis of test data. Most of the indices reported here relate to tests with objective scoring schemes, such as multiple-choice tests (where there is a unique correct answer for each item) or closed-response questions (where the answer is either right or wrong). They are described briefly here:

- *Test/retest reliability* – the same test is administered to the same students at about the same point in time. Scores on the two tests are then correlated. If the correlation is strong or very strong (0.7 or higher), it can be concluded that test scores are consistent.
- *Alternate forms reliability* – if there are multiple forms of the same assessment (for example, Form A and Form B), these forms are administered to the same students and their scores are correlated. If the correlation between forms is strong, it can be concluded that the different forms of the test are consistent with one another.
- *Split-half reliability* – the responses to items taken by the same students on the same assessment are split into two halves, and scores on each half are correlated

to give an indication of the overall consistency of the assessment. A statistical correction such as the Spearman-Brown prophecy formula may be added to estimate the reliability of the full-length test, given that the correlation is based on two halves of the test.

- *Internal consistency* – the results on different tasks (items) or sections of an assessment are correlated to see how well they relate or 'hang' together. A common statistic used for this purpose is Cronbach's Alpha. Similar to a correlation coefficient, this provides an indication of how consistently the items in a test contribute to the overall result and, hence, how well the test forms a coherent whole. Another statistic that is often used for this purpose is the Kuder-Richardson Formula 20 (KR_{20}). On standardised tests, Alpha or KR_{20} values often exceed 0.90, indicating very strong internal consistency.

A number of factors besides the internal structure of the test can contribute to the strength of reliability coefficients reported in test manuals. Kubiszyn and Borich (2013) provide the following general principles related to the evaluation of reliability:

- Group variability affects the size of the reliability coefficient. Higher coefficients (correlations) result from heterogeneous groups (where there is a good spread of performance) than from homogenous groups (where scores cluster together, with small differences in performance between students).
- Scoring reliability limits test score reliability. If tests are scored unreliably (i.e. there are differences between markers), error is introduced that will limit the reliability of test scores (though, in the case of good multiple-choice questions, this source of error is minimised).
- All other factors being equal, the more items included in a test, the higher the reliability of scores.
- Reliability of test scores tends to decrease as tests become too easy or too difficult (again, a clustering effect with students clustering together at the top or bottom of the scale).

Finally, it might be noted that, even if a test has satisfactory reliability, there may still be issues with the validity of test score interpretations. If the underlying construct is undermined (for example, by the inclusion of questions that are not relevant to the curriculum), the validity of test score interpretations will still be threatened.

Standard Error of Measurement

A student's performance on an assessment represents only a sample of his or her performance on a sample of items selected from a large pool of possible items. Arising from this, a student's actual score should be regarded only as an estimate of his or her 'true' score. A statistic that is widely used to estimate the size of the error associated with assessment scores is the Standard Error of Measurement (SEM). The SEM seeks to quantify the error associated with a score, and therefore can be considered as a measure of the unreliability of test scores. Indeed, formulas used to calculate the SEM include a measure of reliability such as the KR_{20} or Cronbach's Alpha.

The score achieved by students on an assessment may be accompanied by an estimate of the SEM. Thus, it might be reported that a student achieved a scale score of 105 on a test (about average achievement on many standardised tests) and that the SEM associated with that score is 3 score points. Since error scores (that is, differences between achieved and 'true' scores) are normally distributed, with a mean score of 0 and the SEM as their standard deviation, we can establish a confidence interval around an achieved score. Thus, we can say that, 68% of the time, a student's score falls into a range between 102 and 108 (the 68% confidence interval, or the student's score plus or minus one standard error). We can also say that, 95% of the time, it falls into a range between 99 and 111 (the 95% confidence interval, or the student's score plus or minus two standard errors). One implication of this is that two scores falling close to one another (for example, 105 and 110) will have overlapping 95% confidence intervals (99–111 and 104–116). Since the intervals overlap, we cannot claim that the two scores, 105 and 110, are different from one another. If the standard error is larger (for example, 4 or 5 points), the confidence intervals would widen, reflecting weaker reliability.

Reliability of assessments marked with scoring schemes or rubrics

Reliability coefficients, such as Cronbach's Alpha, are typically used with tests that mainly include multiple-choice and short-answer (right/wrong) items. A somewhat different situation arises in contexts in which there is no clear right or wrong answer, but, instead, responses vary in quality along a specified dimension (for example, the ability to structure a piece of writing or the ability to produce a drawing related to a given theme). These tasks call for the use of marking schemes or scoring rubrics – descriptions of the criteria for awarding different scores – on a performance-based task such as an exam question that calls for a written response (see Figure 2.2). We return to scoring rubrics in Chapter 7, when the construction and scoring of performance-based measures are considered. Here, we note the importance of moderation procedures in ensuring the reliability of scores or grades based on marking schemes, whether in high-stakes contexts, where thousands of scripts are marked by an examining board or research consortium, or in within-school contexts, where

---

Question: Why did the Cabinet Mission of 1946 fail to achieve a united India?

Level 3 – Explains reasons (e.g., The Muslim League felt that the transfer of power from the British Raj to a League/Congress coalition would result in a Hindu Raj, with Indian Muslims suffering at the hands of a Hindu majority. The initial rejection of a proposed Hindu-majority India and a Muslim-majority Pakistan led to swaths of violence which, ultimately, led to the partition of India.)

Level 2 – Identifies reasons (e.g., Congress and the Muslim League did not agree on a united government).

Level 1 – Simplistic statement (e.g., the Cabinet Mission was a failure, describes the mission).

Level 0 – No valid response

Figure 2.2 Example of a scoring rubric

several hundred scripts are marked by teachers within a subject department. The term 'inter-rater reliability' is often used to describe the reliability achieved by two or more raters scoring the same work.

A number of approaches can be used in implementing moderation to ensure that an assessment is marked reliably and in line with required standards (that is, high levels of inter-rater reliability based on the marking scheme are achieved). These include:

- *Trial marking*, where markers mark a number of questions or papers, and marks are standardised (adjusted) by a marking team, in line with agreed criteria.
- *Double-blind marking*, where two examiners mark or grade the same question or paper independently; a percentage agreement can then be calculated.
- *Sampling*, where a moderator reviews a cross-section of a marker's work to standardise the marks awarded. This may result in the statistical adjustment of marks if they are higher or lower than the required standard.
- *Group moderation*, where a group of markers discuss examples of assessed work in order to share their understanding of the agreed criteria.

Gipps (1994) and others have noted the value of groups of teachers within a subject department working together to establish standards for scoring students' work. In addition to enhancing the reliability of the marks awarded to students, group moderation can enhance teachers' understanding of the criteria that students need to achieve, which, in turn, can impact in positive ways on teaching and learning (see Klenowski and Wyatt-Smith, 2014 for more information on moderating teachers' judgements of student performance).

Reliability of teachers' classroom assessments

An advantage of classroom assessments (such as teacher-made tests or portfolio assessments in primary and secondary education) over other forms of assessment (such as formal exams and tests) is that a teacher has access to outcomes from multiple assessments on which to base grades or scores. The use of multiple assessments (one of the principles of assessment outlined in Chapter 1) could lead to higher levels of reliability as students have more than one opportunity to demonstrate their knowledge or understanding. However, teachers also need to guard against bias in their judgements, such as favouring certain students or negatively stereotyping others, as these actions would undermine the reliability of assigned scores or grades.

Fairness

The *Standards for educational and psychological testing* (AERA et al., 2014) identify fairness as a fundamental validity issue that requires attention at all stages of test development and use. A key issue is the extent to which unfairness or bias could impact in a negative way on the interpretation of test scores. This, in turn, relates to the construct being assessed and whether the construct is the same for different groups of test takers, such as students with a learning disability (versus non-disabled students), female (versus male) students, students with low proficiency in the language of test (versus highly proficient students) or education-ally disadvantaged (versus non-disadvantaged) students. Fairness does not imply that students in different groups should achieve the same average scores. Rather, it implies that assessment practice and the interpretation of assessment results must be fair for all students (Gipps and Stobart, 2009). In a similar vein, Popham (2012) argues that it is unfair to assess a student on a test of English reading if they have not had a reasonable opportunity to acquire the language (that is, the resulting score could not be considered valid).

Fairness and access to the construct being assessed

Careful standardisation of an assessment, clear administration procedures and con-sistent scoring can help to reassure test takers that they have the same opportunity to demonstrate their understanding of the construct underlying the test, even if it is administered in multiple venues and scored by different markers. If an assess-ment is computer-based, examinees should have similar levels of exposure to the technology, and the equipment used in all centres should be the same in terms of the processing speed and clarity of text and images. Nevertheless, whether an assessment is paper-based or computer-based, some adjustments may be required to provide equivalent opportunities to all test takers to demonstrate their standing with regard to the construct being assessed. Access arrangements or reasonable accommodations that may be available to students with certain documented disa-bilities include:

* extra time in which to complete the assessment
* access to a reader
* a waiver from the assessment of spelling, grammar and punctuation in language subjects
* use of a word processor (sometimes with spelling and grammar aids enabled)
* assistance of a scribe (if, for example, the student has a disability that prevents him/her from writing) or speech recognition technology
* large print or braille test forms
* exemption from aural exams.

In all cases, the goal is to ensure greater equality of access, without changing the nature of the underlying construct. In cases where the construct is altered (for example, by providing a waiver from the assessment of spelling on a language test because a student has severe dyslexic difficulties), an explanatory note may accom-pany the grades achieved by the student. Readers are referred to the Joint Council for Qualifications (2016) and State Examinations Commission (2016) for additional information on the types of accommodations that are available to students taking examinations in the UK and Ireland. However, the issue of providing suitable accommodations will arise for a broad range of assessments, including those administered on an ongoing basis in the classroom. Hence, teachers will need to take steps to ensure that their own classroom assessments – whether tests, port-folios or performances – are fair to all students. We return to the issue of assessment accommodations in greater detail in Chapter 10 in the context of students with disabilities and other special educational needs.

Gipps and Stobart (2009) argue that it is important to go beyond access in considering fairness. They argue that differences in performance on an assessment may be due to differences in access to learning and that fairness in access to curriculum and schooling must precede a genuinely fair assessment situation.

Fairness and measurement bias

In addition to a lack of access to assessments, fairness can be compromised if an assessment is biased against particular groups of students. In some cases, bias may be evident in the wording of a problem or question. In other cases, bias may be more subtle. Popham (2012) has identified three common sources of assessment bias that may need to be addressed: racial/ethnic bias, gender bias and socio-economic bias. For example, he argues that the use of 'field' in the sentence 'My mother's field is court reporting', benefits students of higher socio-economic status who might be expected to be more familiar with this use of 'field', and therefore perform better on the associated item, compared with students of lower socio-economic status. He argues that careful sensitivity to these potential sources of bias must be exercised in the course of developing and/or reviewing assessment tasks, with a view to revising or deleting any items that might be unfair. For classroom assessments, he suggests that a teacher's colleagues might act as reviewers, including colleagues from minority groups. This suggests that the contexts in which test items appear, as well as the items themselves, should be based on the shared experiences of all students, and that the language used should not portray narrow or stereotypical representations of sections of society. The Educational Testing Service (ETS, 2009a) provides a useful manual, *ETS international principles for fairness review of assessments*, which can be used as a basis for the systematic review of the fairness of specific assessments.

While careful item review may serve to detect more obvious sources of bias, statistical approaches can also be used. Differential item functioning (DIF) is one such approach. It seeks to find out if a difference between subgroups on an item is sufficiently large and unexpected that the item merits further detailed review. For example, if female students who do well on a test as a whole perform poorly on a particular item, and their equally high-achieving male counterparts do well (or vice versa), that item would be earmarked for further investigation. Approaches to measuring DIF usually require large student samples and therefore it is not feasible to use with class-sized groups.

Ethical assessment

From the foregoing, it is clear that fairness has an ethical dimension, where test developers and test users have an obligation (and sometimes a legal requirement) to ensure that assessment is fair. Indeed, an emphasis on ethics/fairness and the rights of the individual is one of five guiding principles underpinning the European

Framework for Standards in Educational Assessment (AEA – Europe, 2012), outlined in the previous chapter. The Framework draws on the United Nations Convention on the Rights of the Child (which stresses that the rights of the child must be paramount in any endeavour involving children) to support its stance.

Elwood (2013) frames her discussion of equity and fairness around the social consequences of assessment (consequential validity), including possible group differences arising from test bias. For example, she considers how the inclusion of different item types can give rise to differences between male and female test takers, with, for example, boys likely to outperform girls on multiple-choice questions (where students select a correct answer from among several alternatives) and items that are novel (such as problems presented in realistic contexts), and girls more likely to do better on constructed response items (where students write an answer to a question), as well as on items based on prose pieces, poems and stories.

Chapter summary

The key issues discussed in this chapter – validity, reliability and fairness – are important, whether the focus of assessment is improving students' learning in the classroom (assessment *for* learning) or summarising student performance at the end of a course or school year (assessment *of* learning). Moreover, they relate to all aspects of assessment and to all types of assessment.

Validity was presented as a unitary concept, for which various sources of evidence should be provided. The idea that validity evidence should focus on the interpretation of assessment outcomes (scores), rather than on the assessment itself, was emphasised, as was the obligation on test users to justify the uses they make of assessment data, if evidence for those uses has not been provided by test developers. The concept of consequential validity, or the effect of an assessment on teachers, students and other stakeholders, was introduced and linked to fairness in assessment. Threats to the validity of test score interpretations, including construct under-representation and construct-irrelevant variance, were examined. Reliability was identified as a prerequisite for validity rather than being an end in itself. A distinction was made between approaches to evaluating the reliability of fixed marking schemes (such as those for tests consisting entirely of multiple-choice questions) and of scoring schemes or rubrics (such as those used to mark essays or projects). Moderation was identified as an approach to ensuring consistency (and therefore reliability) when assessments are marked using a scoring scheme. The need to take measurement error (a by-product of reliability) into account in interpreting scores or grades was considered.

The concept of fairness in assessment was examined and it was argued that, while access to assessment (and, in particular, to the construct being assessed) is an important dimension of fairness, other dimensions should also be considered, including the effect of assessment on different groups of students. Ethical dimensions of fairness were also considered, including the responsibility on policy-makers, test developers and test users to make decisions that always put the interests of the student first.

Questions for discussion

1.   Some assessment experts concerned about consequential validity refer to the 'backwash' effects of assessments, that is, the negative effects that a particular assessment can have on teaching and learning. Think of an assessment situation that you have experienced as a learner, for example A level/National/Leaving Certificate examination, coursework, portfolio or presentation. What were some of the positive and negative effects of the assessment, including backwash effects? Were the effects the same for all test takers?

2.   A recent photograph in the media showed relatives of students taking a law examination in India climbing the walls of the test centre to provide assistance to the students through open windows. How might this undermine the validity of test score interpretations?

Further reading

Black, P., Harrison, C., Hodgen, J., Marshall, B., & Serret, N. (2010). Validity in teachers' summative assessments. *Assessment in Education: Principles, Policy and Practice*, *17* (2), 215–32.

This article shows how moderation can support teachers in gaining a better understanding of what is meant by validity. The focus is on the validity of teachers' own summative assessments (assessments *of* learning) to assess English and mathematics using portfolios at Key Stage 3. The authors use the term 'assessment literacy' to describe teachers' understanding of assessment.

Elwood, J. (2013). Educational assessment policy and practice: a matter of ethics. *Assessment in Education: Principles, Policy and Practice*, *20* (2), 205–20.

The main focus of Elwood's article is on ethical issues around the use of two different tests used in the transfer of students from primary to post-primary schools in Northern Ireland, with some schools accepting scores on either test for admission. In addition to issues around the comparability of the two tests, Elwood considers the impact of the selection tests on students and their parents.

Newton, P.E., & Baird, J. (eds) (2016). *Assessment in Education: Principles, Policy and Practice*, *23* (2). Special Issue on Validity.

This special issue of the journal provides an opportunity for debate between scholars on the topic of validity. A range of issues is explored spanning divergent understandings of validity across time, geographic locations and philosophical and scientific perspectives.

3

Understanding assessment *of* learning
Purposes, impacts and challenges

What you will learn in this chapter

To arrive at this stage in your education or career, your learning will have been assessed at several key points or transitions. For example, you may have sat national tests such as the Standard Assessment Tests (SATs) at the end of a key stage of learning. You may have completed an examination leading to certification of your learning at the end of compulsory education such as the General Certificate of Secondary Education (GCSE) in England, Wales and Northern Ireland, the Scottish Qualifications Certificate or the Junior Certificate in Ireland. You and thousands of your fellow students may, at some point, have been sampled to take part in international assessments such as the Trends in International Mathematics and Science Study (TIMSS) or the Programme of International Student Assessment (PISA). You may have taken an aptitude test selected by a guidance teacher. The process of assessing students (or indeed adults) at key points in their lives is often referred to as 'assessment *of* learning' (AoL) or summative assessment (that is, a summary of student learning). AoL is typically formal (that is, administered and scored using standard procedures) and can include teacher judgement of performance as well as testing (Isaacs et al., 2013). A key factor distinguishing AoL from AfL (for assessment for learning, see Chapter 4) is the use to which assessment information is put. In AoL, assessment outcomes (results) are typically compared with those achieved by others, whether individuals, schools, districts or even countries. In contrast, the outcomes of AfL typically relate to task performance and are more likely to feed directly into future student learning. Typically, they do not involve a direct comparison with other students but instead focus on the extent to which key knowledge and skills have been acquired.

In this chapter, we look at the origins of assessment of learning and how it has evolved over the past 100 years. We then examine examples of AoL and their main features. We also consider the strengths and limitations of AoL.

When you finish the chapter, you should be able to answer these questions:

- What is AoL?
- Why is AoL important?
- What procedures and technical requirements are associated with the use of AoL?
- How can AoL inform teaching and learning?
- How is AoL linked to the topic of Chapter 4, assessment for learning?
- What are some strengths, weaknesses and pitfalls of AoL?

What is assessment of learning (AoL)?

According to Isaacs et al. (2013: 12):

> Assessment of Learning, also known as summative assessment, is a success measure of the outcomes of the end of a unit, programme, year's study, qualification or school experience (for example, school leaving examinations and certificates). It is almost always a formal process that can include teacher judgement as well as testing.

Typically, AoL involves an examination, a test or an oral or other performance. However, teacher judgements based on evidence, such as quality of homework, work shown in a portfolio, contributions to class work, and attendance and effort, are also examples of AoL. In some contexts, test results may stand side by side with teacher judgements of achievement on a report. In other contexts, such as vocational education, grades based on teacher judgements may be the only focus of AoL. Table 3.1 illustrates some of the purposes of AoL.

Table 3.1   Assessment of learning: purposes

Level	Purposes	Illustration
Student level – internal to school/college	Maintaining records and generating reports for teachers, parents and students	End-of-term summative assessments conducted by teachers (teacher-made tests, portfolio assessments)
Student level – external to school/college	Certifying that a student has met course or graduation requirements Selection of students Meeting statutory needs	Key Stage 2 Assessments (England and Wales); GCSE and A levels (England, Wales, Northern Ireland); Nationals, Highers and Advanced Highers (Scotland); Junior and Leaving Certificate (Ireland); Baccalauréat (France)
School level	Monitoring trends in student achievement; Evaluation of teachers, schools or larger units, by school itself or by national/local authority	Use of standardised test or examination results to evaluate school improvement
System level	Monitoring of achievement – year-on-year or periodic comparisons of students' average performance at regional, national or international level	Key Stage 2 assessments in England and Wales; Programme for International Student Assessment (PISA)

While AoL often occurs in the context of formal tests and examinations, it can also form a part of classroom assessment. Schools and teachers may conduct summative assessments at the end of a term or school year, and report the outcomes to other teachers, parents and students. Students may contribute to these reports by summarising their own performance. The Assessment Reform Group (2006: 5) describes summative assessment by teachers as:

> the process by which teachers gather evidence in a planned and systematic way in order to draw inferences about their students' learning, based on their professional judgment, and to report at a particular time on their students' achievements.

The Group notes that teachers can assess a broader range of achievement and learning outcomes than formal tests and examinations, and can also provide information about students' learning processes. It also notes that such information can be used formatively to support student learning.

AoL can be high-stakes or low-stakes, depending on the context and the actors involved. End-of-term summative assessments that are internal to a school are typically low-stakes for students; results may cause some discomfort when they arrive home, but, generally, there are no long-term consequences for school, teacher or student. Examinations, especially those that take place at the end of secondary schooling and may determine the institutions that students attend and courses they take in further and higher education, are high-stakes for students and their parents. Other assessments, such as Key Stages 2 tests in England, may be low-stakes for students but high-stakes for schools, because schools may be judged on the outcomes. Finally, international assessments, such as the Programme for International Student Assessment (PISA) (see below), may be low-stakes for students and schools (since results are typically not reported at student or school levels), but high-stakes for education systems (represented by national education departments).

Approaches to assessment of learning

AoL encompasses a broad range of assessments, including examinations, tests and moderated assessment tasks and teacher assessments.

Examinations

The earliest recorded evidence of standardised examinations was in China, where the imperial examinations were administered from the Song Dynasty (AD 960–1279) onward, though their roots may date back to the imperial university established in the Han dynasty (206 BC–AD 220) (Encyclopaedia Britannica, n.d.). Candidates for the civil service competed in a series of exams dealing primarily with Confucian texts, and, if successful, progressed from local to provincial and national level. Although the exams tended to emphasise rote learning over original thinking, and form over substance, they produced an administrative corps grounded in a common body of teachings, based on a system of merit. As the system was deemed to be too inflexible to be capable of modernisation, it was finally abolished in 1905.

Examinations were virtually unheard of in England at the beginning of the 19th century, but were quite prevalent by the late 1800s, spurred on by university examinations and legislation to effect open entry to the civil service via competitive examination in 1870 (Roach, 1971).

The terms 'examination' and 'test' can be used interchangeably. An examination (or test) can be defined as 'an attempt to measure a learner's knowledge, understanding or skill within a certain subject or sector domain in a limited amount of time' (Isaacs et al., 2013). Although examinations (and tests) can be administered for both formative and summative purposes, here we are concerned with summative purposes. These include:

- Certifying and accrediting candidates – examinations such as A levels and the Leaving Certificate examination are used to certify an individual candidate's skills and understanding. Examinations may also be used to allow access to the professions (for example, medicine, law, accountancy) or to provide a 'licence to practise'.
- Selecting candidates – end-of-schooling examinations are used to select candidates for further and higher education. Where examinations are used to this purpose, they can be described as 'high-stakes' for the individuals concerned as the outcomes (grades) can determine the examinee's future.
- Maintaining and raising academic standards – examinations can encourage candidates and (more recently) the institutions they attend to meet and exceed established standards. They can hold students, teachers, schools and larger units to account.

There are a number of distinguishing characteristics associated with formal examinations such as GCSEs, A levels, Scottish Nationals, the Leaving Certificate and the Baccalauréat:

- They are administered in a systematic way with strict time limits.
- They are fixed in scope and difficulty.
- They are marked in a consistent way, using a marking guide, applied by a trained marker.
- The outcomes can be examined to ensure reliability, validity, fairness and equity (see Chapter 2).

In theory, examinations give everyone an equal chance of succeeding, as students are required to demonstrate their knowledge and understanding of a given syllabus, at a fixed time and place, under the same conditions that are experienced by other candidates, and the same scoring schemes are applied. In practice, performance on examinations and other assessments may be influenced by a range of inter-related factors such as the quality of the teaching and learning, school and student socioeconomic status, student gender and student motivation.

Figure 3.1 provides some examples of the types of items found on examinations administered to students towards the end of compulsory schooling, and here include the types of items used to assess science. Note that the number of points allocated to each item is clearly specified.

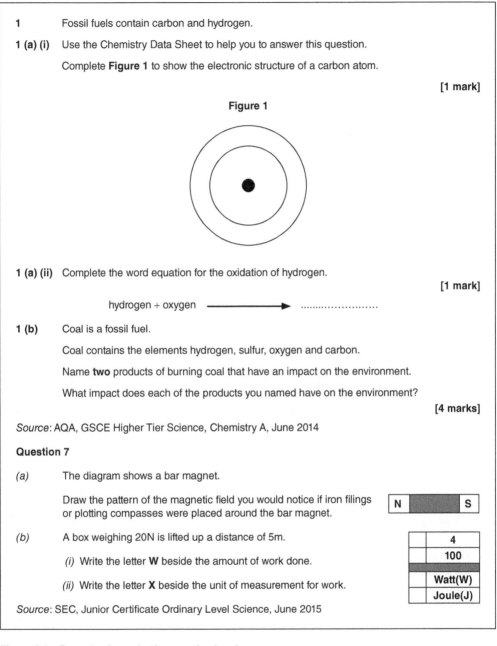

1   Fossil fuels contain carbon and hydrogen.

1 (a) (i)   Use the Chemistry Data Sheet to help you to answer this question.

           Complete **Figure 1** to show the electronic structure of a carbon atom.

                                                                                        [1 mark]

Figure 1

1 (a) (ii) Complete the word equation for the oxidation of hydrogen.

                                                                                        [1 mark]

                   hydrogen + oxygen ———————▶ ....

1 (b)   Coal is a fossil fuel.

           Coal contains the elements hydrogen, sulfur, oxygen and carbon.

           Name **two** products of burning coal that have an impact on the environment.

           What impact does each of the products you named have on the environment?

                                                                                        [4 marks]

Source: AQA, GSCE Higher Tier Science, Chemistry A, June 2014

Question 7

(a)   The diagram shows a bar magnet.

           Draw the pattern of the magnetic field you would notice if iron filings
           or plotting compasses were placed around the bar magnet.

           N [   ] S

(b)   A box weighing 20N is lifted up a distance of 5m.

           (i) Write the letter **W** beside the amount of work done.

           (ii) Write the letter **X** beside the unit of measurement for work.

4
100
Watt(W)
Joule(J)

Source: SEC, Junior Certificate Ordinary Level Science, June 2015

Figure 3.1   Example of examination question in science

The types of items used to assess science include:

- completing diagrams and tables
- completing word equations
- naming items (single-word responses)
- answering short questions.

Other requirements for questions found in examinations include:

- writing extended answers, including essays (language)
- drawing graphs (mathematics)
- writing mathematical proofs and showing calculations (mathematics)
- drawing sketches (art)
- answering oral questions (foreign languages).

Standardised tests

The origin of standardised tests, as we know them today, can be traced back to a number of assessment initiatives in the late 19th and early 20th centuries: written essay-type examinations used for selection purposes (see above); early psychological testing, mostly designed to study individual differences in sensation, discrimination and reaction time (associated with Francis Galton and James McKeen Cattell); the development of statistical methods, in particular correlation methods (associated with Karl Pearson); and testing to diagnose underperformance (associated with Alfred Binet and Theodore Simon) (Du Bois, 1970). The tests of Binet and Simon were particularly relevant to future developments as they consisted of a wide range of separate items, using different types of material, and were designed to assess higher mental processes (some of which are now considered aspects of intelligence), such as memory span, problem solving and judgement (see the profile of Alfred Binet below).

While the earliest standardised tests, such as those of Binet and Simon, were individually administered, it was only a matter of time until tests of achievement that could be administered to groups were developed. A need for large-scale testing arose in the USA during the First World War for the selection and placement of personnel in the US army, leading to the development of the first group test – the Army Alpha test. A parallel nonverbal group test (Army Beta) was developed for use with individuals with literacy problems or whose first language was not English – one interesting early illustration of the type of effort made towards more inclusive assessment, discussed later in Chapter 10. Development of the tests was facilitated by the invention of the multiple-choice format (attributed to American Fredrick J. Kelly) in 1914. Through the 1920s, tests of achievement in a variety of curriculum areas (arithmetic, English composition, spelling, handwriting) were developed for use in American schools. Tests were designed primarily to assess individual students, but test data were also aggregated to assess curricula and later to evaluate the efficiency of teachers and school systems in delivering the curriculum. Another key milestone was 1936 when the first automatic test scanner, IBM 805, was developed. This enabled the scanning and scoring of answer sheets, making it easy to assess large numbers of students efficiently, provided the answers were objective.

A standardised test can be defined as:

> a procedure designed to assess the abilities, knowledge, or skills of individuals under clearly specified and controlled conditions relating to construction, administration, and scoring, to provide scores that derive their meaning from an interpretative framework that is provided with the test. (Shiel et al., 2010: 23)

Personalities in educational assessment: Alfred Binet (French experimental and theoretical psychologist, 1857–1911; the father of intelligence testing)

In the early 1900s, the French government asked psychologists Alfred Binet and his colleague Theodore Simon to help decide which students were mostly likely to experience difficulty in schools. The government had passed laws requiring all French children to attend school, so it was important to find a way to identify children who would need specialised assistance. The aim was to test each child deemed to be at risk using a battery of memory, attention and problem-solving items (a type of diagnostic testing). For example, the 1905 test, designed to assess children starting school, included verbal knowledge of objects, verbal knowledge of pictures, repetition of sentences of 15 words, five weights to be placed in order, and an exercise of memory for pictures. It was observed that some children could answer more advanced questions that older children were generally able to answer, while other children of the same age were only able to answer questions that younger children could typically answer. Based on this observation, Binet suggested the concept of a mental age or a measure of intelligence based on the average abilities of children of a certain age group. This allowed for a comparison between mental and chronological age. For example, a mental age that was two to three years behind a child's chronological age might signal a need for special intervention. Binet's test was extended to older children before his death in 1911.

The tests developed by Binet and Simon were later adopted in the USA, where Lewis Terman developed the Stanford-Binet Intelligence Test (currently in its fifth edition). In addition to identifying children with learning difficulties, the test identifies children and adults with high levels of intelligence.

In England, Sir Cyril Burt, like Terman, a proponent of the view that intelligence is largely hereditary, is credited with introducing the 11+ tests, which were used to select children for entry to Grammar (academic), Secondary Modern or Secondary Technical school between 1944 and 1976. It was subsequently alleged that Burt falsified some of his research results (e.g. Kamin, 1974; Gillie, 1977).

Binet, on the other hand, held the view that intelligence remained an outcome that could be modified. He believed in identifying students' strengths and weaknesses, and addressing weaknesses to improve learning outcomes.

Tests of ability and aptitude, such as the Cognitive Abilities Test (CAT), which may be taken today by students on entry to secondary school, have their origins in the tests developed by Binet many years ago. Stobart (2008) argues that scores based on ability tests, while predictive of later achievement, are often viewed by teachers and others as proxies for intelligence. This may mean that teachers will hold low expectations of students who perform poorly on such tests, and that students themselves may hold low levels of self-worth. Neither attitude is conducive to the types of improvement we might expect to occur in the context of Assessment for Learning (AfL).

Some definitions of standardised tests specify only administration, scoring and interpretation (e.g. Popham, 2011). However, aspects of construction (how the test was put together) are also important, because they are relevant to understanding the meaning of test scores (an aspect of test validity). While examinations can be classified as standardised tests, the focus in the remainder of this section is on standardised norm-referenced tests, primarily consisting of objective test items such as multiple-choice items, short-answer items, true–false items, or similar.

Construction

The construction of a standardised test involves a number of steps. These typically include:

- describing the domain or the construct to be assessed – this is normally exemplified in an assessment framework
- developing test items such as multiple-choice or short-answer items (see Figure 3.2 for examples)
- implementing a pilot study to try out items and select those that work best
- selecting items for the standardisation study, or, in the case of computer-based assessment, developing an algorithm for administering the test to students
- implementing a standardisation study in which a representative sample of students completes the new test (for example, a national sample of several thousand students in Year 9), and test norms are developed. Test norms are derived scores (such as grades or standard scores) that compare a student's performance on the test with that of other students. Thus, a raw score on a test (for example, 30 items correct out of 40) may be converted to a standard score (such as a score on a scale with a mean of 100 and a standard deviation of 15) (see Chapter 8).

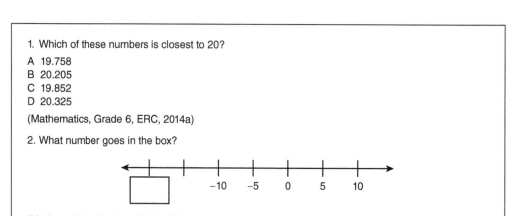

1. Which of these numbers is closest to 20?

A 19.758
B 20.205
C 19.852
D 20.325

(Mathematics, Grade 6, ERC, 2014a)

2. What number goes in the box?

(Mathematics, Grade 6, ERC, 2014a)

3. (Based on text provided) Why were women forbidden from acting in plays? (English reading, Grade 6, ERC, 2014b)

4. (Based on text provided) 'I was totally convinced that the Queen and Ophelia were what they appeared to be.' What did the writer mean by this? (English reading, Grade 6, ERC, 2014b)

Figure 3.2   Examples of standardised test items

The sample items in Figure 3.2 illustrate some of the item formats found in standardised tests. They include: multiple choice, where the test taker selects the correct response from the four options given (item 1); answer supply, where the test taker provides a brief answer such as a number or a word (item 2); and short answer, where the test taker responds to a question by writing two or three lines of text (items 3 and 4). Items 3 and 4 show that even relatively short questions can tap into the higher-level thinking required to respond to some texts, including an understanding of complex language and causal relationships. These issues are discussed further in Chapter 6.

Administration

Standardised tests require a uniformity of procedure in how they are administered. The materials used, instructions given to test takers, preliminary demonstrations (practice questions) and ways of handling queries are all clearly specified. Furthermore, the conditions under which a test is administered relating to comfort, lighting, freedom from distraction and student interest, cooperation and motivation should be the same for all candidates. Deviations in administration or in the conditions of testing will affect the interpretation of examinees' performance. The test manual should provide clarity on any accommodations that can be offered to students, including those with special educational needs (see Chapter 10 for further discussion on assessment accommodations and the inclusion of students with special educational needs in the assessment process).

Scoring

The instructions for scoring in the manual accompanying a test must be followed exactly. Discretion on the part of the examiner is eliminated when selection-type items (e.g. multiple-choice, true–false) are used. Tests with this type of item can be, and frequently are, scored by machine, increasing the speed and reducing processing costs. A further advantage of selection-type items is that they allow the wide sampling of a domain since responding to an item requires very little time.

As illustrated in Figure 3.2, standardised tests may also include supply-type items (e.g. short-answer items). While pre-set criteria are generally provided for scoring such items (much like the marking scheme for an exam question), scoring will not be as objective as is the case with regard to selection-type items, and steps may need to be taken to establish the reliability of scoring (see Chapter 2). While such items can tap into higher-order skills, there are also higher costs associated with scoring them.

Interpretation of scores

Standardised test outcomes are usually presented with one of two interpretative frameworks. In the first, it is possible to locate the position of a candidate's score in a set of scores. In this case, the standard used in interpreting test performance is a relative one, and the score given to an examinee is called a norm-referenced measure. Often, student scores are reported on a scale with a mean (average) score of 100 and a standard deviation (spread) of 15 (see Chapter 8). The second interpretative framework is a criterion-referenced one, where performance is interpreted in terms of the content or skills that a student has mastered or is likely to successfully apply in taking a test. This idea is also taken up in more detail in Chapter 8, where the use of proficiency levels as a method for reporting performance, and as a basis for planning future learning, is considered.

Moderated coursework, assessment tasks and teacher assessments

As noted above, moderated tasks and teacher assessments can also be used for summative purposes. Moderated tasks are assessment tasks that are scored by a student's teacher or by an external marker. According to Isaacs et al. (2013), the purpose of moderation is 'to ensure that the assessment is reliable, fair and consistent with required standards'. Teacher assessments often have assessment for learning or teacher support for students' learning as their main purpose (Chapter 4). However, if certain quality control procedures are followed, they can also be used for AoL. For example, a portfolio of a student's writing or artwork, gathered over a school term, can be used by the teacher as a basis for awarding an end-of-term grade. Teacher assessments, including assessments based on coursework, may or may not be moderated, depending on the context.

In some high-stakes contexts (for example, where coursework contributes to a student's grade in a final examination), moderation may play a key role. The examining body (for example, Edexcel, Scottish Qualifications Authority, Hong Kong Assessment and Examinations Authority) will require evidence that the assessment was conducted fairly and that a marking system was implemented accurately. The examining body may choose to verify the scores awarded to students by examining the underlying work and comparing this to the grade assigned by the teacher. The examining body will be concerned with consistency in marking across teachers so that the same grade is awarded for similar work in different schools. Where disparities arise, adjustments may be made to the marks or grades assigned.

In low-stakes contexts (for example, where coursework does not form part of an examination), a more informal approach to moderation may be employed. For example, groups of teachers within a school subject department may put a system of moderation in place. In both high- and low-stakes contexts, group moderation may be implemented. This typically involves groups of markers discussing examples of students' work and relating these to the marks or grades they have assigned, based on the interpretation of the marking criteria. A significant benefit of involving teachers in scoring their own students' assessments is that teachers become familiar with the strengths and weakness of their students, and can draw on that knowledge to inform subsequent teaching and learning. More formal examinations and tests do not include this feedback loop.

Concerns about the effects of examinations and standardised tests

While examinations and standardised tests are generally regarded as a fair and efficient way of assessing a student's knowledge and understanding, a number of criticisms have been levelled against high-stakes assessments that are used for accountability purposes. These include the following:

- An over-reliance on examination grades or test scores can limit what is on the curriculum and encourage teaching to the test (Jennings and Bearak, 2014), even if this consequence is not intended. Parents, and even students, may put pressure on the teacher to cover exam content.
- Examinations (and tests) can be over-predictable, leading to rote learning, which may be quickly forgotten after the examination has been completed (Baird et al., 2015). Other approaches to learning, such as those based on constructivist and socio-cultural theories, align better with more continuous and student-centred approaches to assessment (see Chapters 4 and 5).
- Grade inflation, where examination grades creep up over time, undermines confidence in the examination process (Coe, 2010).
- Examinations and tests that are used to classify students can lead to labelling and may influence teacher expectations in negative ways.
- Many standardised tests do not provide information on what the student has learned, only how he/she stands relative to other students.
- Externally regulated examinations and tests take the responsibility for assessment of learning away from teachers.
- *League tables* of schools based on examination grades or standardised test scores often fail to take students' initial levels of achievement or their socioeconomic status into account. The use of alternative approaches to assessment (assessment for learning) would strengthen processes such as school evaluation.
- There is potential social and economic inequity associated with examinations and standardised achievement tests, with some social and ethnic groups consistently achieving higher average grades or scores than others.

Join the debate: What are some advantages of AoL?

In the literature on assessment, concerns about the negative effects of examinations and standardised tests abound. Literature supporting such assessment is available but can be harder to locate. Use the internet to access at least two articles, such as those in the further reading section at the end of this chapter, to make a case for AoL. Document four or five points that support the use of summative assessment to improve students' learning. You can draw on the companion website prompts when addressing this task.

Visit the companion website at: https://study.sagepub.com/murchanshiel

International assessments

Many of the summative assessments that students complete at school will be for the purposes of maintaining school or individual student records, reporting to parents and students, or certifying students. However, students may also be asked to take part in international assessments that are specifically designed to compare performance across countries and educational systems. International assessments of educational achievement compare the average performance of students in different countries. Typically, they involve the administration of the same standardised tests to students in different countries, and the scaling of performance so that scores can be compared across countries. Table 3.2 provides summary information about the main international assessments of educational achievement. As part of these assessments, questionnaires are also administered to generate contextual data that can be used to interpret performance outcomes. The regular administration of the same tests allows for monitoring of performance over time.

Table 3.2   Selected international assessments of achievement

Name of assessment or study	Purpose
Progress in International Literacy Study (PIRLS): www.iea.nl/pirls_2016.html	A study of reading literacy that is implemented every 5 years. In 2016, PIRLS was administered in over 50 countries, including England (Year 5), Northern Ireland (Year 6) and ROI[a] (Fourth class)
Trends in International Mathematics and Science (TIMSS): www.iea.nl/timss_2015.html	A study of mathematics and science that is implemented every four years. In 2015, TIMSS was administered in 57 countries, including England (Year 5 and Year 9), Northern Ireland (Year 6 only) and ROI (Fourth class and Second year) (see Mullis et al., 2016 for outcomes)
Programme for International Student Assessment (PISA): www.pisa.oecd.org	A study of reading literacy, mathematics and science that is administered every three years to representative national samples of 15-year-olds. In 2015, PISA was administered in 72 countries/economies including the UK (with separate samples for England, Northern Ireland, Scotland and Wales) and ROI. (see OECD, 2016a; Shiel et al., 2016 for outcomes) Unlike other international studies, PISA aims to assess students' preparedness for their future lives and study, rather than their performance on curriculum-based tests
International Civic and Citizenship Study (ICCS): www.iea.nl/iccs_2016.html	A study of students' knowledge of and attitudes towards civics and citizenship. In 2009, ICCS was administered in 38 countries, including England and ROI. A further round was administered in 2016

Note: [a] ROI = Republic of Ireland

In addition to testing students on their knowledge and skills in international assessments, questionnaires are frequently administered to the students, their parents, their school principals and their teachers. The questionnaire data provide a context for interpreting student performance. The outputs of international assessments include framework documents (where the content and processes underpinning the assessment are described), performance reports (including rankings of countries by average score) and thematic reports (where major themes such as gender and equity in learning outcomes are explored in depth).

In recent years, international assessments have begun to move to computer-based platforms. In 2015, PISA was administered on computer in most participating countries, while a computer-based version of PIRLS (e-PIRLS) was administered in 2016. Studies have also begun to include innovative domains such as collaborative problem solving and financial literacy in PISA 2015.

PIRLS, TIMSS and PISA all have norm-referenced and criterion-referenced interpretative frameworks, though performance is typically reported at the country or regional level rather than at the individual student level. In PISA, for example, the average performance (in reading, mathematics and science) across OECD countries is set at 500 and the standard deviation at 100 when a domain has major status for the first time. Countries are assigned mean scores at, above or below this average. In addition, the skills that students at differing levels of achievement are expected to succeed on are described in terms of proficiency levels, with the highest proficiency levels (Levels 5–6) describing the skills that the highest performers can demonstrate, and Level 1 and below describing those skills that the lowest performers might be expected to demonstrate.

While international assessments can provide useful information on the standing and progress of national educational systems, they too have been criticised on a number of grounds. Criticisms have included the following:

* International studies can have an inordinate impact on policy development at country level because of their high profile. There was evidence of this in the Republic of Ireland in 2009 when performance in reading literacy and mathematics was found to have declined significantly, even though there was no corroborating evidence from other international assessments or from national assessments. A National Strategy to Improve Literacy and Numeracy (DES, 2011b) was launched to address the decline.
* In some education systems such as Norway, Germany and Denmark, the impact of unexpectedly low performance on the PISA assessment has prompted use of the term *PISA Shock* to describe policy-makers' reaction to the results (Nusche et al., 2011; Breakspear, 2012). Perspectives differ on the value of *PISA Shock* to an educational system.
* International studies privilege skills that can be easily assessed and scored, and ignore other important higher-level skills that are more difficult to assess. In response to this, PISA has been implementing newer assessments (for example, collaborative problem solving in PISA 2015), along with innovative item types in reading, mathematics and science. A further response is the intention to assess transferable global competencies as part of the PISA programme in 2018.
* Since there is relatively little or no teacher involvement in international studies, the outcomes of such studies have minimal impact on teaching and learning in schools.

Chapter summary

The focus of this chapter is on assessment of learning (AoL) or summative assessment. AoL provides an outcome measure such as a mark or grade that is awarded at the end of a unit or course of study. It incorporates a range of purposes, including maintaining records and generating reports for teachers, parents and students; certifying that a student has met course or graduation requirements; evaluating teachers, schools or larger units; and monitoring (and raising) achievement from year to year, at school, regional or national levels. These purposes are achieved by administering a range of different assessments, including examinations, tests and moderated coursework, assessment tasks and teacher assessments. The stakes associated with these instruments can be described as high or low. Assessments may have high stakes for schools and teachers, and low (or no) stakes for students, and vice versa.

Examinations and tests include a broad range of tasks. These include multiple-choice items, short-answer items, essay questions, interviews and, in some cases, performances. Where these tasks are used for AoL, they must be administered in systematic and uniform ways, and procedures for scoring and for reporting results must be consistent within and, where relevant, across schools. If coursework or teacher assessments are used as a basis for generating grades or marks, moderation procedures should be put in place. As noted in Chapter 2, reliability, validity and fairness are important attributes of assessment in general, and of AoL in particular.

AoL, and examinations and tests, in particular, have been the focus of strong criticism in the literature, with concerns such as teaching to the test, predictability and grade inflation often raised. Persistent differences in performance among ethnic and socioeconomic groups have also been identified as a problem with some summative assessments. Teachers may not derive sufficient information from examinations and tests to allow them to plan instruction and intervene successfully in students' learning. Approaches associated with assessment *for* learning, outlined in Chapters 4 and 5, are usually more suitable for this purpose.

International assessments of educational achievement such as PIRLS, TIMSS and PISA are used to compare performance across educational systems and to monitor progress over time. These studies report performance using both norm-referenced approaches (where performance is described in relative terms) and criterion-referenced approaches (where the knowledge and skills of students performing at different levels of proficiency are described).

Questions for discussion

1. Many aspects, features and practices associated with education and schooling have changed a great deal in the past few decades, but has the way we assess students changed as much? Try to locate a test or assessment used with students 20, 30 or 40 years ago or more. You might source this in your school, in a book, online, or from someone you know. How different is the assessment from what is used nowadays? In what ways? What similarities exist?

2. How well informed are parents and the public about the breadth of summative assessments in use today within the education system? Write a brief explanatory memo for your school's parents' association that summarises the role of summative assessment.

Further reading

Brown, G.T.L., & Hattie, J.A. (2012). The benefits of regular standardized assessment in childhood education: guiding improved instruction and learning. In S. Suggate & E. Reese (eds) *Contemporary debates in child development and education* (pp. 287–92). London: Routledge. Available at: www.academia.edu/1964802/The_benefits_of_regular_standardized_assessment_in_ childhood_education_Guiding_improved_instruction_and_learning

This book chapter outlines how standardised tests can be used to improve teaching and learning.

Morris, A. (2011). *Student standardised testing: Current practices in OECD countries and a literature review.* OECD Education Working Papers No. 65. Paris: OECD Publishing. Available at: http://dx.doi.org/10.1787/5kg3rp9qbnr6-en

This short paper focuses on how standardised tests that have low stakes for students can be used to improve teaching and learning. In particular, Sections 4 and 5 focus on the potential positive impacts of standardised tests.

Murphy, C., Lundy, L., Emersen, L., & Kerr, K. (2013). Children's perceptions of primary science assessment in England and Wales. *British Educational Research Journal, 39* (3), 585–606.

This article considers how a range of assessments, including standardised tests, impact on students, from the students' point of view. In particular, it explores the effect of tests on students' attitudes towards science.

Understanding assessment *for* learning
Purposes, impacts and challenges

What you will learn in this chapter

You have already seen the various uses to which assessment can be put in school. This chapter expands on some of those purposes, especially in relation to promoting students' learning in class. We first explore beliefs in education and psychology that provide the theoretical foundation for assessment *for* learning (A*f*L). The evolution of this approach to assessment is outlined, highlighting similarities and differences with other approaches to assessment with which you may be familiar. We also discuss research and policy development in relation to AfL, while also highlighting some recent cautionary comments that merit consideration.

When you finish the chapter, you should be able to answer these questions:

- How do students learn?
- How can teachers draw on students' beliefs about learning to promote success?
- How does assessment for learning 'fit' with teachers' instructional practices?
- To what extent does the formative use of assessment relate to other functions of assessment?
- What is the evidence to support AfL and how much faith can we have in that evidence?

What do we know about how students learn?

Learning and development are at the heart of education and schooling. Parents send their children to school with the expectation that the school will accelerate the learning that has already begun in the home. Teachers need to understand how students learn to help realise these expectations and facilitate students' further learning. Along with careful planning and sound instructional methods, assessment is one of the pedagogical approaches available to teachers to help students learn.

Psychologists have differed both in defining learning and explaining how it occurs. Early psychologists such as John Stuart Mill and Edward Thorndike viewed learning as the shaping of understanding and behaviour. This led to teaching practices that emphasised drill and practice, such as memorising spellings and tables. You may well have encountered these approaches in your own education, and indeed many people believe that such approaches are an essential element in ensuring that students acquire the necessary knowledge. Subsequent viewpoints conceptualised learning as a process where change in knowledge, skills and behaviour is understood and modified through changes in one's experience. This idea that knowledge can be changed by new experiences is fundamental to all interpretations of learning.

Pre-cognitive theories

Considerable interest emerged during the late 19th and early 20th centuries in the process of how people learn. Early behaviourist theories of learning by psychologists Ivan Pavlov, B.F. Skinner and others focused on modifying student behaviour. Change in student behaviour, it was argued, could be engineered by the application of reinforcement (for example, rewards that parents and teachers may be familiar with, such as the systematic use of praise, stickers, tokens and toys) and through shaping (directing students towards long-term goals through reinforcing short-term related goals). Key to these behavioural theories of learning was the belief that learners modify their behaviour in positive, predictable ways, to bring about a consequence desirable to the learner.

An alternative social learning theory highlights how learners observe and copy the actions of others. The psychologist Albert Bandura stressed how learners relate their behaviour to that of others and also understand reinforcement and consequences in relation to others.

Cognitive and social-cognitive theories

Those early behaviourist and social learning theories recognised learning as the modification of an individual's behaviour by stimulus–response associations cultivated through reinforcement or by imitation of others. Later cognitive theories explain learning in relation to less observable internal mental processes such as receiving, remembering and using knowledge. Information-processing models focus on how learners process information and represent it mentally. Centred on internal brain activity, this is often confined to specific aspects of processing such as language acquisition, comprehension, arithmetic, visual processing and memory. Stage theory cognitive models of development, illustrated most famously by the Swiss psychologist Jean Piaget, typically suggest chronological sequential milestones at which learners can succeed at cognitive tasks. For example, according to Piaget, a child's thought remains highly egocentric and self-centred until about the age of 7, whereas in the period of 7–11 years this tendency gives way to thinking that is broader than the self.

Social cognitive theories of learning expand the range of factors that may influence learning. Not only might learning be shaped by a person's internal information-processing skills and developmental stage, but the learner's dispositions, emotional state, beliefs about learning, perceptions and motivation may all interplay to impact on learning. You may have seen this in school where some students feel that they are no good at mathematics (a self-belief) and as a result are not motivated to engage with new concepts or persist with difficult concepts.

Constructivist and socio-cultural theories

Typically, young people learn in group contexts such as with family, friends, peers and classmates. A further development of the socio-cognitive models of learning outlined above recognised the possible effect on meaning making of learners' inter-action with their social and cultural environment. Lev Vygotsky, a Russian psycholo-gist, emphasised the influence of group participation on individual learning. Vygotsky formulated ideas about the zone of proximal development (ZPD), repre-senting the difference between what students can learn on their own and what they can achieve with assistance from competent others, such as teachers, classmates or parents (or indeed, nowadays, also from digital adaptive tutoring systems). In addi-tion, it is possible for teachers and others to scaffold students' learning by providing support such as clues, prompts and guidelines without providing direct instruction. This provides students with external support to enable them to reach the next stage in the learning journey. Later in this chapter and in the book, we will see how these two ideas – zone of proximal development and scaffolding – are keystones in the theory and practice of assessment for learning.

Lorrie Shepard (2000: 8) identifies some characteristics of learning that are framed within cognitive and constructivist learning theory:

* Deep understanding is principled and supports the transfer from one learning context (topic, situation, subject) to another.
* Intelligent thought involves 'metacognition' or self-monitoring of one's own learning and thinking.
* Cognitive performance depends on dispositions and personal identity.
* New learning is shaped by prior knowledge and cultural factors and perspectives.
* Learners construct knowledge and understanding within a social cultural context.

A number of these characteristics relate directly to assessment for learning. Students' prior knowledge is recognised as a key influence on learning, a view reflected in the following observation by the psychologist David Ausubel (1968: vi):

> If I had to reduce all of educational psychology to just one principle, I would say this: The most important single factor influencing learning is what the learner already knows. Ascertain this and teach him accordingly.

Teachers need to be aware of the prior knowledge, conceptions and misconcep-tions held by learners and to act on this information when planning and provid-ing instruction. This suggests the need for mechanisms to constantly check on students' learning throughout the instructional process, rather than waiting for defined moments to administer more formal tests. Teachers also need to help students understand the very process by which they learn so that they acquire the capacity over time to monitor their own learning without a specific need for direction by the teacher. Such self-monitoring and regulation of their own learning are considered key goals for students and have been promoted in national and international educational policy (OECD, 2013). Finally, teachers need to recognise that individual dispositions such as emotional state, motivation and self-efficacy impact on learning so that they can take this into account in planning and implementing teaching.

Putting the learner in control of learning

Aspects of the above theories help us understand the process and motivation behind learning. Overlooked until relatively recently, strategies to help learners better understand and control how they learn is now seen as a key competency within 21st-century learning (European Union, 2006). Learners who are self-regulated know how to set targets for themselves, plan how to achieve the targets and evaluate their success in reaching them. Secondary school students might, for example, set a plan to revise three topics in science during a mid-term week. Actively deciding to revise one topic every two days and complete an end-of-chapter test on each topic to check learning is an example of self-regulated learning (SRL). Pintrich (2000: 453) defines SRL as an

> active, constructive process whereby learners set goals for their learning, and then attempt to monitor, regulate and control their cognition, motivation and behaviour, guided and constrained by their goals and the contextual features of the environment.

The pre-flight checklist is an example of SRL and of self-assessment. Learners use a checklist to verify the completion of essential features of an assignment or task, before handing it in to the teacher. These actions, involving active cognitive thinking and planning by learners, are sometimes referred to as cognitive behaviour modification. Strategies to help develop students' SRL are teachable (see Schunk and Zimmerman, 1994; Pintrich, 2000).

Approaches that teachers can use to promote SRL include:

- cognitive strategies – specific study skills such as focusing attention on particular parts of a task or using mnemonics to recall lists
- metacognition – knowing how you learn and when to employ certain cognitive strategies
- willpower strategies – encouraging learners to stay on task by working towards goals, prioritising goals and avoiding distraction
- motivational strategies – evident when students analyse a task, set goals, formulate plans for learning and reflect on their success.

Barry Zimmerman (2002) suggests three distinct phases that self-regulated learners pass through when learning new material or consolidating material already learned:

1. *Forethought*: the learner receives information about the task, sets some goals and plans strategies to realise the goals.
2. *Performance*: this is the actual learning phase, where the student enacts the plans developed during the forethought phase and maintains the willpower to continue towards the goal. The learner needs to monitor learning and change strategies if goals are not being realised.
3. *Self-reflection*: this is a crucial phase of learning. Students reflect on learning, think about specific reasons for success or failure and adjust the approach to the next learning task in light of such self-appraisal.

Such strategising requires the self-activation of students' own internal cognitive traits, emotions and motivation, approaches to learning and teaching that are quite different from the behavioural and social learning theories outlined earlier.

Effective AfL requires the active involvement of the learner. This assumes that the student is motivated to learn and believes that success comes as a result of personal effort rather than luck or some other uncontrollable factor. Students need to choose to engage seriously with learning that is directed towards some specific goal. They need to make an effort in response to that choice and maintain that effort over a period of time. Without this, effective learning is difficult and students will not realise their potential.

Activity 4.1

Try this out – Implementing self-regulated learning

Consider the four approaches to self-regulated learning listed above (cognitive, meta-cognition, willpower and motivation). Identify a number of cognitive strategies that you could use to revise the section on *What do we know about how students learn* earlier in this chapter. Devise a plan to gauge how successful your revision is. The companion website to the book includes some prompt sheets to aid you in developing strategies. Each sheet contains prompts to help you try some strategies with students in class. Record your experience on the sheets.

Visit the companion website at: https://study.sagepub.com/murchanshiel

Self-efficacy and attribution theories

Teachers sometimes assume that students in their class can organise and pursue a particular course of action. As a teacher or student teacher, how often have you said to a student experiencing difficulty, 'you can do it'? As teachers, we sometimes assume that the learner believes in their own personal competency and effectiveness to learn. Self-efficacy theory (Bandura, 1997) helps explain why some students are motivated to achieve on a task and some are not. Students with poor self-efficacy simply do not believe that they can plan and follow the steps required to succeed in a specific task. A related idea is best understood by an example. Consider two students, Alex and Youcef, of more or less equal ability who receive similarly poor results on a mid-term history test from the teacher. Despite not having really revised in advance,

Alex feels that the test was unfair and the teacher really did not reward him for what was a good answer. Youcef, however, recognises that he hadn't really revised well for the test. Alex attributes his lack of success on the test to external factors outside his control (unfair test, biased teacher), whereas Youcef takes responsibility, attributing his poor result to lack of preparation. He recognises his own capacity to determine the outcome and in this case believes that his lack of engagement, time and effort resulted in a poor performance.

The above scenario fits with Bernard Weiner's (2000) attribution theory. Here, learners perceive their success or failure in a task under three categories:

- *locus* – outcome is caused inside or outside of the individual
- *stability* – cause is likely to stay the same or is modifiable
- *controllability* – can the learner control the cause?

Depending on the manner in which a learner attributes success or failure, the motivation to put in the effort to succeed is affected. Self-efficacy and attribution interact with each other and influence motivation in complementary ways. For example, if Youcef believes that tardy preparation (internal locus) caused his poor result, then his self-efficacy is preserved. He can study better for the next test and succeed.

Differentiated instruction and AfL

How schools are organised, with class sizes of anywhere between 15 and 30 pupils, creates a challenge for teachers. The work of David Ausubel (1968), mentioned earlier, highlighted teachers' need to ascertain what students already know. This might be reasonably straightforward if all the students were identical in their prior knowledge, interest level and motivation. Of course, they are nothing of the sort. In order to vary the teaching pace and emphasis in class for different students, we first need to diagnose how different they are. Identifying students' levels of ability, achievement, motivation and interest is essential for tailoring instruction to student needs. In contrast, whole-class teaching occurs when teachers pitch instruction to some middle ground, somehow hoping that all students will benefit. In reality, this practice under-challenges some in the class, while resulting in frustration, de-motivation and poor achievement for lower-ability learners.

The term differentiated instruction has gained popularity in recent years in describing an 'organised yet flexible way of proactively adjusting teaching and learning to meet kids where they are and help them to achieve maximum growth as learners' (Tomlinson, 1999: 14). Though the term may be relatively new, the concept is not. For years, effective teachers have sought to place students at the centre of teaching and learning and have shaped planning and instruction around student needs. Authors such as Tomlinson (1999), Schumm and Vaughn (1995) and Heacox (2002) describe the benefits, challenges and processes of differentiated instruction. As a way of thinking about teaching and learning, key elements include: providing optimal challenge to individual learners; giving students choice in what they learn; implementing flexible grouping based on ability and interests; and increasing the depth of learning by introducing different levels of content for different ability levels.

A number of models exist to highlight how differentiation can be used by teachers. In Ireland, the NCCA (2007b) identifies seven means by which teachers can teach to the differing needs of students. Teachers can vary learning based on:

- task to be completed
- outcome expected
- resources used
- complexity of directions
- support offered
- pace of teaching/learning
- choice (students select work appropriate to their own needs).

In England, Ofsted inspectors, while not expecting to observe any one standardised instructional methodology in classrooms, nonetheless equate the outstanding quality of teaching with teachers using 'well-judged teaching strategies that … match pupils' needs accurately' (Ofsted, 2015: 61). In Scotland, key aspects of the curriculum include meeting the learning needs of students and embracing assessment for learning to enable appropriate progress for all learners (HM Inspectorate of Education, 2007) and ensuring 'personalisation and choice' in curriculum and learning (Scottish Government, 2008: 13). Whether by name or not, such indicators of sound teaching reflect in part Carol Tomlinson's (1999, 2000) categorisation of differentiation by:

- content – individual students or groups explore different topics simultaneously in class
- process/task – what students are asked to do, perhaps giving different activities and tasks to students to suit their particular needs
- product/outcome – students are given choice in demonstrating learning through written, oral, visual, role play or other means
- learning environment – classroom spacing, resources, routines.

Benefits linked with differentiated instruction include enabling students to regulate their own learning (Van Bramer, 2011) and improving their engagement with school-work (Painter, 2009). When differentiating instruction, the teacher needs to first identify the appropriate learning outcomes. In addition, it is necessary to know to what extent students are already familiar with some of the content and skills relevant to the outcomes. They then need to develop learning experiences likely to bridge the gap between what they already know and what they should know next. This gap is similar to the zone of proximal development (ZPD) highlighted by Vygotsky. Aided by a knowing peer or adult, students can bridge the gap between what they know and what they should know. This suggests a crossover between differentiation, the ZPD and AfL.

Differentiated teaching and learning require systematic, ongoing assessment of students' learning. The teacher ascertains students' readiness, motivation, interests and knowledge, and builds learning outcomes and experiences around that insight. As teaching and learning progress, the teacher and students move through continual cycles of identifying learning levels and interests and basing subsequent learning approaches on that information. Many forms of assessment can be used as part of differentiated teaching and learning – baseline tests, informal logs of outcomes achieved, questionnaires to assess interest, and so forth – and these will be discussed in later chapters.

Paul Black and Dylan Wiliam, in developing a theory for formative assessment (2009: 9), noted that:

> Practice in a classroom is formative to the extent that evidence about student achievement is elicited, interpreted, and used by teachers, learners, or their peers, to make decisions about the next steps in instruction that are likely to be better, or better founded, than the decisions they would have taken in the absence of the evidence that was elicited.

Differentiated instruction involves 'changing the pace, level or kind of instruction you provide in response to individual learners' needs, styles or interests' (Heacox, 2012: 5).When combined, formative assessment and differentiation bring together three important dimensions of pedagogical practice: teaching, classroom management and assessment. This highlights the intertwined and shared purpose between differentiation and formative assessment. It is difficult to envisage successful differentiation without formative assessment. Through employing informal assessments embedded in day-to-day instruction and learning, teachers can ascertain current learning levels and facilitate learners in taking their next steps. Therefore, assessment, as a necessary tool for unlocking the potential of differentiation, is central to current concepts of effective teaching and learning. The application of differentiation approaches in relation to students with special educational needs, including students with exceptional ability, is developed more fully in Chapter 10.

Assessment purposes

Background to AfL

When reading about assessment for learning in books, articles, reports and online, you will encounter a wide variety of related terms. In 1967 Michael Scriven coined the term formative evaluation, indicating the process of critically reviewing the effectiveness of educational processes, for example an alternative approach to teaching mathematics or a new curriculum, while it is under way as a means to improve its functioning. Rather than wait until the programme has finished or is long-embedded, review is undertaken during the programme. This concept, later applied to student assessment by Benjamin Bloom, suggested that teachers can identify students' learning levels during the teaching process 'directly affecting both the quality of the instruction and the student's ability to understand the instruction' (Bloom, Hastings & Madaus, 1971: 53). Such in-class approaches to assessment contrasted with a policy emphasis on measurement and external testing, such as a minimum-competency approach to testing in the USA and term or end-of-year exams in systems within the British Isles, continental Europe and Asia. Interest in pedagogical uses of assessment and assessment information evolved, accelerated by the work of the Assessment Reform Group (ARG) in England and Wales from the mid-1990s. Researchers associated with the ARG identified specific factors and features associated with assessment that has as its primary function the improvement of learning, and sought to ensure that government policy, especially in the UK, was informed by research evidence.

Assessment for learning (AfL) contrasts with assessment of learning, or summative assessment. This contrast occurs on a number of dimensions: the use to which assessment information is put (AfL stresses the learning needs of the student); how frequently this information is communicated (in AfL, students are constantly apprised on how they are doing); and the role of the students where the task of self-assessment in helping students regulate their own learning is central to AfL.

The evolution of AfL can be understood by reference to the different functions of assessment as outlined in Figure 4.1. Rather than describing assessment or assessment formats, these terms highlight the main traditional purposes of assessment – formative, diagnostic, summative and evaluative – and the uses to which they are put. All purposes are relevant, to varying degrees, for learners in school systems. Whether we look at the micro (student), meso (classroom and school) or macro levels (educational system), the interplay between different purposes of assessment is evident.

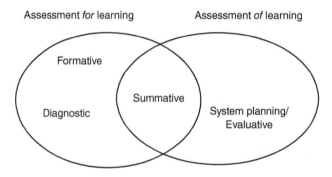

Figure 4.1   Relating purposes and types of assessment

Evaluative assessment

As mentioned already in Chapter 3, assessments are sometimes used to provide descriptive information about the functioning of a system such as a school or a broader educational structure (eg. LEA, region). Often, this information is based on the assessment of samples of students, such as those selected for national monitoring tests and international assessments, for example PISA and PIRLS. Summative assessments are varied in form and scope, often aiming to provide a succinct snapshot of student learning that has occurred during a defined time period, such as the learning gained during a topic, a term or a course of study. Often, the results of summative assessment are expressed in the form of grades or levels that relate student attainment to expected levels represented in a curriculum or set of standards. Examples include end-of-term grades compiled by teachers and results on public examinations. Summative assessment may be based on specific tests, tasks and exams, but also on the retrospective judgement of teachers in relation to a body of the student's work, such as entries in a portfolio assessed summatively.

Formative assessment

Formative differs in purpose from summative assessment, aiming to inform and form the learning as it proceeds. Waiting until the unit or course has finished to assess students cannot fulfil this purpose. Formative assessment occurs during learning and offers the teacher and student information about how learning is progressing. Many types of 'informal' classroom assessments (observation, questioning, self-assessment, teacher-designed tasks) can provide this information. Timely interpretation of the results of tests, portfolios and projects can also contribute useful formative information that can help guide the next steps in learning. Formative assessment involves using interactive assessment approaches to better understand student learning and then intervening during the learning process to gather feedback, which is used to guide teaching and learning in the direction of the intended learning outcomes. Key to this process is the generation of information for the learner who actively uses this to improve learning.

Diagnostic assessment

Figure 4.1 also highlights the diagnostic use of assessment. All teachers recognise instances where a student's difficulty with learning is hard to explain. This may occur, for example, when a student consistently fails to answer simple number operations in mathematics, perhaps due to an inadequate formation of the concept of place value, or when a student makes frequent errors of reversal of letters in early writing. Such scenarios are often first encountered and addressed through formative assessment where teachers try to identify the problem and introduce some corrective measures. Sometimes the learning difficulty may not be amenable to easy identification by teachers and diagnostic tests are employed to investigate further and try to pinpoint the specific learning errors. Diagnostic tests are typically commercially produced and reference a student's performance on the test or task to specific pre-set criteria (criterion-referenced) or to the performance of other students of the same age in the population (norm-referenced), similar to the interpretation of standardised test scores highlighted in Chapter 3. Purposes of diagnostic assessment include:

- identifying disabilities among students
- identifying students in need of special education provision, either special support or more challenging provision
- identifying students with specific learning difficulties, especially difficulties in language and numeracy, and pinpointing the specific nature, causes and potential ways of overcoming those difficulties. This can expand beyond language and mathematics to investigate students' performance, conceptions and misconceptions about a range of topics and curriculum areas.

The overall purpose of diagnostic assessment is to help the teacher differentiate the learning experience to best meet the needs of the student, through establishing a learner's specific knowledge, skills, strengths and weaknesses. This illustrates a similarity of intention between diagnostic and formative assessment. Both have individual student learning as the focus, both emphasise providing relevant, timely information or feedback and both assume subsequent action by the teacher, in conjunction with the student (Murchan, 2011). The main difference between the two functions of assessment is the formality of the procedures, tests and assessment instruments employed.

Another related term that you might encounter in your reading on assessment is classroom assessment, used especially in North American systems. In contrast to the externally developed standardised tests, classroom assessments highlight the key role of the teacher in developing, administering and interpreting assessments in the context of normal day-to-day classroom activities. Clearly, there is a strong overlap between formative assessment, classroom assessment and AfL, and Wiliam (2011) explores the nuanced relationship between different terms. Fundamentally, AfL highlights the potential of a wide variety of approaches to assessment that can be embedded within teaching and learning practice in class. A voluminous and growing literature describes the application of AfL in many different contexts and provides evidence to support the practice.

Feedback

A key feature of AfL is the provision of feedback to learners and how this feedback can inform student (and teacher) actions. Feedback is 'information provided by an agent (e.g. teacher, peer, book, parent, self, experience) regarding aspects of one's performance or understanding' (Hattie and Timperley, 2007: 81). Feedback is task-specific and should provide specific information that fills the gap between what is understood at present and what ought to be understood in relation to the learning task (Sadler, 1989). A distinction is made between offering praise (not considered to be particularly effective) and providing information about a student's performance in relation to a specific task, content or learning. Effective feedback provides cues or reinforcement to learners, whereas praise, punishment or extrinsic rewards (stars, stickers, grades) are less effective. The role of the student and the focus of the feedback are crucial: students must be committed to the goals of learning and the feedback must relate specifically to that learning, rather than to personal characteristics of the students such as their effort or general orientation to study. Three questions are often asked to reflect students' engagement with AfL:

1. Where am I now?
2. Where am I going?
3. How do I get there?

In answering these questions, a number of actions are necessary for the learner and teacher. To gauge the present learning level (Question 1), the teacher and/or learner needs to gather relevant evidence about students' current level of functioning in relation to the intended learning, analogous to understanding prior to learning in the context of differentiated teaching. To know where learning is going (Question 2), students need to receive information that enables them to relate their current level of learning to the intended learning outcome or state and understand also what success on relevant learning tasks will look like. Typically, there is a gap between where students are now and where they need to be. Such feedback provides information to enable the student to self-regulate their learning. Once the nature of the gap between actual and intended learning is made clear, the learner needs to receive feed forward in the form of information to help adapt learning approaches and processes to generate enhanced learning. The above steps, while appearing straightforward, require the adjustment of practice by teachers and students, rather than the mere application of a few assessment techniques to traditional teaching. The blending of specific assessment techniques with teaching and learning practice in class is discussed in the next chapter. Issues discussed include the articulating and sharing of learning goals, the effectiveness of marking and feedback, the use of questioning strategies in class and the deeper involvement of students in assessment through self- and peer assessment.

Assessment as learning

Ideally, the student should be an active participant in assessment rather than someone to whom assessment is *done*. Motivation and willingness are required on the part of students to actively engage with the process, share the development of learning goals, attend to the feedback and monitor their own learning (Dann, 2014). Thus, engagement with assessment is itself learning, coining the term assessment *as* learning (A*a*L). Normal classroom activities such as questioning, role-playing, completing a worksheet, working on projects and tasks or designing a model can all be used to generate information of formative use to students and teachers alike. Given the right conditions, students come to see assessment as a natural part of how they learn in school, thus assessment as learning. This interpretation highlights the inter-relationship between AfL and the concepts of motivation, attribution of cause and self-regulated learning discussed earlier in the chapter. Whereas assessment can help the teacher to evaluate and redirect the focus of the planning, teaching, organisational strategies and teaching methods, fundamentally formative assessment offers feedback to students that can motivate and promote learning.

Understanding assessment for learning as part of a wider pedagogical context is central to proper understanding and to its successful implementation. AfL requires fundamental adjustments to teaching practices and students' engagement with learning, rather than merely attaching some novel assessment methods to teachers' existing practice. One of the key elements in understanding assessment as formative is that the results (feedback) are systematically used as part of the instructional system in the class or school to promote further learning (Wiliam, 2011: 4). In this regard, it is unhelpful and artificial to separate formative assessment from teaching pedagogy and classroom management.

AfL in policy and research contexts

One historical backdrop to the emergence of formative assessment internationally was the drive to improve educational standards through the administration of externally developed tests, especially in England and in the USA. Though intuitively appealing to policy-makers, the effects of these tests did not flow as intended, with declines in achievement in the USA, for example (Darling-Hammond and McCloskey, 2008). In England, the introduction of national testing at key stages coincided with a narrowing of the curriculum by teachers, some of whom focused disproportionately on what was tested, a phenomenon well identified in educational research internationally. Part of the problem with externally designed assessments is the mismatch between what policy-makers see as desirable learning and the views of teachers in class. Teachers make the real difference to what students learn, not assessments, so it is important that teachers are centrally involved in the design of the assessment and how it is implemented in class. Tests *brought in* from outside can reduce the role of the teacher in appraising the learning and planning the next steps. The legitimisation of formative assessment within education is evident in many systems. In England, formative assessment was promoted in the Primary National Strategy (DfES, 2006). Both Finland and Sweden adopted similar approaches, moving from centralised systems of assessment, so that now much of the assessment undertaken in primary and secondary schools in those countries is conducted by the teacher and used to provide immediate formative feedback to students to inform and enhance their learning. In Scotland, policy surrounding Assessment *is for* Learning followed from national debate in 2002 and was embedded in the recent Curriculum for Excellence. The revision of the Scottish curriculum into National 1 to 5 has reinforced the central role of the teacher in making professional judgements about students' achievement, skills, attributes and capabilities. Central to the message in Scotland is the holistic, informative nature of assessment whose most important function is to support the learner. In Ireland, the adoption of largely formative approaches to assessment (NCCA, 2007a) has provided a re-envisioned emphasis on assessment as a seamless part of what the teacher does on a daily basis in the classroom.

Analyses by the Organisation for Economic Cooperation and Development (OECD, 2005, 2013), possibly best known in education as a sponsor of large-scale international surveys such as PISA, also highlight the increasing importance of formative assessment as part of overall educational practice and reform. Amongst six key policy directions identified by the OECD (2013), one focuses on student assessment and 'putting the learner at the centre' (p. 9). Policy across member countries of the OECD now focuses on formative assessment, the active role of the teacher in assessment and building 'students' capacity to engage in their own assessment':

> Students should be fully engaged with their learning, contributing to the planning and organisation of lessons, having learning expectations communicated to them, assessing their learning and that of their peers, and benefitting from individualised support and differentiated learning. To become lifelong learners, students need to be able to assess their own progress, make adjustments to their understandings and take control of their own learning. (p. 13)

That position, strongly aligned with the basic tenets of AfL, is based on evidence for the value of such practices. Research suggests that the effective implementation of AfL has a positive impact on student learning and achievement, motivation, behaviour and ownership by students of their own learning (Wiliam, 2011; Faragher, 2014), with evidence of particular gains for low-achieving students. Benefits for teachers are also evident, with more positive, dynamic and collaborative relationships with students, improved relationships in class, fewer behaviour problems and greater teacher control over all aspects of professional practice, including assessment (in contexts where assessment was often imposed from the outside).

Some cautionary voices have been raised, however, about over-interpreting the potential of AfL to provide achievement gains that have been described as 'amongst the largest ever reported for educational interventions' (Black and Wiliam, 1998: 61). Bennett (2011), Dunn and Mulvenon (2009) and Kingston and Nash (2011) explore the research evidence of the past few decades on AfL in a wide variety of contexts, educational levels and formats. Their conclusions highlight the complexity of implementing truly formative assessment in practice and illustrate the need for focused research so that practice is evidence based. The reservations do not dismiss the potential of AfL to positively impact on learning; rather, they suggest that achieving such potential is perhaps more complicated than it might appear.

Join the debate: How strong is the evidence for AfL?

Use your library's online journal service to access the papers by Wiliam (2011) and Bennett (2011) listed in the further reading at the end of this chapter. With a colleague, role-play the two authors to advance 3–5 points that might capture the essential position of both. Try to frame a small number of key points of agreement between the authors in relation to the potential and effectiveness of AfL.

Chapter summary

Assessment that is designed to support learning needs to be framed and understood within the many dimensions, features and practices of teaching and learning. Theory on the nature of learning, learner attributes and the processes of teaching and learning shape and are themselves shaped by formative assessment. Tailoring instruction to the needs of students resonates well with policy in many modern education systems and has spawned many instructional programmes in the past few decades. Most initiatives require timely assessment of student learning to reveal the optimal next steps in learning. Whether diagnostic or formative assessment, it is clear that focused just-on-time assessment intuitively complements efficient and effective learning. For years, the use of assessment to measure what students had learnt dominated policy, with effects evident in classroom practice, not all of them as intended. More recent policy emphases support assessment by teachers as part of their professional role and the use of these assessments to direct teaching and learning. There is a considerable but not uncontested research base for the policy shift. We encourage you to engage with that debate on AfL with a view to incorporating evidence-based best practice in your professional practice.

Questions for discussion

1. Develop a lesson plan or strategy for a topic you hope to teach in one lesson. How will students know what is expected of them at the end of the lesson? What feedback (oral and/or written) will students get from you? How does this feedback relate to what is expected of students?

2. Imagine you are asked to make a presentation to a staff meeting on the topic of AfL. Make five slides for a PowerPoint/visual presentation showing how AfL links to the following:

    -   the instructional approach/pedagogy
    -   the self-regulation of learning by students.

3. Table 4.1 presents a number of definitions related to assessment. Consider how each definition relates to the three main questions underpinning AfL: Where am I now? Where am I going? How do I get there? Work with a colleague if possible.

Table 4.1   Assessment-related definitions

Definition of assessment	Question
'in the service of learning – the necessary intertwining of testing and teaching … woven into learning environments … offering executable advice to both students and teachers.' (Glaser, 1990: 480)	
'a process of collecting data for the purpose of making decisions about individuals and groups' (Salvia and Ysseldyke, 2001: 5)	
'specifically intended to provide feedback on performance to improve and accelerate learning' (Sadler, 1998: 77)	**Where am I now?**
'use of a diverse set of data for a purpose. That purpose is the modification of the learning work to adapt to the needs that are revealed by the evidence. Only when assessment evidence is acted upon in this way does it become formative' (Black, 1998: 105)	**Where am I going?**
'any assessment for which the first priority is to serve the purpose of promoting students' learning … it is usually informal, embedded in all aspects of teaching and learning, and conducted by different teachers as part of their own diverse and individual teaching styles' (Black et al., 2003: 2)	**How do I get there?**
'assessment that supports the learning process in contrast to assessment that measures the outcomes of learning' (Shepard, 2006: 626)	
' the process of gathering, recording, interpreting, using, and reporting information about a child's progress and achievement in developing knowledge, skills and attitudes' (NCCA, 2007a: 7)	

Further reading

Bennett, R.E. (2011). Formative assessment: a critical review. *Assessment in Education. Principles, Policy and Practice*, *18* (1), 5–25.

This is an analysis of assumptions, research and interpretations made about formative assessment. While not dismissing the claims made for AfL, the article highlights the contestable nature of some of the policy narrative in relation to AfL.

Clarke, S. (2005). *Formative assessment in action: Weaving the elements together*, and (2008). *Active learning through formative assessment*. London: Hodder Murray.

These two books provide accessible illustrations of some of the key practices associated with formative assessment, particularly in primary education. The work draws on collaborating teachers in a number of schools who provide worked examples of lesson plans featuring strong elements of formative assessment.

Swaffield, S. (ed.) (2008). *Unlocking assessment: Understanding for reflection and application.* Milton Park, Oxford: Routledge.

This edited volume contains chapters drawn from a range of authors in the field, many of whom are associated with the Assessment Reform Group in the UK. The book highlights formative approaches, issues of quality and the use of teacher judgements about students for summative purposes.

Wiliam, D. (2011). What is assessment for learning? *Studies in Educational Evaluation*, *37*, 3–14.

This article explores the nuanced differences in interpretations across terminology and practices related to formative assessment. The paper argues that clearly defined assessment in support of teaching and learning can improve student engagement and attainment.

Implementing assessment *for* learning
Techniques and illustrations for classroom use

What you will learn in this chapter

The previous chapter highlighted the richness and complexity of learning and the need for teachers to understand how to accommodate content, teaching methods and classroom management to the needs of students in class. Understanding students' previous learning, selecting appropriate content and creating suitable learning experiences are essential elements of teachers' craft. Systematic approaches to planning, classroom management, teaching and assessment help ensure that classrooms and the work of teachers and students are directed, enjoyable and productive. Good planning requires the consideration of curriculum guidelines, available resources, student characteristics and specific instructional/learning intentions and methodologies. Evaluation of the success of teaching is also important, both in terms of what and how the students have learned and the teacher's reflection on the process. The successful implementation of assessment for learning (AfL) requires that decisions about assessment permeate all stages of planning, teaching and learning. There is no one AfL event in a lesson or in a topic. Instead, we can look at assessment itself as learning, a seamless part of students' experience in class. This chapter illustrates the interconnected links between AfL and teaching. Readers who are enrolled in teacher education programmes may find some of the approaches outlined similar to the instructional methods content of some of their other modules and readings. This is the strength of AfL – it can and should be seen as part of teaching, not as something appended at the end of the class, topic or term.

When you finish the chapter, you should be able to answer these questions:

- What informal or semi-formal assessment opportunities exist in widely used teaching practices and methodologies?
- To what extent do existing instructional approaches require modification to yield real-time information of value to teachers and learners?
- How can I involve learners more in their own learning?

- How can learners understand their learning better and act on this information effectively?
- What feedback can assist both students and teachers in making learning more effective?

Effective teaching, learning and assessment

Chapter 1 explored the increasing role of professional codes of practice and their influence in shaping expectations of teachers in school. Such codes draw, in part, on evolving research on effective teaching, such as studies by Brophy and Good (1986), Kyriacou (2014), Mortimore (1993), Harris (1998), Marzano (2009), Ko et al. (2013), OECD (2014) and Schleicher (2016). This research highlights certain teaching behaviour, practices and skills that are associated with enhanced student learning, summarised in Table 5.1.

Table 5.1 Factors associated with effective teaching and learning

Teacher knowledge of subject matter and pedagogy	Students experiencing success
Well-organised teaching time	Quality of teacher questioning
Active instruction by teacher	Pacing of instruction
Coverage of relevant content	Designing activities suitable for students' ability and needs
Students engaged in learning	Teacher adaptability during lessons

Students learn better where teachers are highly structured in their approach, cover more content and allocate class time to relevant academic activities; where students and teachers are on-task in active student-oriented teaching approaches; and where students are enabled to achieve success in class. Teachers need to be knowledgeable about the content to be taught and how to teach it, and to think reflectively about the decisions to be made before, during and after instruction (Harris, 1998). Assessment plays a central role in influencing what and how students learn. The New Zealand educator, John Hattie, undertook a fascinating meta-analysis of over 800 different studies that themselves reviewed other research exploring what influences student achievement in school. Drawing on data based on millions of students worldwide, he explored variables identified as having an influence on achievement (most influences were positive, some negative). The review found that practices associated with formative assessment are amongst the most powerful correlates of student achievement. In a ranking of 138 potential influences, Hattie (2009) found that the contributions of formative evaluation, of feedback and of teaching meta-cognitive strategies were ranked third, tenth and thirteenth respectively. Figure 5.1 presents effect sizes associated with the top 10 influences on student achievement.

These influences are not trivial. For example, feedback was associated with a 'high' effect size of 0.73, indicating a three-quarters of a standard deviation increase in achievement where teachers draw on feedback about students' learning in class.

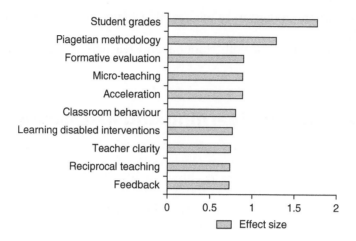

Figure 5.1   Influences on student achievement

Source: Adapted from Hattie (2009)

A one standard deviation increase in achievement is equivalent to accelerating a student by two to three years (Hattie, 2009). Therefore, such effects are clearly important, and distilling AfL approaches that can be incorporated into teaching practice is worthwhile.

Research has converged on a number of useful AfL strategies centred around sharing learning goals, providing effective feedback, the effective use of questioning and self- and peer assessment (Black and Wiliam, 1998; Clarke, 2005; OECD, 2005; Thompson and Wiliam, 2008). This list is reflected in guidelines and advice provided to teachers by a number of national educational agencies, as highlighted in a snapshot of education systems in Table 5.2. These and other strategies have become widespread across the globe and reflect a research-led desire to embed assessment within instruction.

This advice for teachers illustrates the extent to which AfL strategies have been mainstreamed into educational policy. In the remainder of the chapter, we will focus on a range of AfL strategies that are promoted frequently in education systems worldwide.

Table 5.2   Emphasis on key AfL strategies in selected education systems

	Ireland[1]	Northern Ireland[2]	Scotland[3]	New Zealand[4]	Norway[5]
Making learning goals explicit for students	✓	✓	✓	✓	✓
Providing useful feedback to students	✓	✓	✓	✓	✓
Questioning	✓	✓	✓	✓	✓
Self-assessment	✓	✓	✓	✓	✓
Peer assessment	✓	✓	✓	✓	

Sources: 1. NCCA (2015); 2. CCEA (2009); 3. Scottish Government (2011); 4. New Zealand Ministry of Education (2011); 5. Nusche et al. (2011)

In some recent development work with teachers, we sought to build teachers' capacity to develop, implement and successfully draw lessons from AfL in their teaching (Shiel and Murchan, 2011; Murchan, Shiel, et al., 2013). We facilitated a whole-school community-of-practice approach with associated external support provided to participants. This involved introducing teachers to possible AfL approaches and supporting the try-out and reflection on these ideas in school. This model provides a framework for embedding AfL in classroom practice by focusing on limited dimensions of assessment and creating opportunities for sustained practice with and discussion of the approaches. The approaches highlighted in the next sections of the chapter are a structured snapshot of a small number of methods. These will allow you to try out ideas, enjoy some successes, perhaps see some challenges, and then give you the confidence to embrace wider practice in the area of AfL. The further reading at the end of the chapter provides signposting to a number of additional sources worth visiting. Table 5.3 provides an overview of key dimensions of AfL with selected associated techniques. Many of these approaches will be outlined in the following sections.

Table 5.3   Selected AfL approaches for use in class

Dimension of AfL	Illustrative techniques
Identifying and communicating learning intentions	• Sharing learning intentions • Rapid student share/recap at end of lesson
Identifying and communicating success criteria	• Sharing criteria with learners • Sharing exemplars of work at different levels of quality
Providing useful feedback	• Comment-only marking • Using rubrics
Effective questioning	• Collaborative generation of diverse questions • Private–Intimate–Public
Peer assessment	• Two stars and a wish • Pre-flight checklist
Self-assessment	• Traffic lights • Know–Want–Learned (KWL)

Source: Adapted from Thompson and Wiliam (2008)

Using AfL approaches with your students

Successful implementation of AfL involves professional learning, whether as part of initial teacher education or continuing professional development. We found that individual try-out coupled with collaborative reflection provides incremental success for teachers, that in turn leads to a more successful and productive learning experience for students. Throughout the chapter, therefore, we prompt you to try out some ideas and reflect on experiences with your study group or colleagues in school. The website accompanying the book provides useful material and templates to assist in this reflective learning.

Personalities in educational assessment: Paul Black

Paul Black's work has spanned formative and summative assessment, though it is for the former that he is probably best known. An emeritus professor in the school of education, communication and society of at King's College London, his work with Dylan Wiliam influenced a generation of assessment researchers and educational policy-makers. Their co-publication *Assessment and Classroom Learning* in 1998 collated existing literature on classroom formative assessment, concluding that such assessment had immense potential for the improvement of educational practice. Black was an active member of the Assessment Reform Group in the UK, a group dedicated to the formulation of educational policy informed by research. He has been a champion of formative assessment through his research, writing and professional speaking worldwide and has been active in research and advisory roles since his retirement.

Letting learners in on the secret: identify and communicate learning intentions

The need for careful planning for teaching is emphasised in initial teacher education programmes and as part of continuing professional development for teachers. Like other professionals, teachers are encouraged to plan their work carefully so that the likelihood of success is increased. Imagine the lawyer who comes into court to take a case for which there has been little advanced planning, or the nurse who approaches a patient without being first familiar with the relevant patient history! Consider the application of sports stars, musicians and artists to their craft. Few remarkable achievements are founded on the basis of luck. The great South-African golfer Gary Player, once characterised by an onlooker as lucky in holing three bunker shots in a row, famously quipped: 'the more I practice, the luckier I get'.

In teaching, planning helps guide its direction and provides a coherent strategy, context and resources for the development of learning opportunities for students. Some of the features of AfL presented below require very few extra resources on the part of teachers, other than some adjustment to the use of time and methodology in class. Research on the psychology of learning highlights benefits in using advanced organisers, including learning objectives in class, helping students to understand and prepare for the work that is to come (Stone, 1983; Joyce et al., 2000). Applied to AfL, this encourages teachers to share their own understanding of what students should learn with students themselves. This can take a variety of formats, including general discussion with students and highlighting the expected learning on a whiteboard, PowerPoint slide or a combination of both. Teachers can facilitate students in activating their prior knowledge to enhance attention, motivation, understanding and retention. In introducing a new topic, for example, you can encourage students to discuss what they know about it and make predictions about it. This can give students more control over their learning and enables them to assimilate new learning more effectively within their existing mental schemas.

Research supports the sharing of learning outcomes/intentions with students. Shirley Clarke (2005, 2008), working with a number of schools in England, found that this seemingly simple action was recognised by both teachers and primary students themselves as a valuable step in enhancing students' understanding of learning. Sharing the learning intention provides a clearly understood reference point that students can use in reflecting on their learning. By converting the teacher's lesson objectives or learning outcomes into learning intentions phrased in a more student-friendly way, the teacher can then facilitate suitable lesson activities, relevant resources and opportunities for reflection to support the intention.

Case study   Lena and the youth club

Geoff teaches English as a second language to lower-secondary students. He wished to reinforce the concepts of 'used to', plus the infinitive, then and now (before and after), using a story about a teenager's life (Lena) before and after she joined a youth club – for instance, Lena used to *stay* at home and *play* computer games; used to *watch* TV; used to *talk* to friends on the phone. Now, after joining the youth club, Lena *plays* basketball every Friday night, *helps* out with a drama group and *travels* to other clubs in the area.

To prepare students for this learning, Geoff prepared a *learning intention*, as follows, and wrote it on the whiteboard:

'We will use the idea of "then and now" to learn how to say sentences using the correct form of verbs.' He spent about 4 minutes at the start of the lesson talking about the intention, encouraging students to talk about what they used to do then and what they do now, using primary school and secondary school as the contrasting contexts. Then he read the story about Lena and posed some questions to the class. At the end of the class, the students referred back to the learning intention to consider their progress in this language concept.

This case study illustrates the importance of activating students' awareness of, interest in and possibility of engaging with the learning by sharing the purpose of the lesson with them. This is important because students often feel that lessons happen and then end without their really understanding and appreciating the purpose or direction of the lesson (Earl, 2013). Learning requires the active engagement of students themselves and a willingness and motivation to persevere and succeed. The chances of this happening are increased when teachers clearly communicate to students what they are expected to know in language that they can understand. Furthermore, once students are aware of what they should learn, the teacher needs to scaffold the learning process and provide explanations, illustrations or exemplars of the expected learning. This demonstrates an important concept in the use of learning intentions as part of AfL. Learning intentions are designed to help students understand what they will learn about during an instructional period. Because they are primarily aids to student learning rather than to teacher planning, learning intentions should be phrased in terms such as: *We are learning to understand how electrical currents work; we are learning how to use a calculator to solve complex calculations; we are learning about the importance of nutrition for health; we are learning to use adverbs to improve our creative writing.*

In our own professional development work with teachers and also in working with student teachers, participants report that their students do engage with beginning-of-class discussions around learning intentions and that the intentions provide students with a language and framework for discussing their learning at the end of the lesson. The more the learning intentions describe the learning rather than the task, the richer the post-lesson discussion and self-appraisal by students. Furthermore, the shorter the learning intention and the more accessible the language used to describe it, the easier it is for students to remember it.

Activity 5.1

Try this out – Identify and communicate learning intentions

In this chapter, we provide some strategies to get you started using AfL. The first two are presented below. The companion website includes some prompt sheets to lead you through use of the strategies. Each sheet contains prompts to help you try the strategy with students in class. Record your experience and reaction to the prompts and follow your own learning. Good luck, and remember, there are no right answers to the prompt sheets. We've tried these activities out with student teachers and experienced teachers and know that it can take a few attempts to become comfortable with the strategies. What really works is if you can discuss your experiences with one or more colleagues and learn from each other.

Putting learning intention on board	End-of-lesson rapid student share/recap
Convert teacher's learning objectives into a student-friendly format. Generally, present one or two clear learning intentions. If needed, clarify with a small number of sub-intentions. Write on one section of board and discuss with students (2–5 minutes)	Briefly revisit learning intention as part of lesson conclusion. Ask a small number of students to briefly tell the class (share) something they learned in the lesson. Teacher and other students can evaluate these comments in relation to the lesson intention written on the board. Be sensitive in dealing with any student misconceptions identified. If possible, address misconception on the spot. Otherwise, note and address at start of next lesson

Visit the companion website at: https://study.sagepub.com/murchanshiel

Creating expectations: Helping learners understand their progress

Students need to know what success is if they are to become self-aware as learners and regulate their own learning: How will I know that I have learned? How will I know if I have achieved the learning intention? Teachers can help students recognise the type of learning that is expected (the finish line) and scaffold their journey towards that goal. Teachers, in addition to taking responsibility for classroom management, resources and lesson scope and sequence, also need to help students understand the nature and level of work required to achieve the learning goal. In other words, teachers need to explore with students the success criteria that will enable them to know to what extent they are successful in learning. At its simplest, sharing success criteria (or, better still, involving students in the development of success criteria) helps students know what to aim for. Students benefit from illustrations of successful learning, whether through rich discussion, provision of exemplars of student work or looking at the work of their peers in class. Many teachers use rubrics to assess work, where dimensions of the work are assigned to different levels of quality. Success criteria should then be visible to students, for example written on a whiteboard. Teachers sometimes use strategies such as WALT (We Are Learning To…) and WILF (What I'm Looking For) to simplify and aid students' understanding of the desired learning.

Ideally, success criteria should not be interpreted or presented like a 'solution' to a test question. Rather, you should offer students clarity about what constitutes achievement of the learning intention without giving step-by-step guidelines to follow. Success criteria provide more general statements about what strategies to use and about what the evidence of success will look like. As highlighted in Chapter 4, students need to monitor their own learning and take responsibility for that learning in class. Simply telling students in minute detail what they must do is not the same as fostering students' independent learning. Through careful discussion of success criteria, the teacher and students come to an understanding of the type of strategies and performances that will demonstrate that students have learned.

Teachers often identify the success criteria at the same time as the learning intention and both are communicated to students at about the same time, that is, at the beginning of the lesson. It may be preferable sometimes to delay an extensive discussion of the success criteria until students have had an opportunity to engage with the learning through the context of the lesson and/or the assigned tasks. Sometimes only when students have engaged with the task will they be able to comment more fully on the evidence for successful learning. This provides a solid opportunity to involve students more fully in the process of establishing the success criteria. One teacher we worked with shared her rationale for delaying the introduction of success criteria in a specific lesson developed as part of a set of lessons on a topic in Business Studies, noting that 'success criteria give students a goal and confidence. Students had already covered the topic up to a certain point so they came up with the success criteria themselves'.

Case study   School club

Ms Johnson wanted students in her Spanish class to learn vocabulary related to teenagers' pastimes. She wanted students to engage in conversation about starting a school club. The learning intention for a lesson was: 'We will be able to develop ideas in Spanish for a conversation about setting up a new school club.' Developing this lesson, Ms Johnson asked the class to listen to an audio clip where two students discussed setting up a photography club. Following this, students in her class were to work in groups of 3–4 to come up with ideas for setting up a new club in the school. Students and teacher agreed on the following success criteria:

(Continued)

(Continued)

- Identify a new club that would be of interest to some students in the school.
- Write at least one rule in Spanish for joining the club.
- Write some text in Spanish for a short conversation about the club.

The class listened to the recorded conversation and the teacher led a class discussion identifying the three success criteria evident. Student groups then engaged with the task, writing joining rules and conversational text in relation to clubs for baking, journalism, dancing, the environment, mathematics and singing.

Activity 5.2

Try this out – Explore success criteria

Use the companion website prompts when trying out the following strategies in class. Reflect on your experience with a colleague. Remember, there are no right answers to the prompts, only experiences to reflect on. Avoid defining too many success criteria. Otherwise, you will essentially provide minute instructions to students in how to complete tasks. The responsibility for learning rests with students and they need to make the decisions to help them decide whether or not they have achieved the learning intention.

Write criteria on board	Teacher shares exemplars of work at different levels of quality
For a lesson of your choice, develop one main task or learning activity to support the learning intention. What criteria can students use to gauge their success in relation to this activity? Through discussion, help your students to understand the main criteria. Record criteria on the board alongside the learning intention. Express criteria simply and clearly to let students know how they can demonstrate their learning in relation to the intention	Examples of work related to the learning intention and success criteria are shared with students. The examples might be newly developed by the teacher or, over time, sourced from students who have completed similar tasks previously. Try to provide examples that clearly show different quality levels in the work, perhaps using two or three levels of quality. In addition to providing examples, discuss the characteristics of the examples with the class to ensure that they can identify (i) the success criteria and (ii) the differences in quality evident in different examples

Visit the companion website at: https://study.sagepub.com/murchanshiel

Using questions effectively to elicit and promote learning

Teachers spend a lot of time asking questions of students in class and many generally believe that this is one of the most powerful forms of assessment that they use. Purposes and benefits of teacher questioning include the following:

- Keep students engaged in the lesson.
- Clarify important points in a lesson.
- Reinforce ideas.
- Scaffold learning.
- Establish baseline knowledge.
- Monitor progress and check understanding.
- Challenge misconceptions.
- Provide feedback to teachers during learning, thus allowing for immediate intervention to address misunderstandings.
- Assist in judgements about students' thinking and learning processes.
(Ofsted, 1996; Harris, 1998; Nitko and Brookhart, 2014; Kyriacou, 2014)

Wrong answers may be as useful as correct answers since they provide teachers with opportunities to probe students' understanding in greater depth and enable scaffolding of learning. What we also know about questioning by teachers is, however, that in the form practised it may not be as effective as teachers think. Teachers typically ask 200–400 questions per day (Wragg, 1997; Hattie, 2009), of which half focus on students' recall of facts and information and 20% focus on analysis (Stiggins, Griswold & Wikelund, 1989). Nor do teachers wait long for students' answers – some estimates being only about 1 second, despite the obvious fact that waiting for answers conveys the impression to students that teachers are genuinely curious about the question and the answer (Hattie, 2012; Kyriacou, 2014). Increasing the 'wait time' by even a few seconds can result in an improved length and quality of response by students. The challenges with questioning strategies are also illustrated by research that shows that 70% of student answers are less than 5 seconds in duration, or only about three words. Wragg (1997) reported that in a study of 1000 teachers' questioning practices in the UK, one-third of students' answers met with no response at all by teachers. All this does not suggest the coherent application of a powerful pedagogical tool by teachers, and we can conclude that much questioning practice at present is not really a recipe for rich dialogue and debate in class.

More systematic yet creative approaches to teacher questioning are required if it is to provide usable information and feedback to students and teachers to optimise the next steps in learning. For this reason, getting questioning right goes to the heart of getting AfL right. Below, we identify a number of ways and approaches to maximise the chance that the questions that are posed in class are of high quality and can contribute useful information to teachers and students about student learning.

Teachers need to distinguish between 'open' and 'closed' questions. Closed (convergent) questions typically require short 'correct' answers reflective of lower-order thinking such as memorisation and recall. Typically, there is only one correct answer, as in 'Is seven a prime number?' Sometimes we draw on the 'W' questions: what, who, when, where, as in the examples: What is Guy Fawkes night? Who was Guy Fawkes? When is he remembered each year? Where was the gunpowder stored? We need to realise, however, that many of these are closed questions, encouraging the student to 'converge' on one correct answer. While such recall is undoubtedly important as a first stage in learning material, exposure only to lower-order questions will certainly restrict students' capacity to engage in deep and meaningful learning. In contrast, 'open' questions typically assume a number of possible correct answers, promote more elaborate responses and link with higher-order thinking such as organisation, analysis, problem solving and speculation. For example, asking a student 'Why is 7 an example of a prime number?' helps the teacher to explore better the student's understanding.

Question prompts with rich assessment opportunities

How can we be sure that...?

What is the same and what is different about...?

Is it ever/always true/false that...?

How would you explain...?

What does that tell us about...?

What is wrong with...?

Why is ... true?

A widely established method of classifying questions draws on Bloom's Taxonomy of Educational Objectives (Bloom et al., 1956). Curricula, teaching materials and teachers themselves across the world have drawn on this taxonomy for decades. Bloom's taxonomy of objectives has undergone various revisions since it was published (Anderson and Krathwohl, 2001; Krathwohl, 2002). The case study below illustrates a number of questions matched to the six different levels of one such revision by Anderson and Krathwohl (2001). The revised taxonomy is noted in the further reading list at the end of this chapter (see the article by Krathwohl). Though designed originally for the specification of instructional objectives (the forerunner to learning outcomes and intentions), the principles underpinning the taxonomy apply equally to developing test questions in traditional testing and to oral questioning by teachers as part of AfL.

Case study   Questioning at different skill levels

Mr Remous introduces the poem 'The Snare' to his P4 class. He asks questions to the class and they have to use Think–Pair–Share to address the questions. The teacher uses Anderson and Krathwohl's category system in developing some questions:

1. *Remember*: Where is the rabbit? What noise is the rabbit making?
2. *Understand*: Why is the rabbit crying? Why is the rabbit wrinkling up his face?
3. *Apply*: What do you think will happen next?
4. *Analyse*: What evidence in the poem suggests that the poet will be unable to help?

The Snare

I hear a sudden cry of pain!

There is a rabbit in a snare:

Now I hear the cry again,

But I cannot tell from where.

But I cannot tell from where

He is calling out for aid!

Crying on the frightened air,

Making everything afraid!

Making everything afraid!

Wrinkling up his little face!

5. *Evaluate*: How suitable is this poem for younger children such as those in P1? Why? What might they get from it?
6. *Create*: The rabbit can speak and calls out directions to the poet to find him. Write up the conversation between the rabbit and poet.

As he cries again for aid;

And I cannot find the place!

And I cannot find the place

Where his paw is in the snare!

Little One! Oh, Little One!

I am searching everywhere!

James Stephens

Table 5.4 provides further information on how Anderson and Krathwohl's taxonomy can be of help to teachers at primary and at secondary school levels in developing diverse questions to assess different types of thinking and learning.

Table 5.4   Higher- and lower-order question types based on Anderson and Krathwohl's (2001) taxonomy

Category	Illustrative questions as part of AfL
Remember material (content, procedures, patterns previously learnt)	Who are the main characters in the story?
	Name three types of triangles.
	How many elements in the periodic table are acidic?
	When was the Magna Carta written?
Understand or grasp the meaning of material	Based on the passage you've just read, is the story set in the town or in the countryside?
	I will play two bars of music on the keyboard. I will play them twice. Then tell me what notes you heard.
	Tell me one example of air pollution discussed in the YouTube video we have just watched.
	Look at this invitation to a party, written in Italian. Translate it into English.
Apply what students have learned in concrete or new situations	We have discussed different types of friendships that people have: tell me how these relate to the friendships you have.
	Nicola wants to follow a high carbohydrate diet. Suggest some foods she could eat for dinner.
	Tell me how you might use the mathematical concept of the median (average) in a history project.
Analyse the details and structure of material being learned	What patterns can you see in the way these verbs change when you are using the future tense?
	What might explain the results you presented about how different materials float in water?
	What dramatic techniques does the author use to create a feeling of despair in the play?
	From your reading of the newspaper article about the UK's Brexit negotiations with the EU, what are the main obstacles to future British membership of the European Economic Area (EEA)?

(Continued)

Table 5.4   (Continued)

Category	Illustrative questions as part of AfL
Evaluate or judge the purpose or value of material	What makes this a good piece of handwriting? How could it be improved?
	We will look at [one of the students in the PE lesson] demonstrate a mat roll. Afterwards, tell me three criteria we could use to judge that roll.
	Which of these three slogans is likely to have the greatest impact in the TV ad for mobile phones?
	Now that you have looked at the case study, should the company build the new shopping centre on the green-field site or the brown-field site?
Create or synthesise different aspects of the learning	Think of a suitable name for the piece of music we have just heard.
	How might you encourage the school principal to let our class go on a trip to see the [history event]?
	Tell me some different ways you could check a prospective company client's credit history.
	Think of some ways you could check if a demand exists for introducing chocolate milk into the school's canteen.

Selected strategies for effective questioning in AfL

Effective questioning increases the quality of information flow about student learning and enables a better targeting of instruction. It also creates a richer, more stimulating environment in class where students are more likely to become motivated and engage. Interesting detail about different types of questions and useful questioning strategies for teachers are available in Cohen et al. (2004), Walsh and Dolan (2009) and Kyriacou (2014), for example. Below, we outline some approaches that you can use to improve and diversify your questioning techniques, and therefore to generate richer information about student learning. One approach, developed by Husbands (1996), focused on providing students with separate sequential opportunities for developing and sharing their ideas in class – in private, then in small groups, and finally in open plenary discussion. This process is sometimes termed Private–Intimate–Public (PIP). A strategy that teachers can easily embed in normal classroom interaction, PIP discourages hands-up by students. A number of simple stages are followed in sequence:

- Stage 1: *Private* – students individually write down their responses to the teacher's oral or written question
- Stage 2: *Intimate* – students compare responses with each other through pair or group discussion
- Stage 3: *Public* – the answers become public, when the pairs or groups are invited to report back. Students can assess each other's answers.

A number of variants to this approach are possible. You can ask pairs or groups to provide an 'agreed' answer, or to pick the best one for communication to the teacher or class. *Think–Pair–Share* is very similar in format to PIP. The Think–Pair–Square variant involves recording individual answers within each group of, say, four students on a sheet of paper. The group then agrees the 'best' of the answers which is recorded in a square drawn in the middle of the sheet. Whatever variant is used, the aim is the same:

increase the amount of time that each student spends engaging with questions posed in class, and thereby increase the quantity and quality of information available about student learning. A number of additional strategies are provided below.

Activity 5.3

Try this out – Promoting more effective questioning

Use the companion website prompts when trying out the following strategies in class. Reflect on your experience with a colleague.

Generating more diverse questions (collaboratively)

Teachers pose questions (oral and written) in class that probe students' learning in relation to a variety of content and skill areas. Some questions may check students' factual knowledge and understanding; other questions should focus on more high-level cognitive skills, requiring deeper reflection and possibly multiple correct answers. It can be helpful for teachers to use a relatively limited number of questions in any one lesson, but plan the questions more systematically; perhaps beforehand in writing to ensure that they are actually presented to students as intended. If possible, work with a colleague or a group of colleagues to generate a pool of high-quality questions that are tried out in class over time.

Students identifying easy and difficult questions

This activity is designed to build students' metacognitive knowledge. The ultimate goal is that students will reflect more on the questions they are asked to respond to, and on what is needed to answer a question correctly.

Provide students with a set of questions based on work under way in class. First, ask them to answer the questions individually or in pairs. Then, ask them to categorise the questions using a two-point scale (easy, difficult). Ask students to explain why they think questions are easy or difficult. For older students, a four-point scale might be used (very easy, quite easy, somewhat difficult, very difficult).

Student-generated questions

Students spend a lot of time answering questions posed by the teachers. They can benefit greatly, however, from developing their own questions, to reflect on what they already know, to identify further information they need to discover and to relate their understanding. Students are divided into pairs or groups of 3–4. Each student is asked to write a few questions related to the lesson – perhaps two easy questions and two more difficult ones. Students work in pairs to answer each other's questions:

- Students explain why questions are easy or difficult.
- Students suggest changes to the question they wrote to improve them.
- Students summarise what they have learned from taking part in the activity.

Question–answer relationships (QARs)

An adaptation of Raphael and Au's (2005) work involves asking students to categorise questions according to the level of *thinking* that the answer requires. Students first categorise questions according to where they believe the answer is located, either:

- in the text/diagram/resource/stimulus (the answer is clearly evident *or* requires me to think and search the stimulus to locate it); or
- in my head (I can get the answer by drawing on previously encountered information *or* I need to combine information contained in the stimulus with my own knowledge).

Students then use this metacognitive information to respond to the questions.

Visit the companion website at: https://study.sagepub.com/murchanshiel

Peer assessment

Two key theories explored in Chapter 4 relate significantly to peer and self-assessment practices.

First, social constructivist interpretations of learning highlight the collaborative nature of effective learning and the role that students as a cohesive group play in their own development in school. Embedding constructivist principles in classroom practice is facilitated by approaches such as using knowledge of student pre-conceptions, student inquiry, active learning, collaborative learning, and self-reflection by students and teachers. Given the inter-related nature of planning, teaching, learning and assessment, constructivist interpretations of learning need to be reflected in the assessment approaches used by teachers and students. The worthwhile effort that goes into creating communities of active inquiry-oriented learners in classrooms is undermined if approaches to assessment do not involve students in collaboratively engaging with assessment tasks, interpretations and reporting. Creating opportunities for students to review the work of their classmates fosters coherence across teaching, learning and assessment dimensions. If we view assessment *as* learning (Dann, 2014; Hayward, 2015), then the work of students in assessing their peers *is* learning, and thus, both assessor and partner should benefit from the process.

Second, there is an obvious parallel between peer and self-assessment and self-regulated learning and the processes by which students themselves increasingly take on the role of their own teachers in monitoring and adjusting their own learning. In separate studies of Dutch children in upper-primary classes and at lower vocational level, Pat-El et al. (2011) and Baas et al. (2015) focused on two dimensions of AfL: its monitoring and scaffolding functions. In these studies, AfL practices helped students to monitor their own learning and engage in appropriate subsequent steps with the result that metacognitive strategies and cognitive outcomes were improved. This 'ceding [of] responsibility to students in taking control of their own learning' (Baas et al., 2015: 33) can be facilitated through strategies such as peer and self-assessment. This is a useful way to conceptualise peer assessment. On a practical level, it can be very challenging and inefficient for teachers to act as the sole assessor of learning in class. Sharing the assessment role with the students themselves allows teachers to place more of the onus for learning and for monitoring learning on the students themselves, enabling them to achieve greater levels of intrinsic motivation and knowledge about and control over their learning. Transferring some responsibility for assessment to students themselves also fits with the socio-cultural perspective on assessment, as well as ensuring that individual students receive more feedback more frequently and more swiftly (Topping, 2013).

For peer assessment to work in class, the learning pairs or groups must be clear about the learning intentions and associated success criteria. Peer assessment should involve students in manageable chunks of assessment, whereby both the specific aspect of learning to be assessed and the criteria and approach to assessing it are clear. A summary of some important points about peer assessment is presented below:

- Peer assessment can provide students with the confidence, skills and tools to constructively monitor the learning of other students and also their own learning. It should benefit both assessor and assessed.

- Students need support and structure for appraising their work. This support should provide clarity about the learning intention(s) and success criteria, along with advice on how to provide feedback to their peers.
- Feedback to peers should be specific, linked to the learning outcomes and success criteria, and should be fair and sensitive.
- Students may need help in distinguishing between friendship groups and learning groups. Peer assessment is most effective with learning groups where the purpose of the group is to learn.
- Students need to see themselves as working in a positive learning environment that promotes a culture of mutual respect and learning.
- Peer assessment offers an increased opportunity for on-task dialogue amongst all students in the class in relation to specific learning.

These criteria require considerable commitment and skill on the part of students and we cannot assume that students will already possess such traits and expertise. Depending on students' prior familiarity with peer assessment, you may need to model and coach sound peer-assessment practice. For example, ensure students focus on the work rather than on the person; ensure critique is positive and constructive; and ensure that learning groups rotate over time so that students get the opportunity to work with several different peers and to see a range of work. Topping (2013) recommends against putting together in pairs or groups students who are very friendly or those who do not relate well to each other in class or socially.

Below, we introduce a few strategies to get you started on peer assessment, beginning with a case study of one lower-secondary teacher who used a simple checklist to enlist the help of her pupils in assessing each other's learning of English poetic technique.

Case study   Using checklists to scaffold peer assessment

Ms Allen's first-year English class completed three lessons on poetic technique. A homework exercise asked the students to apply their understanding by writing a short piece of poetry using different poetic techniques. In class the next day, the teacher discussed a checklist, presented on a PowerPoint slide, to assist learning partners in identifying and assessing poetic technique in each other's work. Students looked for the presence of onomatopoeia, alliteration, simile and other features of language. Application of the checklist involved placing sticky notes on examples of the poetic techniques and also required dialogue between the partners. For example, if a student was unable to find a use of simile, they asked their partner if it was included and, if so, to identify it. The teacher circulated amongst the students as they engaged in the peer assessment: 'I could walk around and see how everybody got on – it allowed me to see very clearly if people had problems with specific terms or techniques. Students were quick to say to each other "I just can't see that!"'

The case above illustrates an interesting feature of peer assessment, identified by Black et al. (2003) and Topping (2013). Students often quickly 'withdraw' from the teacher's probing about whether they understand something or not, pretending that they understand when, in fact, they do not, thus missing a rich opportunity for addressing misconceptions. This can be the result of not wishing to reveal that they still don't know after a concept has been explained a second time. Ms Allen's reflection on the checklist assessment shows that genuine and sustained dialogue about learning and misconceptions are possible in class, though it may happen more amongst students than between students and teacher!

Activity 5.4

Try this out – Promoting peer assessment

Use the companion website prompts when trying out the following strategies in class. Reflect on your experience with a colleague.

Two stars and a wish	Pre-flight checklist
This technique provides a positive, developmental structure to enable students to evaluate and provide feedback on each other's work. Students swap work and reflect on what they see.	This strategy, promoted by Thompson and Wiliam (2008), helps ensure that work submitted to the teacher meets at least minimum standards in relation to the success criteria. Students swap work (diagram, artefact, essay) and the partner cross-checks the work against a clear set of criteria established and known to all students. The check is to ensure that essential, oftentimes structural, elements are included. The reader is not asked to judge the quality of the work, but rather to report back to the author (other student) on what is included and what is missing. The author has an opportunity to act on this report prior to the final submission of the work.
The reader seeks to identify two positive elements/ideas that are evident in the work (two stars). He/she also tries to identify one aspect of the work where some development could be achieved. It is important not to be too prescriptive about the tasks facing the reader. Perhaps only one star is evident, or perhaps there are more than two? Perhaps the reader is satisfied with the work and no wish is recorded? In any event, it is the process of viewing others' work using structured evaluative tools (stars, wishes) that make the technique worthwhile. Communicating the stars and wishes can be in oral, written or other form (e.g. drawing, image, with younger students). This technique can also be used by the teacher in assessing and providing feedback to students and it can be used by a student in relation to his/her own work (self-assessment).	

Students construct and apply a scoring rubric. The following steps may be used:

1. Students complete some learning or product (e.g. dramatic activity, speech, piece of writing, project, report on experiment).
2. Teacher and students together develop a scoring rubric. Students have some say in deciding what the components of the rubric are.

3. Students break into cooperative learning groups or into pairs and apply the rubric to each other's work.
4. Students reflect and report on what they learned from applying the scoring rubric. For example, they might describe how they will improve their work on the next occasion.

An example of a scoring rubric assessing one dimension of a writing task:

Criteria – Structure of a Narrative Text

5	Elaborated story – well-developed sequence of episodes
4	Extended story – clearly defined sequence of episodes
3	Developed story – sequence of episodes developed but incomplete
2	Basic story – series of events – lacks cohesion
1	Undeveloped story – list of unrelated events

Visit the companion website at: https://study.sagepub.com/murchanshiel

There are many advantages associated with peer assessment, in terms of improved student awareness, monitoring, confidence, self-esteem, motivation and self-regulation. An additional benefit is the immediacy of the feedback for all students. The comment by one learner in further education surely applies also in both primary and secondary schooling: 'our teacher takes so long to mark our work, we've forgotten what it was about by the time we get it back' (Armitage et al., 2012: 162). Peer assessment enables students to remain actively on task in relation to both assessment and learning while reviewing a peer's work, providing feedback, receiving feedback and discussing the work. While no class could exclusively use peer assessment, its judicious use releases the responsibility from the teacher to review every piece of work and instead allows more time to observe the process of assessment, with nobody 'waiting' to hear about their work from the teacher. In your own teaching, you won't be long in also discovering the challenges. Students can be reluctant and uncomfortable in assessing each other's work, perhaps expecting that this is the teacher's role. This suggests the need for training and ongoing support for students, in part through the provision or co-development of rubrics. Enabling students to see the value of an assessment culture in class is vital. When students understand that sharing their work with other students is a normal part of their learning, they come to see that they learn from the peer comments and have the opportunity to actively discuss their work in class, much more than if the assessment and monitoring role is reserved solely for the teacher.

Self-assessment

Teachers sometimes find it easier to introduce students to peer assessment before self-assessment. This helps students to gauge the quality of other students' work prior to applying similar procedures and rubrics to their own work. Once embedded in classroom practice, self-assessment can provide a vehicle for directing students' thoughts, feelings and behaviours in working towards specific goals.

It seems obvious to say that students need to know what they are learning in order that they may assess their own progress. The targets of the learning need to be made clear to students if self-assessment is to be successful. Formative use of self-assessment assumes that the process will yield insights for the student or teacher to enable further learning.

For students, self-assessment involves a number of important tasks and stages. These include: initially recognising the nature of the work completed or the student's own academic ability; describing that work or ability; and making qualitative judgements in relation to their own learning by engaging with the feedback and actions suggested by that judgement. The latter element might not necessarily be present for summative assessment, but is central to the use of self-assessment for formative purposes. Self-assessment can be used for formative and summative purposes, but its most valuable use is in relation to helping students take more responsibility for their own learning. Self-assessment promotes engagement, achievement, self-esteem, confidence and self-regulation of learning (Sebba et al., 2008; Flórez and Sammons, 2013). It can contribute to richer dialogue between teachers and students and between students and their peers, focusing more productively on learning and standards.

As with peer assessment, students need to be provided with appropriate knowledge, skills and tools if they are to succeed with self-assessment. Simply encouraging students to assess their own work without detailed guidance will not succeed in the absence of appropriate scaffolding by the teacher. Students require clear criteria to use as a basis for describing, judging and learning from their own work. If we consider that without the use of rubrics, teachers' judgement of student work is subject to error (Harlen, 2007), it is obvious that students need sound scaffolding processes such as clear criteria and rubrics when assessing their own work. The introduction of normative dimensions to self-assessment (comparing my work with illustrations of the work of other students) can further help a student understand better and judge his/her own work, thus illustrating the usefulness of peer assessment as an aid to training students for self-assessment. The use of rubrics (and samples of other students' work) enables the student to link their judgement to specific elements or indicators of quality in the work. For example, one language teacher at secondary level used a very simple checklist rubric to assist students in peer-assessing essays on the topic of alcohol abuse. Use of basic criteria such as evidence of an essay plan or guiding points, presence of title, essay length, length of sentences and unclear syntax gave students clear criteria for approaching the task. The teacher noted that the students wished to go further and apply the same criteria in self-assessing their own essays subsequently. Research in Scotland with students both at the end of primary and beginning of secondary school showed that students could successfully appraise the quality of their own science investigations (ASG South Ayrshire, n.d.). This study contrasted the quality of students' own self-assessment where some students related their work to success criteria, but other students used rubrics in addition to the criteria. Use of the rubrics resulted in better assessments, a finding consistent with the benefits for teachers of using rubrics.

Promoting self-assessment by students is a priority learning skill in an increasing number of education systems. The list below highlights five student characteristics associated with effective teaching and learning identified by education authorities in one state in the USA. Review this list and note the importance attached to self-assessment:

- recognises good work and identifies steps for improving own work
- monitors progress towards reaching learning targets
- periodically assesses own work or that of peers
- uses feedback (teacher- and peer-generated) to improve own work
- reflects on work and makes adjustments as learning occurs.
  (Kentucky Department of Education, 2015)

Activity 5.5

Try this out – Self-assessment

Use the companion website prompts when trying out the following strategies in class. Reflect on your experience with a colleague.

Traffic lights

This technique has the advantage of (i) promoting students' self-reflection on their learning and understanding, while at the same time (ii) efficiently communicating information to the teacher in relation to the progress of each individual student and the class as a whole. Each student has three discs: Green signifies *I understand*; Yellow *I am not sure*; and Red *I don't understand*. At various points (not always at the end of the lesson), the teacher invites students to indicate, by a show of cards, their level of understanding of the topic or concept. Variations of this can be used, for example one large 'set' of traffic lights in the classroom which is used by the teacher to elicit student responses or smiley faces (very happy, confused, sad) for use with younger learners. The teacher needs to make concrete use of the information gleaned from the traffic lights. Try to address issues where difficulties in learning are indicated by the self-assessment process. Be aware of student apprehension about disclosing a lack of understanding of topics to their peers. Some teachers we have worked with occasionally ask students to close their eyes during traffic-lighting assessments. What will you do if you observe many red lights amongst your class?

KWL chart (What I know, What I want to know, What I learned)

At the beginning of the lesson (or topic), ask students to record in writing what they already know about a topic and what they want to know. At the end of the lesson (or topic), the students record what they have learned. The teacher reviews the written responses for further discussion with students and to plan the next steps in instruction (possibly involving revision or clarification). A variant of this involves a true–false game at the start of class. The teacher provides various statements about the topic and students identify whether the statements are true or false. This encourages rich debate in class about a topic and allows for the correction of misconceptions by students themselves.

(Continued)

(Continued)

Learning logs or journals

Learning logs or journals are a good way of encouraging students to reflect on what they have learned and to identify aspects they want to find out more about. Learning logs may be read by the teacher, or by peers, depending on what has been decided in advance. Logs as a self-assessment approach can provide valuable feedback to the teacher as they offer insights into how the student is thinking about a topic, a task or other learning experience. Logs also allow students to record their thoughts and feelings about what they have achieved and what they have learned. They can help pupils to set short-term targets for themselves, which describe what they need to improve and how they can improve it.

A log can be simple or complex, short or long but should belong to the student who has time in class to complete it. Teachers should not grade logs when used formatively. Instead, they should analyse students' comments and respond to them; use the log to carry out sustained conversations with students about their learning; and probe, prompt and challenge students to reflect more deeply on their learning over time. The website prompts associated with this chapter are structured in the form of learning logs. These prompts illustrate the use of learning logs and also provide an opportunity for you to reflect on your own learning in relation to concepts introduced in the chapter.

Take a ticket

At the end of a lesson, ask students to respond to short prompts about the lesson. Answers can be written on a ticket/card containing space for a response and left with the teacher at the end of class. Prompts might include:

- Today I learned…
- One thing I could teach someone after today is…
- A new idea in the lesson is…
- I had a difficulty with…
- I tried to overcome the difficulty by…

Occasional use of this method provides teachers with valuable feedback about student learning, thereby informing subsequent teaching. A variation involves the use of sticky notes, where students write a note about what they found easy/difficult and post it to a board at the end of class.

What was the most important idea you learned today?

_____

_____

Name: _____ Date: _____

Visit the companion website at: https://study.sagepub.com/murchanshiel

Ways to improve the effectiveness of student self-assessment:

- Involve students in developing a rubric and train them in its use.
- Ensure that students apply the rubric accurately and actively engage with it.
- Encourage students to justify their assessment to others (teacher, peers) and take on board any feedback provided, especially where the self-assessment is weak or incomplete.
- Retain an active role in student self-assessment, providing training and support throughout the process, rather than leaving the assessment solely in the hands of the student.
- Encourage a culture of learning disclosure and improvement in the classroom where students are comfortable discussing the quality of the work and where stakes associated with the outcomes do not distort the honesty of the judgements. (Adapted from Brown and Harris, 2013.)

Role of feedback

Scores and grades have a function in education. There are many contexts where it is appropriate that the performance of students on tests and assessments is communicated to learners and others in the form of scores, marks or grades. Students in many education systems routinely receive information about how they are achieving in the form of public exam grades, standardised test scores, levels of achievement and other formats. The purpose and processes of grading are explored in detail in Chapters 3 and 8, especially in terms of public exams, reporting to parents and system accountability. This chapter focuses on a different function of assessment in education and therefore we explore a different form of communication to students. You will recall from earlier in the chapter that feedback is one of the most significant factors influencing student achievement (see Figure 5.1).

Feedback to students is sometimes viewed as a more user-friendly form of grading or marking. Instead of giving grades to students, teachers provide more qualitative and helpful commentary, orally, in writing, or otherwise. There are two difficulties with this interpretation. The burden on the teacher, as provider of all formative information, is great and the value of feedback to the teacher about students' learning is underestimated. In fact, feedback to teachers about students' learning, coupled with the appropriate teacher response, is key to student learning. Hattie and Timperley (2007: 102) define feedback as 'information provided by an agent (e.g. teacher, peer, book, parent, experience) regarding aspects of one's performance or understanding'. One such agent is the student who, through informal and formal mechanisms, provides feedback in relation to learning to the teacher who can respond appropriately in terms of adjusted instruction and experiences (Hattie, 2009).

It is important to recognise that not all feedback is equally effective. More effective forms tend to focus students' attention on specific aspects of the work or learning, as in commentary on the way in which a student made a persuasive argument or the approach taken in relation to texture in a work of art. General statements of affirmation do not constitute feedback at all. Table 5.5 highlights some ineffective feedback with suggestions for how it might be improved. What is noticeable is that the helpful feedback tends to be somewhat longer, though not excessively so. This additional length, however, provides much more clarity for the learner about how learning can develop.

The approaches below and on the website highlight some of the ways that you can create a feedback culture in class.

Table 5.5   Focusing formative feedback to guide learning

Unfocused feedback (less helpful)	Focused feedback (more helpful)
You've done a good job	It is interesting how you linked the Fairtrade logo on chocolate bars to equality for farm workers in developing countries
You need to put more effort into learning the verbs	There are sentences that are written in the future tense, but you used the past tense form of many verbs instead. Can you spot where this happens?
Improve your diagrams	Can you work out a way to make your diagram more clearly understood for the reader (e.g. add labels)?
You could play the part of Cinderella's sister better	Can you think of suitable clothes to take from the costume box? How can you make the sister's voice sound different to Cinderella's?
Come on! Respond to the music better	The beat to the song was syncopated in a number of places. Can you spot where and add some additional shoulder-drop or other movements?

Activity 5.6

Try this out – Feedback

Use the companion website prompts when trying out the following strategies in class. Reflect on your experience with a colleague.

Create time for providing and receiving oral feedback

The timeliness of clear feedback to and from students is a key principle of assessment for learning. Feedback can be oral or written. In the context of a busy lesson, perhaps with large numbers of students, it can be challenging to find the time to engage with students individually. A useful approach is to provide feedback to students on a rolling basis, perhaps targeting one fifth of the students per lesson over a sequence of five lessons (or other systematic pattern). In this way, you can at least ensure that you engage individually with each student in the class over a specified time frame. This oral feedback or discussion can occur while the rest of the class is engaged in some desk work, appropriately differentiated so that students can complete it with minimal requirements for seeking the teacher's help.

Act on feedback from students

The teacher receives a voluminous amount of feedback from students in relation to their learning during the course of a day. This does not mean that you cannot act on feedback – the opposite is true. In the course of reviewing students' work in class during the day, take brief notes of key insights requiring action. Before the end of the lesson (or day), prioritise the top two and address them in the conclusion, either with individuals or with the class as a whole. This will help ensure that your teaching is continually informed by recent assessment information from students.

Provide comment-only marking

There are many worthwhile reasons to provide grades in relation to student work. Equally, there are other times when grades are neither needed nor helpful. Identify some specific student tasks where comments alone are used instead of grades and discuss this policy with students. Such comments should relate back to the success criteria, focusing the student's attention on the extent to which the work presented is consistent with the criteria. The comments should focus on the specific nature and qualities of the work rather than on the students' attitude, motivation and other personal traits. The comments should encourage the students to think again about or reflect on the work and provide guidance on what to improve. Don't assume that students will devote time at home to reflecting on the comments and taking corrective action. Try to build this time into the lesson or the subsequent lesson. Set aside some time to allow students to digest the comments and to act on them to improve their work.

Use rubrics

Rubrics are rules (oftentimes illustrated as short statements) that teachers use to rate the quality of separate elements of students' work, such as the success criteria. For simplicity initially, it may be helpful to present rubrics as tables, where the different expected elements of the work (success criteria) are listed vertically and where different quality levels are established (and listed horizontally). Rubrics can also be established in relation to one dimension that attempts to capture the overall quality of a piece of work.

Use colour coding or 'plus, minus, interesting'

When reviewing student written work, teachers can use a small number of colours to identify and communicate to students particular aspects of the work. In general, colour coding should be identifiable in relation to the learning intention and success criteria. For example, a green highlighter or marker might communicate to students a part of the written work or an idea contained within it that is sound evidence of learning. A section of the written work highlighted or coloured pink, for example, could communicate to students a part of the written work that requires further consideration and review. It can be useful to provide, on some occasions, brief specific comments to help students understand why the written work is so coloured and to help direct them to reach the success criteria. In other situations, it may be preferable to let the students themselves try to interpret the reasons for the colours (with some checking by the teacher subsequently to see if they have understood the purpose and reason).

(Continued)

(Continued)

An alternative to colour coding is to use +, − and I codes (Plus, Minus, Interesting). This can also be used as a self-assessment method by students, identifying positive, negative and more neutral but nonetheless interesting aspects of their written work.

Visit the companion website at: https://study.sagepub.com/murchanshiel

Join the debate: Might feedback do more harm than good?

Not everybody is so enthusiastic about clear criteria and specific feedback! Harry Torrance (2007) conducted a study involving nearly 600 learners and assessors involved in the learning and skills sector in England. Respondents were drawn from sixth form, further education colleges and adult education settings. He concluded that excessive emphasis on specifying objectives and providing detailed feedback can reduce, rather than increase, student autonomy and that students can become dependent on teachers. Taking particular aim at the provision of feedback and communicating criteria to learners, he warns of assessment 'procedures and practices [coming] completely to dominate the learning experience, and "criteria compliance" [coming] to replace learning' (2007, p. 282).

If you can, access the article through your library's online journal service (see further reading at the end of the chapter).

Consider the views of Torrance in light of the ideas presented thus far in this chapter. Though Torrance's critique is in relation to AfL practices in post-secondary education, are some of his points relevant to primary and secondary levels? Make a list of the advantages and disadvantages associated with AfL from your reading. When you look at your list, what are the implications for your own teaching?

Opportunities and challenges in fostering AfL in teaching

We noted in Chapter 4 that implementing formative assessment in class requires more than an application of some techniques that might somehow transform student learning. Effective formative assessment requires shared buy-in by teachers, students, school administrators, policy-makers and parents. There are always instances of inspiring teachers who undertake innovation that results in positive change for students. Film makers have for years tapped into this positive image, as epitomised in the film *Dead Poets Society* (1989). The hero, Mr Keating (played by Robin Williams), takes a group of students and transforms their learning and life experiences with alternative teaching methods. The common ingredient in most such films is the isolation of the innovative teacher amongst his or her peers and the suspicion of school authorities. This illustrates one challenge of formative assessment, namely ensuring that the culture, intention and approaches are the mainstream rather than the remit of a few committed, charismatic but isolated individual teachers. Teachers in many countries see this in the tension that exists between the requirements for summative testing for certification or school accountability (possibly in the form of league tables) and the wish to empower students' own love for learning and their progression through formative approaches.

The recent educational journey of two exam-dominated education systems – Singapore and Hong Kong – illustrates the challenges and possible solutions to resolving the tension between formative and summative assessment. Ratnam-Lim and Tan (2015) note how the implementation of 'holistic assessment' in Singapore was predicated on the need for more constructive feedback to students to support all aspects of their development. However, teachers had difficulty in providing a high frequency of such feedback and couching it in terms that primary-age students could understand. Teachers still favoured the use of frequent 'bite-sized' summative tests that contributed to a cumulative grade per student. So whereas teachers were enthusiastic about formative assessment, even within a high-stakes examinations culture, the need for a significant mindset change by all stakeholders, including parents, should not be underestimated.

Similarly in Hong Kong, where a strong tradition of summative assessment exists, the Ministry of Education has been attempting to promote more AfL by teachers. However, the 'target-oriented curriculum', introduced in the 1990s, fell foul of teachers who felt that the record keeping required for providing feedback to students was too time-consuming (Berry, 2011). Further refinements and some change in nomenclature from 2002 onwards saw greater emphasis on identifying problems that students experience with learning and providing appropriate feedback to enable them to improve their work. This has required a more explicit articulation of formative assessment policy by government, along with stronger efforts to foster a greater balance between formative and summative approaches in senior secondary school, strategies designed to ensure the active involvement of students in the assessment process.

Experience in Singapore, Hong Kong and many other education systems suggests that changing assessment practices requires a shift in the teaching and learning culture of classrooms and schools. Any educational change needs to be sufficiently close to teachers' existing practice to encourage engagement, but far enough away so that some effort is required to implement it (Murchan et al., 2009). This presents a dilemma for some teachers who may view formative assessment as a heavy burden that is added to what they already do.

Addressing and resolving the tensions and challenges associated with introducing and maintaining effective AfL in schools requires the involvement of all key stakeholders in education. Teachers on their own cannot 'implement' AfL without concomitant support from the other players, including students, parents and policy-makers. A number of challenges are presented in Table 5.6, with suggestions for resolution. What is obvious is that whereas teachers can effect some change, the system and broader school and system cultures must change also.

Table 5.6   Obstacles to implementing AfL and suggested solutions

Challenges with AfL	Policy and practical implications
Time-consuming to implement properly	Teachers may feel they need to assess everything students do all the time. Try out specific AfL approaches with some targeted students on a rolling basis. You can also implement specific AfL approaches for selected lessons or on selected days. Create time within class to dialogue with specific students
Practicality of 'recording' assessments	Given the importance of transmitting feedback from students' work back to the teacher, place more emphasis on students showing how they have learned from teacher feedback. Foster peer and self-assessment and empower students with checklists, rubrics and portfolios
Insufficient resources	School systems, schools and publishers can help. A lot of strategies and material are available online
Teachers' lack of belief in AfL	This is sometimes manifested in teachers not wishing to share a responsibility for assessment with students. We need to embrace a new vision of teaching that emphasises students' responsibility and self-regulation. We also need to recognise that AfL is not a panacea for all challenges in education and society. Work with colleagues in your school to identify AfL approaches that are particularly helpful and prioritise these
Teachers' lack of confidence or competency	Share practice with colleagues whom you feel are 'about the same' as you and with others whom you feel 'know AfL'. Try out some ideas, just as you are invited to do in this book, and reflect on your experience with others. Look for video examples of AfL online, from your local educational or curriculum agency and other providers; look at AfL as a combination of teaching, learning, assessment and classroom-management practices and culture – it's not only about specific techniques
Social pressures to provide grades	Talk with colleagues within your school and with parents. Discuss AfL with your students and explain about finding an appropriate balance in assessment. Create a non-threatening, inquiry-based culture in class where students feel safe in monitoring their own learning, in responding to and sharing what they find from this process
Washback from exam-dominated system	Most systems now promote AfL, even those systems with high-stakes examinations or accountability systems. There are always opportunities to practice AfL with your own students
Tension between formative and summative purposes of assessment	Move away from a position where one purpose of assessment is better than another. There are different purposes that often, but not always, involve different methods. Include a blend of purposes and approaches in your professional practice

Case study   Teachers collaborating together can overcome obstacles to AfL

The authors were invited to provide support to an initiative aimed at enabling primary and secondary teachers to make effective use of AfL with students. Taking incremental steps, teachers, selected from a number of schools, learned about some of the principles underpinning AfL and how it might work in their classes. They tried out some approaches, recording their experiences along the way. These experiences were shared with other teachers in their schools. Though this process unearthed many 'obstacles' facing teachers, the collaborative in-school dialogue with teachers and school leaders provided solutions to many of the roadblocks. Teachers working within communities of practice can collaboratively solve problems that seem unsolvable to the individual.

Chapter summary

The history of educational change is littered with examples of initiatives that, though theoretically sound, were difficult to implement in practice, or were modified to such an extent that classroom practice bore scant resemblance to the intended policy. Assessment for learning certainly has the potential to transform learning, but, to do so, it may also have to transform teaching. Most education systems now include AfL as a significant component of practice in primary and secondary education. For some, there is considerable tension between AfL and other expectations for assessment. This chapter introduces some of the opportunities and challenges associated with embedding AfL in classroom practice. Six dimensions of AfL are explored and the reader is invited to try out a range of approaches associated with each one. A general theme throughout is the need to make assessment practical, manageable and worthwhile for students and teachers. The sustainability of incorporating AfL into your professional practice can be enhanced by transferring some of the responsibility for assessment from the teacher to the students themselves, individually and collectively.

Questions for discussion

1. Identify one subject or learning area from the curriculum you intend to teach and focus on a specific grade or class or year level. Note one student competency you wish to promote in one or a series of lessons. Develop a specific learning outcome or instructional objective (in adult wording) related to the targeted learning. Re-write this outcome as a learning intention in student-friendly language appropriate to the target age or grade level. Ensure that the statement describes what students will learn from engaging with any task or content. Ask a colleague to evaluate the learning intention.

2. Write criteria to show students how they can demonstrate success in relation to the learning intention(s) developed in question 1 above. Try not to simply repeat the learning intention or give the answer. Focus on evidence of learning. Your success criteria may be in the form of statements or rubrics. What do you notice about writing learning intentions and success criteria?

3. See if you can obtain access to the assessment policy for a primary or secondary school. Describe the relative emphasis placed on formative and summative assessment. Identify some specific formative approaches to assessment that are articulated in the policy and relate them to the six dimensions of AfL presented earlier in Table 5.3.

Further reading

Gershon, M. (2014). *Assessment for learning toolkit.* A website hosted by the Times Educational Supplement. Available at: www.tes.co.uk/teaching-resource/assessment-for-learning-tool kit-6020165

This is a free resource offering many practical classroom-based ideas for implementing AfL within your class.

Krathwohl, D.R. (2002). A revision of Bloom's taxonomy: an overview. *Theory into Practice, 41* (4), 212–18.

Bloom's taxonomy, developed in the 1950s by a group of educators in the USA, remains one of the most widely used frameworks for categorising cognitive learning aims and objectives. The taxonomy has influenced curriculum development, at national and at individual teacher levels, in many countries worldwide. A revision of the taxonomy in the late 1990s sharpened the focus on knowledge and cognitive processes within the taxonomy and provided greater illustrations of applicability to primary and secondary education.

Torrance, H. (2007). Assessment as learning? How the use of explicit learning objectives, assessment criteria and feedback in post-secondary education and training can come to dominate learning. *Assessment in Education: Principles, Policy and Practice, 14* (3), 281–94.

Set in the context of post-secondary education and training in the UK, this article offers an alternative vision of assessment as something that may undermine rather than support genuine learning and inquiry by students. It is a thought-provoking article that challenges some of the dominant narrative around formative assessment.

Designing and implementing summative written assessments for classroom use

What you will learn in this chapter

The previous chapter illustrated a range of techniques enabling you to embed assessments seamlessly and relatively informally in classroom practice. Many of them offer students a structured opportunity to learn through engagement with the assessment approaches: the assessments themselves promote enhanced learning. This chapter introduces some techniques more traditionally associated with summative assessment, where the purpose is largely, though not exclusively, to gather information about students' learning at a particular time. Chapter 5 illustrated some alternative ways in which students can demonstrate their learning. The emphasis in this chapter focuses largely on assessments that primarily call on students to write. Many assessments developed by teachers and contained in commercially-produced teaching material and textbooks involve writing. For the teacher, the judicious use of such methods reflects a key professional competency. The chapter explains and illustrates the role of written measures of student learning and helps you to learn how to construct and use such measures. You will hopefully also become a better user of tests produced by commercial publishers and national or statutory agencies.

When you finish the chapter, you should be able to answer these questions:

- How do I optimise the form of assessment to suit students' learning best?
- How can I ensure that what I assess is worth assessing?
- What forms of written tests are available and how can they be constructed and used effectively with my students?
- What characteristics should I look for when selecting assessments for use with my class?

Ensuring a fit between assessment formats and learning outcomes

In Chapter 2, we discussed validity in educational assessment, noting the need to ensure that the interpretations made of assessment results are accurate, reasonable and fair. When we infer from students' assessment responses what students know or can do, there needs to be a clear relationship between the 'results' and the interpretations of these results. One way to increase the validity of assessment interpretations is to ensure that there is a close match between the specific learning being assessed and the methods we use to assess it. Therefore, before you decide on any type of assessment to use with your students, you need to clearly understand the learning itself. Review the learning outcomes presented in Table 6.1 and reflect on how best to assess the learning in each case.

Table 6.1   Illustrative learning outcomes in selected subjects at different levels

Outcome	What students should be able to do	Subject and level
1	Examine evidence to draw conclusions about school life in the early 20th century	History, primary
2	Solve a practical problem requiring the addition and subtraction of kilograms and grams	Mathematics, primary
3	Relate an artist's use of colours to the subject matter in a painting	Art and design, primary
4	Know and understand specific terminology in relation to plant metabolism	Science, secondary
5	Develop a persuasive argument for increased afforestation based on scientific knowledge of global warming and the greenhouse effect	Geography, secondary
6	Understand the rudiments of grammar	Language, secondary

In learning outcome 4, students are required to know and understand the terminology related to plant metabolism, such as nutrition, transport, photosynthesis and phototropism. This represents reasonably low skill levels in the subject area and might therefore be assessed using simple assessment approaches such as short-answer or matching exercises that can be administered and graded efficiently. Outcome 5 also requires that students know specific information (plants take in carbon dioxide and emit oxygen), but they must also use this information in a per-suasive way to argue a point of view (the benefit of planting trees). This represents more complex learning and necessitates a different form of assessment such as an essay, a written speech or an active debate. Finally, we need to be careful in inter-preting student understanding of grammar, particularly given the re-emphasis on functional building blocks of language within initiatives to promote literacy in many countries (see DfES, 2006; DES, 2011b). Whereas students may recognise certain rules (forming plurals of nouns, use of commas and phrasing in syntax), they may lack the capacity to apply these principles consistently in practice in their writing. Therefore, conflating the grammar and content when assessing a subject-based essay (for example, on the merits of tolls on motorways) may lead to confusion in interpreting what a grade means. Teachers need to be very clear with students and others when they apportion weighting to grammar and writing mechanics in essays.

There is usually no one absolute way to assess any outcome. For practical reasons, we often cannot use what might seem to be the best option. To assess a student's oral competency in a foreign language, creating an environment where the student would converse with a native speaker would be ideal. However, this is rarely practicable. Alternative methods are sought and compromises need to be made. However, attention needs to be paid to the validity issue of how well inferences about test scores reflect students' knowledge, skills and ability on the construct of interest. All assessment methods have advantages and disadvantages and you must weigh these up in selecting suitable approaches. Look at the specific type of learning you are trying to assess and match the learning to the approach most likely to let you make sound judgements about pupils.

Recognising cognitive skill dimensions

We referred above to knowledge and even understanding as simple learning outcomes. This assumes that there are more complex learning outcomes, which leads to the question, is all learning the same? Is all knowledge the same? Are different types of learning equally challenging? Of course, the answer to these questions is no. Asking students to recall the names of the nine (or is it now eight?) planets in the solar system is not nearly as challenging as asking them to critically evaluate, from scientific evidence, the likelihood of life forms on any one of the planets other than Earth. When you compare the subjects you studied in school with what students study nowadays, it is clear that learning changes not only in terms of content, but also in terms of what students are expected to do in relation to that content.

Ideas about what constitutes learning and achievement in learning continually evolve. Such change also exists in our views on intelligence. In Chapter 3, we noted that early concepts of intelligence framed in the late 19th and early 20th centuries emphasised one general construct, represented by the Intelligence Quotient, evident in the work of Charles Spearman, Alfred Binet and Lewis Terman, amongst others. Over time, refinements to the IQ index resulted in the identification of separate measures relating to verbal comprehension, working memory and reasoning, as in the work of David Wechsler, author of the widely used Wechsler Adult Intelligence Scale (WAIS) and the Wechsler Intelligence Scale for Children (WISC). That there is disagreement or at least ambiguity about the very nature of intelligence is reflected in alternative conceptions by psychologists such as Louis Thurstone (seven primary mental abilities), Joy Paul Guilford (150 specific abilities) and Howard Gardner (eight multiple intelligences).

Whereas students' intelligence (setting aside ambiguity about its meaning) influences their educational experience, school curricula provide a structured basis for a somewhat different construct – achievement. This is most easily understood as what is learned as a result of instruction (Salvia and Ysseldyke, 2001). Teachers focus largely on ascertaining what students have achieved, assuming that they have had adequate opportunity to learn through instruction and careful classroom management. Like intelligence, achievement is considered to be multi-faceted so teachers need to recognise and promote the different elements of achievement if they are to fully mediate the curriculum.

Achievement can be categorised and differentiated in many ways. Stiggins (1992) identified five separate elements of achievement: knowledge, thinking, behaviours, products and affects, summarised in Table 6.2.

Table 6.2   Elements of achievement and illustrations

Knowledge	Knowledge, facts, concepts and principles in subject areas
Thinking	Cognitive operations, higher-order problem solving – for example, knowing the accounts for a company for the past three years, modelling its future financial outlook
Behaviours	Giving a speech, playing a piece of music or role-playing a situation
Products	Creating achievement-related products such as an exhibit for engineering, a research report based on data or a model from clay
Affects	Acquiring and developing specific dispositions such as academic self-concept, attitude, empathy or increased motivation

Source: Adapted from Stiggins (1992)

Students can engage with most areas of learning from the perspective of any one or a combination of these elements. For example, a child in primary school can learn some basic facts about homelessness but also form attitudinal dispositions in relation to people who find themselves in that situation. These are two separate but related aspects of learning the same content, suggesting that approaches to assessment are also likely to vary.

Three achievement domains have been traditionally identified: cognitive learning, focusing on knowledge, thinking and mental reasoning processes; affective learning, related to attitudes, dispositions, feelings, interests, motives, values and beliefs; and psychomotor learning, associated with students' motor skills, perceptual processes, movements and skills. Usually a mixture of two, or even three, domains of achievement is reflected within the activities that students undertake in school, even though there may be one dominant kind of behaviour required. Bloom's taxonomy (Bloom et al., 1956), mentioned in Chapter 5, represents one way of categorising cognitive learning into six somewhat different dimensions, while a refinement by Anderson and Krathwohl (2001) was also used in that chapter to illustrate questioning as part of AfL. In reality, any reasonable taxonomy or categorisation system can be used to conceptualise and structure learning so that students can engage with content in a way that transcends the mere learning of isolated facts.

Large-scale assessments such as standardised tests and national monitoring systems use test blueprints or tables of specification to ensure that items on a test reflect and sample a wide range of learning in the domain of interest. Though the more elaborate blueprints are beyond the needs of teachers in class, they illustrate how such systematic approaches to test development work. For some samples, see the Key Stage 1 English grammar, punctuation and spelling test framework (Standards and Testing Agency, 2016b) or the Framework for the National Assessment of Second Class Mathematics (Shiel et al., 2014: 17, Table 2.4). Nitko and Brookhart (2014) provide a good overview for developing tables of specifications. In general, such approaches allow teachers to identify both the learning content and the different ways in which students engage with this content (using dimensions such as those of

Table 6.3 Table of specifications for mathematics assessment: Operations and money

Topic	Learning outcome: Students should be able to...	Understanding and recalling	Using procedures	Reasoning and problem solving	No. of items
Operations	Understand subtraction as complementing 0 to 20	3		1	4
	Apply mental strategies for subtraction 0 to 20		3		3
	Add numbers without and with renaming within 99		3	2	5
Money	Recognise, exchange and use coins		3		3
	Calculate how many items may be bought with a given sum			3	3
		3	9	6	18

Stiggins, Bloom and Anderson). Table 6.3 presents a test blueprint for a mathematics assessment developed for use with children in the early years of primary school. This provides clarity for the teacher about the different topic areas included in the test and also about the specific cognitive dimensions of students' mathematics learning covered by the assessment. Eighteen items are presented to students, covering two topic areas and three cognitive dimensions in relation to those topics, thus resulting in a test with a known balance of items.

Moving beyond the specification of content and process skill matrices in single subjects, school systems increasingly promote complex cross-subject competencies or skills. These initiatives stem from a number of large-scale efforts, such as the OECD's Definition and Selection of Competencies – DeSeCo initiative (OECD, 2001) and the Partnership for 21st Century Skills (2015). These promise a more holistic education for students across cognitive, social, emotional and physical dimensions. Such changes in curriculum require a change in assessment, a point well illustrated by the American psychologist Lorrie Shepard (2000), who highlighted a disjoint between current theories of learning, curriculum and assessment. She made the compelling argument that whereas our understanding about how students learn has led to changes in what and how we teach them, approaches to assessment have been much slower to change.

A glance at mission statements from education ministries worldwide highlights the widespread aim that schools would provide challenging subject matter that emphasises deep and meaningful learning and that students should acquire competencies relevant to real-life contexts. These include the capacity to think creatively, flexibly and critically; to identify, interpret and solve problems; to relate and communicate effectively; and to use technology seamlessly in learning. Large-scale testing programmes struggle to adequately capture these complex skills. Accordingly, a greater onus is placed on teachers to assess students at local level so that there is a great opportunity to widen the types of learning that are promoted and rewarded in class (Collins et al., 2010; Baird and Black, 2013).

Activity 6.1

Try this out – Developing assessments related to key skills

Table 6.4 presents a list of selected key competencies promoted in four national education systems across all subjects. For a particular lesson or topic you are going to teach at a particular age level, develop one or two learning outcomes related to any competency and outline how you would assess students in relation to it.

Table 6.4 Extracts from key competencies specified in selected education systems

England[1]	• Develop pupils' numeracy and mathematical reasoning in all subjects
	• Develop pupils' English spoken language, reading, writing and vocabulary in every subject
Scotland[2]	• Use literacy, communication and numeracy skills
	• Use technology for learning
	• Think creatively and independently
	• Make reasoned evaluations
Ireland[3]	• Gather, record, organise and evaluate information and data
	• Think creatively and critically
	• Reflect on and evaluate own learning
	• Use digital technology to access, manage and share information
USA[4]	• Analyse how parts of a whole interact with each other to produce overall outcomes in complex systems
	• Analyse and evaluate evidence, arguments, claims and beliefs
	• Synthesise and make connections between information and arguments
	• Reflect critically on learning experiences and processes

Sources: 1. Department for Education (2014a); 2. The Scottish Government (2008); 3. NCCA (2014); 4. Partnership for 21st Century Skills (2015)

Personalities in educational assessment: Lorrie Shepard

Lorrie Shepard, a professor of research and evaluation methodology at the University of Boulder Colorado, has contributed widely to our understanding of assessment practices. Her research has explored theoretical, technical, policy and practical issues related to assessment, including statistical analysis, the impact of high-stakes testing and AfL. Her recent work emphasises the role of schools and classrooms as social spaces where students learn and are influenced by their peers. Framing her ideas about assessment around a cognitive, constructivist and socio-cultural perspective, she raises fundamental issues about the extent to which current assessment approaches are consistent with current insights about learning.

Constructing traditional test forms

Educational policy increasingly emphasises the value of teacher-based assessment as a complement to more formal external assessment (OECD, 2013). Teachers need to acquire and continually develop their assessment knowledge, skills and expertise, including the capacity to develop, administer and interpret their own assessments (Brookhart, 2011; Australian Institute for Teaching and School Leadership, 2014). Therefore, knowing how to craft valid and reliable assessments for use with your students is a key goal of your professional and continuing education.

Before we move on to consider some ways to develop and use more traditional, written assessments, let us look first at some key considerations when planning for assessment:

- Clarify the purpose of the assessment.
- Identify specific learning outcomes to be assessed.
- Sketch a framework or plan for the assessment.
- Develop the tasks/prompts/questions for students.
- Review the quality of the assessment.

Determining the purpose of the assessment is essential. Will the assessment be used to inform parents about students' progress or to scaffold the next steps in the learning of a topic? Assessing for reporting to parents may require a careful sampling of what has been learned in the previous term or year, whereas assessment to scaffold future learning will require a clear focus on a small area of the curriculum. The intended purpose of an assessment influences many features of the assessment process, including: the approach to preparation by teachers and students; methods of assessment; and approaches to analysing student performance and the 'results' of the assessment.

Assessments should be built around clear learning outcomes that may be drawn from statutory curriculum statements or from outcomes that are specified by the teacher, school or municipality. Often, it is helpful to develop a plan for an assessment that identifies the range of content and skills to be included. Using assessment frameworks or specifications helps ensure that the breadth of student learning is reflected in the assessment and that there is no inadvertent over-emphasis on one or some aspects of learning over others. Education systems increasingly include learners with special educational needs or who come from diverse backgrounds, and this should inform the planning of the assessment (see Chapter 10). Creating the assessment stimuli themselves (questions, prompts, tasks, tests) is a complex process that requires care to ensure that student responses can be interpreted accurately and consistently. Finally, once an assessment has been given to students, it can be helpful if the teacher critically evaluates the quality of the approach before using the findings. The following list summarises some general considerations for developing and administering written assessments to students:

- There should be an appropriate balance of easy-to-assess aspects of the learning and elements that are more difficult to assess.
- Assessment items should be appropriate for the learning outcomes.
- Directions to students should be clear.

- Reading vocabulary and sentence structure should be age-appropriate.
- Items or tasks should be carefully constructed.
- Items or tasks should, where possible, be presented in order of difficulty with the easiest ones first.
- Time limits should be adequate.
- An assessment should be of sufficient size and duration to provide a representative sample of learning.

In the remainder of the chapter, we present ideas for developing and using a number of assessment formats suited to written tests in class, namely: fill in the blanks or short answers; essays and other extended constructed response tests; and objective items such as true–false, multiple-choice and matching.

Fill in the blanks/short answers

Short-answer item formats are widely used by teachers and in commercially published educational material. These typically consist of a short prompt for learners, who respond succinctly with a word, phrase, number or symbol. Spaces are often provided for students' answers. These items are especially suitable for assessing relatively simple levels of learning such as recall and basic computation, though they can also be used where students in mathematics, science, business studies or accounting, for example, are required to engage in more complex calculations to arrive at a correct solution.

Short-answer items can be structured or formatted in a number of different ways, some of which are illustrated in Figure 6.1.

Format	Illustration
Question	What is the common name for Beethoven's Sixth Symphony? _____
Completion	The common name for Beethoven's Sixth Symphony is the _____
Identification/Association	On the lines opposite the numerals, write the popular names that identify these symphonies by Beethoven:

Symphony number	Popular name
3	_____
5	_____
6	_____
9	_____

Figure 6.1   Selected short-answer formats

With the question format, a direct question is posed and the student provides a short answer. A benefit for students is the clarity provided by the question itself, presented as a complete sentence. Provision of a clear, intact sentence in question form reduces the potential reading difficulty for younger students or students with a more limited reading ability, an important validity consideration when interpreting student responses. Where the learning intention being assessed does not relate directly to linguistic skill (e.g. in the case of the music knowledge outcome in Figure 6.1), students' probability of answering correctly should not depend on their reading level. An incomplete sentence with a blank at the end can increase the reading burden on students unnecessarily. Items that require the identification of information or ideas offer an efficient way to assess a number of concepts based on one prompt. A stimulus (such as a list of terms, a diagram, a photograph) is presented to the student, who is required to respond appropriately by writing labels, numbers, symbols or other terms. This format is frequently used to assess basic knowledge in science and geography.

You may have also taken some cloze tests in your own education, as in the example in Figure 6.2. These formats are frequently employed for use in assessing language skills and reading comprehension (Wall, 2004). By filling in the missing words or terms, students' understanding of the content is assessed. Although they are widely used, some concerns arise about the comparability of results when different rules for deleting words are used. In developing such a test, the teacher might delete every fifth word, every tenth, all nouns, all verbs, all key content words or function words, for example. However, student scores can vary depending on the deletion method chosen (Alderson, Clapham and Wall, 1995; Henk, 1981). Some teachers use cloze tests in relation to subjects other than language, sometimes to check for knowledge of specific vocabulary or terminology.

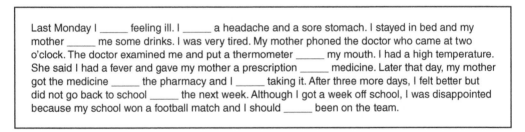

Figure 6.2   Illustration of cloze test measuring language

One positive feature of short-answer items such as cloze and completion is the requirement on students to produce a correct or acceptable answer rather than merely recognise one from a list of possibilities. This offsets the risk of students using partial knowledge triggered by seeing plausible alternatives in, say, a multiple-choice question. However, whereas the correct answer may seem obvious to the teacher who crafts the item, scoring can be complicated by unexpected but plausible answers and even by mis-spellings. See, even in Figure 6.2, how some blanks could have a number of acceptable answers.

Whereas short-answer questions typically involve the insertion of a word, phrase or symbol, some varieties offer students limited scope to write a sentence or two. However, the objectivity of scoring may be more challenging. Review the items in the box overleaf, relating to secondary school geography and consider the quality of each item in relation to any ambiguity in the item as written and the challenges in scoring.

1. Name the four processes of river erosion:

       _____

       _____

       _____

       _____

2. Name the three directions a river erodes in:

       _____

       _____

       _____

3. Why does deposition occur in a river?

       _____

       _____

Key tips for developing and using short-answer items

- Develop the item to assess important knowledge, concepts or skills that students are expected to have learned.
- Word the question yourself rather than copying it directly from textbooks or other material. Students can recognise and remember such previously seen material.
- Be precise in phrasing the prompt so that only one answer is correct and students are clear about the desired nature of the response.
- Avoid providing unintended clues about the answer in the question through grammatical structure, words used or length of blanks.
- Use direct questions rather than incomplete formats, where possible.
- Don't place too many blanks in a question. One is preferable, located at the end. Keep all blanks the same length when a series of questions is used.
- Anticipate mis-spellings by students and consider how important accurate spelling is in relation to the learning outcome being assessed.

Advances in technology mean that student responses to short-answer items can be made digitally on computers, laptops and tablets and captured by scoring software. Whereas initial versions of many computerised tests used multiple-choice items, recent interface and software advances permit the use of a much wider range of items on tests that can be administered and scored digitally (Scalise and Gifford, 2006; Bridgeman, 2009; Murchan, Oldham, et al., 2013). This reduces the scoring burden and can facilitate the objective scoring of responses and faster feedback of results to students.

Activity 6.2

Try this out – Scoring cloze tests

Select a couple of paragraphs from an article in a magazine or newspaper. Delete every fifth word and have a colleague 'replace' each word exactly as it was written in the article.

Repeat this exercise where only every noun is deleted. Now score both tests by giving one point for every word correctly 'replaced' exactly as it was written in the article. Convert the two scores to percentages. What do you notice about the results? What issues arose for you in scoring the tests?

Essays and constructed response formats

Essay questions are often used as a direct measure of writing ability in language classes where, for example, teachers focus on narrative, expository, persuasive and other forms of writing. Language teachers also use essay assessments to gather insights on students' writing processes through the use of pre-writing activities such as discussion, listing, organising ideas and outlining. Wider use for essays is also found throughout the curriculum, in subjects as diverse as biology, economics and art. In these non-language subject areas, the emphasis is likely to be on high-level engagement with subject matter content and skills through assessing outcomes such as summarising, reasoning, critical analysis and evaluation. In these cases, assessment focuses on some of the learning outcomes that are not readily assessed by other means. Recent emphasis on literacy as foundational to all learning has renewed educational policy-makers' focus on students' capacity to express themselves in writing across the curriculum. This is reflected in the national literacy and numeracy strategy in the Republic of Ireland (DES, 2011b) and in advice for teachers in the national curriculum in England that they 'should develop pupils' spoken language, reading, writing and vocabulary as integral aspects of the teaching of every subject' (DfE, 2014a: 11).

The wider term, constructed response tests, is sometimes used to include essays and a range of related item formats that require students to develop and provide responses of varying length and complexity. The response, therefore, might not be a written essay but might include working out mathematical proofs, developing book-keeping responses such as profit and loss accounts or outlining solutions to problems in physics or construction studies. In this chapter, we use the general term essays to apply to all constructed response items that do not fall within more long-term assessment forms such as projects and portfolios.

We can distinguish between restricted response essays and extended response essays. Restricted response items include essay prompts or instructions that restrict or limit the substantive content or form of the written response (Nitko and Brookhart, 2014). The nature of the expected response is overtly explained or should be apparent to students, as in a description of concepts (identify the theme in a poem), an explanation of procedures followed (give an account of an experiment conducted), cause–effect relationships (explain the impact of currency devaluation on exports) and a justification of action (why you selected a pie chart to represent data). A specified length might be suggested, for example two lines or a paragraph, or the response might be limited to a number of points. An example of a restricted response answer, applicable to primary mathematics, is provided in Figure 6.3.

Many curricula, including Scotland's Curriculum for Excellence, promote wider interpretation of the word *text*, as evident in English specifications from Education Scotland (2015, 2016). Broader views of texts include print texts, electronic texts,

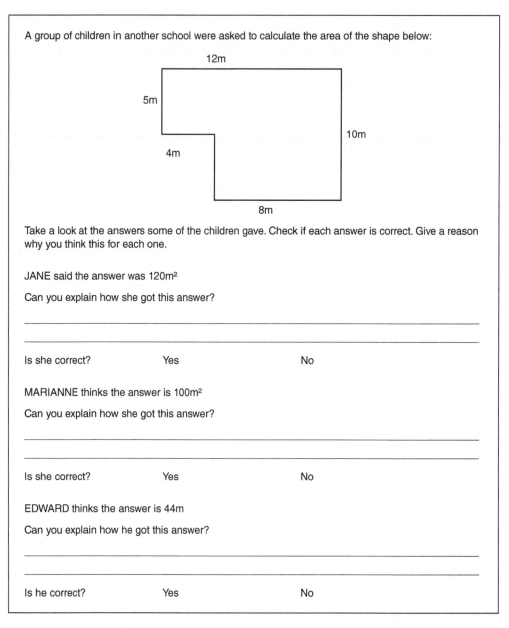

A group of children in another school were asked to calculate the area of the shape below:

Take a look at the answers some of the children gave. Check if each answer is correct. Give a reason why you think this for each one.

JANE said the answer was 120m²

Can you explain how she got this answer?

_____

_____

Is she correct?   Yes   No

MARIANNE thinks the answer is 100m²

Can you explain how she got this answer?

_____

_____

Is she correct?   Yes   No

EDWARD thinks the answer is 44m

Can you explain how he got this answer?

_____

_____

Is he correct?   Yes   No

Figure 6.3   Restricted response item: mathematics

films, games and TV programmes. The following outlines a restricted response item designed to focus students' responses on specific dimensions of one such digital text:

Briefly describe a recent film that you have watched under the following headings:

- *Title*
- *Genre and atmosphere*
- *Cinematography, including any special effects*
- *Use of soundtrack*

In contrast, extended constructed response items offer students the opportunity to organise the form and nature of their answers, to express and expand their ideas and to show inter-relationships between ideas. In the case of extended response essays, usually no single answer is considered correct. Such essay formats are typically used to assess students' capacity to integrate learning in an original form across a number of learning outcomes within a subject and possibly across curriculum areas. Students' creative writing falls within this format, as does a range of other expository and persuasive essays. Extended response essays can enable students to demonstrate more integrated learning skills in planning an individual response, drawing on any information that they consider relevant and communicating their response in a coherent and convincing manner. The prompt below leaves to students the decisions about what information to draw on and how to use that information in framing a response that they consider appropriate:

Examine the defeat of Churchill's government in the 1945 general election in Britain.

Advantages and challenges with essays

As you see from the chapters in this book, all assessment approaches have advantages and disadvantages and essays are no different in this regard. As a measure of writing ability, the essay offers a direct insight into students' ability to write in a variety of genres and for a variety of purposes and audiences. Writing is inextricably linked with literacy and so essays offer a window into students' writing at technical, grammatical and stylistic levels. Essays are used widely across a broad range of subjects and thus allow for the assessment of complex learning skills in various content areas. Students are required to integrate information and to communicate complex ideas clearly – two key skills for modern life.

Teachers often find the creation of essay tests to be relatively straightforward and not time-consuming. However, be warned that creating valid and reliable essay prompts and tests requires much careful thought if the process is to yield accurate, credible and useful information about students' achievement. Whereas essay assessments may be quick to create, administering and scoring such assessments is time-consuming. In comparison with some other forms of assessment, reliability can be low. Different teachers or raters might judge an essay differently. One teacher may be inconsistent in judging essays of similar quality. Where a choice of questions is given to students, the questions may not be of equal difficulty or address the same learning outcomes. Some of these challenges can be addressed by the use of robust scoring rubrics that offer clarity to raters (and students) about the characteristics being sought and about what constitutes achievement at different levels. This process is conceptually similar to the specification of success criteria in Chapters 4 and 5 in relation to AfL. One of the most stubborn challenges with essay assessments centres on the limited number of essays that a student can write in typical test sessions. This can lead to a restricted sampling of learning outcomes. Add in concerns about additional challenges or obstacles for students with special educational needs (for example, fatigue, the suitability of stimulus material or prompts), and we see that the use of essay formats requires careful consideration if the potential of this assessment type is to be realised. These considerations should inform the development of essays, which is the next topic in this chapter.

Developing essays

We will look now at the development and scoring of essays. Some key tips for development are presented in the box.

Key tips for developing and scoring essay items

- Develop the essay prompt to capture specific knowledge and skills that are identifiable in the learning outcomes and that are not more easily assessed by other methods.
- Unless dealing with ambiguity is an aspect of skill to be assessed, phrase the essay prompt so that the meaning and intention are clear to students.
- Students should be given some guidance as to the scope of the task through an indication of time to spend on the essay.
- Avoid or minimise the use of choice in essay titles.
- Use an appropriate analytic or holistic scoring guide.
- Where there are a number of essays to be completed on a test, grade all the answers to one question for all students before moving on to the next essay.
- Conduct a check on your scoring consistency by re-scoring some essays yourself or enlisting the help of a colleague to do so.
- Score on the basis of writing mechanics only if this is warranted by the learning outcome and if students are aware that this is included in the rubric. In content-based essays, it is preferable to score analytically so that a separate score can be provided for writing mechanics, if wished.

Teachers sometimes assign essay questions that are under powered in relation to the learning intention. For example, the extended essay question: *Describe and explain the functions associated with parts of a flowering plant*, really only asks students to remember specific facts and write them out in narrative form. It is little more than recall and translation into the students' own words, indicating nothing more than basic comprehension of a set of facts related to plant life. Depending on the guidelines, students may spend pages and a whole-class period writing out these facts, which might be much more easily assessed using a series of short-answer or objective items (objective items will be discussed in the next section of the chapter). Many assessments offer students some choice about what items to attempt. Typically, this is either to provide scope to students to choose, or it reflects a curriculum so broad that there is tacit understanding that students cannot 'cover' all the content and skills. However, offering a choice of items may not necessarily advantage students in the way envisaged and may lower the validity of inferences made about the student results (Murchan, 1993; Crookes, 2007; McMillan, 2011). Whereas this is less of an issue in formative classroom assessment where the teacher is quite familiar with students' work and has multiple opportunities to assess, it is more significant in summative assessment where students' performance is compared to their peers. If a wide choice is offered to students, they will choose different combinations of questions, with the result that no two students might take the same exam. This is reasonable if all the items are of equal difficulty, which they may not be. Furthermore, grading students where they have all essentially taken individual exams chosen by themselves makes a comparison of overall results problematic – an issue if results are used to formally certify students' achievement or to select students.

Activity 6.3

Try this out – Evaluating essay tests

Write a prompt for an essay designed to assess some aspect of students' language or other subject-based learning. Either review the essay prompt yourself or get a colleague to review it, drawing on the checklist below. If necessary, re-develop the prompt based on the suggestions below. Prompt sheets on the companion website will guide you in this task.

1. Write out the specific learning outcome(s) that the essay is designed to assess.
2. To what extent is your essay the best way to assess the outcome?
3. Identify the dominant cognitive skills expected of students to complete the essay (knowledge, summarising, reasoning, creativity).
4. Are students aware of the relative importance of language competency in the essay (spelling, punctuation, syntax, flow)?
5. Is the task clear to the students? (Is the task appropriate for all students to whom it will be given? Is the prompt written in accessible language, pitched at students' reading level?)
6. Are the expected length of the essay and probable/available time limit clear to students?
7. If the essay is part of a wider assessment, are students aware of the weighting (marks) to be allocated to the essay?

Visit the companion website at https://study.sagepub.com/murchanshiel

Reviewing and scoring essays

One of the main advantages of essays – the space given to students to organise and create original answers – leads to one of their chief disadvantages, namely the challenge in scoring them. Besides the diversity of essay formats, both restricted and extended formats, the approaches to reviewing and scoring also vary. As a formative tool, essays offer an opportunity to teachers to gain insight into students' achievement of certain learning outcomes in a way that more objective methods cannot. The use of writing checklists, such as the pre-flight checklist highlighted in Chapter 5, by students themselves enables students to audit their learning against specific criteria, lessening dependence on the teacher and fostering self-regulated learning. The checklist might require students to review specific structural features in an essay, such as title, appropriate length, syntax, presence of an introduction or a clear conclusion. You can also encourage your students to engage in the sequential drafting of an essay. This encourages students to reflect on each draft individually, with peers or through advice from the teacher, so that each subsequent draft builds formatively on the previous one.

This process of drafting and re-drafting the same essay mirrors the real-world writing of reports in the workplace, where people are seldom expected to produce a final document or report without having the opportunity to amend it. Chapters 4 and 5 explored comment-only grading, an AfL practice well suited to essays. If, prior to working on an essay, students are clear about the success criteria, teachers' comments and annotations on the essay can help students understand the extent to which their response adequately meets these criteria, along with some suggestions for development in their learning. Conferencing with students offers a further opportunity to discuss student work with the students themselves. Meeting individually with students in busy classrooms can be challenging, but alternative group sessions can also be beneficial, particularly where the comments are reasonably uniform across a group. Think of student conferences as brief but frequent opportunities to affirm the quality of the work of individual students, to help the students identify a small number of improvements that can be made and to support them in achieving those goals. Such targeted sessions offer a great opportunity to involve students in shared reflection on their own work and in collaboratively planning the next steps in their learning.

When used summatively, grades are frequently assigned to essays. Two main approaches are typically used when grading essays. Analytic approaches focus separately on a number of features within the essay, 'rewarding' performance on each feature separately. In contrast, teachers using holistic methods focus more on the essay as a whole, identifying an overall impression of the response. Key features of the two approaches are summarised in Table 6.5.

Table 6.5 Common approaches to scoring essays

Analytic	Holistic
Fine-grained analysis of detail in essay	Offers an overview or impressionistic evaluation of the essay
Marks awarded for individual elements	May use a number of level descriptors
Frequently used for content-based essays (history, environmental studies)	Generic rubrics often applicable to a range of different essay topics
Scoring rubric may be unique to the specific prompt/content	

Two essay prompts and associated scoring rubrics are presented in Tables 6.6 and 6.7. The first example, relating to business studies, assesses students' capacity to relate knowledge and concepts about consumer rights to a practical skills-based scenario. An analytic scoring rubric is employed that provides detailed feedback in relation to a number of key features expected in the response. Scores for individual elements can be summed to get an overall score for the essay.

The second example, aimed at students recently arrived in secondary school, focuses on students' narrative and reflective skills in English composition, combining powers of observation within a reflective communication. A more holistic scoring rubric is used that provides levels (grades) based on more aggregated criteria.

The advantages of analytic rubrics include greater clarity for teachers and students about what is rewarded in the scoring and an increased likelihood that the student can draw on the mark to address specific lacunae in the response. Disadvantages

Table 6.6 Essay prompt with analytic scoring rubric

You purchased a second-hand smartphone from a local retailer. Within a few days you notice that some of the features are not working properly. Write a detailed letter to the retailer explaining the problem in terms of consumer rights and requesting that the matter be resolved.

Success criteria	Level of quality (description of the problem and request)			
	1	2	3	4
	Vague description	Simple description	Detailed description	Detailed description with illustrations
Reference to consumer rights law	Little or no mention	Only alludes to existence of such rights	Links consumer rights to one of either the problem or the resolution	Links consumer rights to the problem and approaches to resolution
Request for solution	Unclear request evident	Simplistic evidence of request	Provides for only one solution (e.g. refund)	Outlines the range of redress provided for in law and prioritises one of them
Letter structure	Largely narrative	Contains limited elements of a business letter	Clear focus to letter	Structure and layout of letter appropriate and provides clarity to request

Table 6.7 Essay prompt with holistic scoring rubric

Welcome to secondary school! Now that you have been in your new school for a few months, write an account of your experience so far, describing how it is different to your primary school.

Level	Success criteria
Highly proficient	Identifies a large number and breadth of ideas
	Ideas are organised effectively
	Ideas lend coherence to the narrative and relate to all aspects of the prompt
	Advanced evidence of and correct use of writing conventions in relation to vocabulary, syntax, grammar, punctuation and spelling
Proficient	Identifies a reasonable number of ideas
	Ideas are reasonably well organised, reasonably coherent and largely focused on the prompt
	Reasonable evidence of and correct use of writing conventions in relation to vocabulary, syntax, grammar, punctuation and spelling
Developing	Presents a small number of poorly expressed ideas
	Ideas are poorly organised
	Ideas do not constitute a coherent set
	Weak focus on the prompt
	Significant difficulties evident with some elements of vocabulary, syntax, grammar, punctuation and spelling
More support needed	Few or no ideas presented
	Response displays little or no organisational structure
	Most or all writing conventions very weak and make meaning difficult to follow

include the time involved for teachers in scoring, resulting in a possible delay in returning scores to students. Holistic rubrics can often be applied to a range of essays or/prompts and can speed up scoring. However, they generally offer little formative feedback to students about how they can improve their performance. Another approach, known as Adaptive Comparative Judgement (Pollitt, 2012), represents a variation of holistic judgement, where a teacher or rater compares two pieces of work (two essays) and decides simply which of them is better. This process is repeated to include all essays in a set and enables a ranking of all the essays on a scale. While encouraging levels of reliability have been yielded by this method, it is difficult to provide formative feedback to students.

Regardless of which scoring methods you use, it is good practice to review the accuracy of scoring, with a colleague if possible. This can involve re-checking all or a sample of essays that have been assigned the same score or category to see if they all share similar characteristics in terms of quality. This is generally easier to do in holistic scoring where broad score bands are used, as in Table 6.7, rather than where percentages or a large number of narrower grade bands are used. The more grade bands you use, the more likelihood there is that essays will be misclassified (receive a B instead of a B+; a C1 instead of a C2) – a potentially significant reliability issue (see Chapter 2). The recent reduction in grade bands in the Leaving Certificate in Ireland from 14 to 8 reflects, in part, concerns about the reliability of scoring near the cut scores between grades, especially when many grades are used. Overall, it is important to remember that some form of rubric is essential when scoring essays, perhaps combined with sample answers at different levels of quality.

Join the debate: Back-to-basics and the impact of students' writing skills on assessment in subjects other than language

In Ireland, the national literacy strategy (DES, 2011b) highlights the need for guidance on how teachers in all subjects can develop literacy. Similarly, the revised national curriculum in England requires teachers to develop pupils' spoken language, reading, writing and vocabulary as integral aspects of the teaching of every subject (DfE, 2014a). Does this mean that students should be marked on language skills in other subjects? How would this impact on student performance? Would it be fair? Consider this issue from a validity perspective (see Chapter 2). Develop a position on this in relation to assessments in primary or secondary school. If you are a student teacher, should your language skills be graded as part of assessments in different modules?

Objective items

The final type of assessment format we will look at in this chapter is objective items. Objectivity in scoring is assumed in the name of these items – it is expected that there is one agreed answer to the question and that, therefore, different teachers or raters can come easily to the same conclusion about the quality of a student's response.

Whereas constructed response items such as short answers, essays, orals and even practical exercises have a long history, objective items have increased in popularity over the past century or so, particularly since the development of IQ tests in the early 20th century (see Chapter 3). Studies have queried the consistency of the scoring of essays, leading to an interest in forms of tests that might prove more objective, in that they can provide higher levels of scoring precision than the older forms of testing, judged to be 'subjective'. Objective forms are often used with large cohorts of students as they can usually be scored more efficiently and reliably. There is evidence that objective forms of assessment can measure complex learning as well as more subjective methods (Lukhele, Thissen and Wainer, 1994). A number of reviews by Lukhele and colleagues concluded that essays are very expensive to score and that the information yielded by such tests is often not very different to that which can be obtained from far less-costly but carefully-crafted objective items.

True–false items

This format may be useful if you wish to quickly assess some relatively simple knowledge such as recognition of previously learned material, the recall of historical facts, definitions in science or basic concepts in mathematics. True–false items are usually presented to students in written form, on an exam paper, in a textbook or digitally but, as indicated in Chapter 5, they can also be used orally as part of AfL to gauge students' knowledge about a topic in advance of instruction. True–false tests can enable teachers to assess a broad range of knowledge without exploring the depth of that knowledge. Students can move swiftly through the test, thereby allowing the teacher to include more items and obtain a broader snapshot of students' learning. The writing burden on the students is minimal and scoring by teachers or students themselves is quick. An obvious disadvantage is the potential for student guessing, thus complicating teachers' ability to draw reasonable inferences from the test results. We will return to this matter in more depth later in the chapter. Activity 6.4 outlines some tips to consider when developing true–false items, along with some scenarios to evaluate.

Activity 6.4

Try this out – Evaluating and improving true–false items

Here are some tips for developing and scoring true–false items:

1. This item format is generally designed to assess lower levels of learning so keep the questions short and simple.
2. Ensure that the correct or best answer is unambiguous.
3. Avoid the tendency to use negative phrasing in questions to make them more difficult.
4. Ensure that there is a mix of true and false statements, without a correct response pattern that is obvious to students.
5. Avoid the introduction of irrelevant clues in the questions through careless wording.

(Continued)

(Continued)

Now review the sample true–false items below. Evaluate them in relation to the tips highlighted above, finding one major flaw in each item. Can you think of some ways to improve the items? Re-write them. Then develop three true–false items that you could use with a class to assess some aspect of learning. Prompts on the website will assist you.

Candidates are elected to the European Parliament that meets in Strasbourg	True	False
The Trade Winds do not blow from the north east	True	False
Owls always hunt at night	True	False

Visit the companion website at: https://study.sagepub.com/murchanshiel

Variations on true–false items include Yes–No; True–False–Opinion and Multiple True–False. Popham (2011) advocates the use of multiple true–false items where a number of questions are based on one prompt, thereby speeding up students' progress through the test. True–False–Opinion items offer students an opportunity to judge whether a statement or prompt is definitely true, false or merely an opinion, a skill with application in subjects such as history, civics and environmental studies.

Multiple-choice items

Many of the strengths of true–false tests are retained when teachers use multiple-choice questions (MCQ), while some key disadvantages are minimised. MCQs are widely used in standardised tests such as the Drumcondra Primary Reading Test, SIGMA Mathematics Test, Wide Range Achievement Test and Cognitive Abilities Test. They have been an integral element of large-scale testing programmes in many countries for decades, and are widely used, along with other item types, in international assessments such as PISA, TIMSS and PIRLS. The basic architecture of a MCQ consists of three components, as illustrated in Figure 6.4.

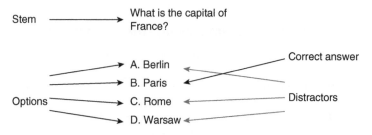

Figure 6.4   Structure of a multiple-choice question (MCQ)

MCQs encompass a wide variety of related formats that facilitate the assessment of a range of learning from lower-level recall to quite complex cognitive processing. They can of course be used to test the recognition and recall of facts and concepts, but can also assess higher-level cognitive skills, such as comprehension, making connections and inferences, the application of concepts and principles, analysis and evaluation (Haladyna, 2004; Downing, 2006; Haladyna and Rodriguez, 2013). Many of you may be familiar with the use of MCQs in testing on the rules of the road. For example, the Driver and Vehicle Standards Agency in Northern Ireland requires learner drivers to take two theory tests containing a total of 100 MCQs (visit www. nidirect.gov.uk/theory-test if you would like to try out some sample items testing your knowledge of the rules of the road). These formats can also be found at college level and in accreditation processes for a number of professions, for example in medicine and accountancy (see certification by the Association of Chartered Certified Accountants at www.accaglobal.com/uk).

Students in primary and secondary education frequently encounter MCQs. The format is flexible and enables the assessment of a wide range of cognitive outcomes. MCQs are efficient in facilitating the assessment of a broad range of content as writing by students is minimised, a factor that also helps minimise an adverse impact on students with writing difficulties. They can be scored quickly and accurately, a process that can be easily automated, especially in the case of computer-based assessment where students and teachers can receive results immediately after the test. When combined with the affordances of computer-based assessment, MCQs offer the potential to provide complex questions based on multi-media stimuli that go far beyond the traditional perception of MCQs as merely assessing recognition and knowledge (Scalise and Gifford, 2006; Sireci and Zenisky, 2006; Kreiter et al., 2011). Multiple-choice items can be constructed to provide powerful diagnostic information about students' learning misconceptions based on the careful analysis of specific distractors chosen by students (Eggen and Lampe, 2011; Murchan, Oldham and O'Sullivan, 2013).

However, quality items are more difficult to develop than people generally think. Many of the criticisms of MCQs are on the basis of poorly constructed items where trivial material is frequently assessed, that ambiguity exists in the question or the options, or the best answer is not clear. The answer to an MCQ is presented to the student amongst a set of possible alternatives, meaning that students do not necessarily have to conceptualise an answer – it is there within the question. There are, of course, many aspects of learning, such as collaborative working, the organisation of knowledge and concepts, original thinking and effective communication that cannot be assessed with MCQs. In keeping with our view in this book that teachers need to use a variety of assessment methods to reflect the variety of learning, MCQs, therefore, like essays, portfolios and performance tasks, contribute to, but are not the totality of, teachers' assessment repertoires.

Criticisms of MCQs by teachers and others sometimes focus on the risk of obtaining high scores through guessing. This is a concern, though less so than with true–false items where there is a 50% chance of guessing correctly on any given item, with an expected chance score of 50% on a test containing only true–false items. With multiple-choice tests, the chances of obtaining high or even moderately high scores by random guessing is much reduced due to the number of options in each item, typically four or five. Therefore, the chances of guessing all or even a large number of items correctly on a test, is remote. If a student were to guess at random on a ten-item MCQ test with four options per item, the expected chance score is 25% or two and a half questions. The probability of a student guessing all ten items correctly on that test is one in a million. On a 20-item MCQ test, the chance of guessing 40% of the items correctly by random guessing is 10 in 100. To obtain 80% or better, through guessing the probability drops to one in a million. However, in reality, students are more likely to use whatever information they have to work out the answer to each item, and, if they are motivated at all, blind guessing is the exception rather than the norm. As outlined in Chapter 2, procedures exist for estimating the reliability of objective tests. High reliability of test scores is evidence that guessing by students is minimal.

While Figure 6.4 highlighted the basic structure of an MCQ, variations exist for different purposes. Some of these include Correct answer, Best answer, Multiple response, Combined response, Negative variety and Incomplete statement. Use of best answer options requires students to choose an answer where a number of reasonable possibilities exist but where one is preferable. This enables the item to tap into students' capacity to know content but also to be able to judiciously weigh alternatives to provide an optimum solution. Figure 6.5 illustrates some common types of MCQs. Opinion differs on the ideal number of options on MCQs. Many tests use four options, including the keyed answer. However,

Correct answer	Best answer
Circle the shape that is divided in half.	What was the basic intention behind the establishment of the European Coal and Steel Community?
	A. Reduce tariffs on basic materials of production B. Avoid further war in Europe C. Improve collaborative decision making amongst member states D. Provide cheaper goods to consumers
Multiple response	**Combined response**[a]
Which two terms are associated with insurance? A. incorporation, mortgage B. maturity, proposal C. demarcation, premium D. policy, deficit	 Look at these photographs, showing different kinds of energy used in the modern world. Which two photographs show **renewable energy sources**?: A and B ☐ B and C ☐ A and D ☐ C and D ☐
Negative variety	**Incomplete variety**
Study the regional map provided. Which of the following transport options is NOT available to residents of the region? A. Air B. Rail C. Road D. Water	An object dropped from your hand falls to the ground due to the effect of: A. Acceleration B. Force C. Friction D. Gravity

Figure 6.5   Selected MCQ variants

Note: [a] SEC, Junior Certificate Ordinary Level Geography, June 2008

Michael Rodriguez (2005) reviewed a range of studies conducted over many decades that investigated this question. His analysis concluded that three options are often enough.

Activity 6.5

Try this out – Evaluating and improving multiple-choice items

Here are some tips for developing and scoring multiple-choice items:

1. Match each item with an intended learning outcome and try to design items that measure higher-order learning outcomes as well as knowledge of facts.
2. Present a single, clearly formulated problem in the stem.
3. Put as much of the wording as possible in the stem: ideally, a capable student should be able to answer the question without seeing the options.
4. Eliminate unnecessary wordiness in the question overall: over-elaborate questions containing unrelated content can confuse weaker readers.
5. Avoid negatively worded stems, sometimes included to make the item more difficult, for example 'Which of the following is not ...?'.
6. Lay out the item in a clear, logical, systematic manner: list options vertically where possible, in a logical order (alphabetical, chronological or by size).
7. Vary the positioning of the correct answer in a set of items to avoid students spotting a pattern (perhaps designed to make correction easier for the teacher).
8. Use homogeneous and plausible options. Sometimes teachers have difficulty in coming up with a last option and include a choice that most students immediately know to be unrealistic.
9. Avoid the introduction of irrelevant clues in the questions through careless wording: make all options grammatically consistent with the stem and ensure consistent punctuation.

Now review the sample multiple-choice items below. Evaluate them in relation to the tips highlighted above, finding at least one major flaw in each item. Can you think of some ways to improve the items? Re-write them. Then develop two other multiple-choice items that you could use with a class you intend to teach to assess some aspect of learning.

The lungs in mammals are examples of:	Lara is 7 years old. She has lovely red hair. She has 4 big red apples. Jan has black hair. Jan has 7 green apples. How many more apples has Jan than Lara?
A. Breathing	A. 2
B. Organs	B. 3
C. Reptiles	C. 4
D. Species	

Visit the companion website at: https://study.sagepub.com/murchanshiel

Join the debate: Is there a place for 'traditional' test formats in 21st-century education systems?

Many academic authors and commentators bemoan the backwash effect of assessment on curriculum and teaching. A study by Stuart Buck and colleagues (2010), however, found surprising support for testing amongst teachers in the US state of Arkansas. The study revealed that articles critical of testing in educational policy journals outnumbered positive papers by nine to one. Teachers interviewed as part of Buck's study held more favourable views of testing than commentators. Teachers felt that tests provide useful information about the extent to which students grasp concepts. They help provide focus to teachers' planning and instruction and do not compromise teachers' and students' capacity to be creative in their teaching and learning. Also according to the study, tests can actually encourage teachers to be more collaborative with colleagues, and some measure of accountability provided by tests is useful. Teachers in the sample frequently used traditional test formats and standardised tests as part of state-wide testing mandates.

Review the recent issues of two educational journals with which you are familiar, ideally one academic/scholarly journal and one professional journal, perhaps from a teacher union or professional association. Identify articles that discuss use of the type of traditional items discussed in this chapter. How are these test formats perceived? By authors/researchers? By teachers? What are the implications for your own practice as a teacher?

Other forms of objective tests

A number of other forms of objective tests are available to teachers. One of the most popular is matching exercises in which students are required to make associations between sets of stimuli. The accuracy of the associations made by students allows teachers to make inferences about students' knowledge and understanding. Normally, a set or list of premises is presented, along with a matching set of options, with the options usually being greater in number than the premises. An advantage is efficiency in both administration and in scoring: many association items can be presented to students in a testing session and there is a minimal writing burden on students. These items enable the teacher to assess students' ability to identify associations between: concepts and definitions, images and labels, abbreviated symbols and meanings, and words and their translation. Whereas these items are useful, they are restricted to a small number of specific elements of learning, mainly involving the capacity to associate. Matching items come in varied formats and Figure 6.6 presents an example using a visual stimulus rather than two lists of words. In this example, the image and four questions about the eye represent the premises, while the list to the left of the image represents the options. Note that there are more options than identified premises. Some authors consider the matching exercise to be an extended form of multiple choice, where each premise is, in fact, a multiple-choice test with options (Nitko and Brookhart, 2014). Generally, it is better to have an unequal number of premises and options, so that students cannot identify the last association by a process of elimination.

(b) The diagram shows the human eye. Examine the diagram and answer   (15)
the questions that follow.

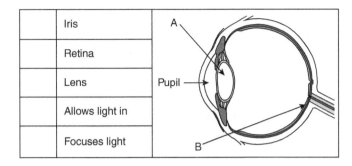

Iris	A
Retina	
Lens	Pupil
Allows light in	
Focuses light	B

(i) In the table write the letter **A** beside the **name** of the **part** labelled **A**.

(ii) In the table write the letter **B** beside the **name** of the **part** labelled **B**.

(iii) In the table write the letter **C** beside the **function** of the **part** labelled **A**.

(iv) In the table write the letter **D** beside the **function** of the **pupil**.

Figure 6.6   Illustration of matching item

Source: SEC, Junior Certificate Ordinary Level Science, June 2008

Chapter summary

The item formats explored in this chapter have been widely used in schools and assessment systems for decades. As such, test developers and teachers have built up considerable knowledge and expertise about how they are best developed, used and interpreted. Some formats, such as multiple choice and essays, are frequently criticised as being traditional and incapable of assessing the type of skills required by students in the 21st century. However, this criticism misses the point that teachers need to use a diversity of assessment approaches and formats. The chapter highlighted the varied dimensions of learning that modern curricula and schools are expected to foster in students, indicating the need to match approaches to assessment with educational intentions. No one approach to assessment can universally capture information on all aspects of students' education and development. It would be as inappropriate for a teacher of primary or secondary students to use only essays as it would be for that teacher to use only in-class presentations. What is needed is a diverse mix of approaches that, together, can help teachers, students and other stakeholders to acquire greater understanding of students' level of achievement and, therefore, of possible next steps in their development.

The chapter explores a number of traditional item types, including essays, short-answer, true–false, multiple-choice and association items. Possibilities for use are identified and advantages and disadvantages are discussed. Readers are invited to review guidelines for developing quality items and to apply these guidelines in evaluating some items and in developing their own items for use with their own students. A number of general implications and recommendations for teachers can be inferred from the discussion in this chapter. There is no one perfect test or assessment approach suited to all learners and occasions. Rather, teachers need to select and/or develop assessments that align as reasonably and as practically as possible with the intended learning outcomes. In preparing assessments, you could usefully share your items with colleagues, craft items using clear, simple language and feel free to use a mixture of formats, even within one assessment. When using tests that require students to write, such as essays, consider to what extent students' language ability does and should relate to the intended learning. When using test formats that require students to select a pre-determined response, such as multiple choice, consider the possible effect of guessing on scores and your interpretation of student performance on the test.

Questions for discussion

1. Make a list of the test formats that you experienced as a student in primary or secondary school (all that you can remember). Group them under a number of format headings (written, oral, practical, traditional, alternative). What conclusions can you draw?
2. Authentic assessment is a term widely used to identify approaches to assessing students that emphasise depth, challenge and real-world contexts in relation to student learning. Frey et al. (2012: 14) identify key elements of authentic assessment. These include: a cognitively complex task, a task that interests the student, and one that relates to skills or abilities that have relevance beyond the assessment itself. To what extent are any of the item formats discussed in this chapter 'authentic'? In particular, can essays support the authentic assessment of 21st-century skills? What are the counter-points that critics might make?
3. Your teaching colleague, Mr Walsh, uses some true–false and multiple-choice tests to assess students. At a recent parent–teacher meeting, a parent told him that these types of tests are too simplistic and the students can probably do fine by just guessing. What advice would you give your colleague in responding to the parent's comments?

Further reading

Haladyna, T.M., Downing, S.M., & Rodriguez, M.C. (2002). A review of multiple-choice item-writing guidelines for classroom assessment. *Applied Measurement in Education, 15* (3), 309–33.

This article explores in detail the arguments for and against many of the guidelines for writing MCQs that are frequently advanced in the literature. The paper also provides useful illustration and evaluative commentary on a range of MCQ formats frequently found in teacher-made tests and in textbooks.

OECD (2005). *The definition and selection of key competencies: Executive summary.* Available at: www.deseco.admin.ch/bfs/deseco/en/index/02.parsys.43469.downloadList.2296. DownloadFile.tmp/2005.dskcexecutivesummary.en.pdf

This article outlines the result of an OECD project lead by Switzerland to investigate the key competencies required by individuals and by society to live successfully and ensure a well-functioning society in the future. DeSeCo identified three broad competencies: using tools effectively; interacting in heterogeneous groups; and acting autonomously. Though not addressing assessment per se, the competencies identified by the OECD have influenced educational policy in many countries and have implications for the ways in which student learning should be assessed. Proponents of traditional written tests need to evaluate how such approaches can be used or need to be modified (perhaps using computer-based assessment with multi-media stimuli) if these approaches are to remain relevant in the future.

7

Performance-based assessment

What you will learn in this chapter

In Chapter 6, we saw how the choice of assessment formats can be linked to expected learning outcomes. This chapter builds on that idea, illustrating many occasions when traditional written tests cannot be directly aligned with learning. Many current curricula focus on developing transferable skills, such as using information interactively, cooperating with others to solve problems and managing one's own learning. Such learning requires the adoption of more varied authentic or performance assessments. This chapter focuses on planning, constructing, marking and evaluating performance assessments. Topics include (a) the move towards '21st-century skills'; (b) the process of conducting performance-based assessments; (c) approaches to scoring such assessments, including the use of checklists, rating scales and rubrics; and (d) the format of performance-based assessments (oral exams and presentations, projects and portfolios and coursework).

When you finish the chapter, you should be able to answer these questions:

- How can I develop and implement reliable, valid, performance-based assessments tailored to address important learning outcomes?
- How can I assess basic skills in literacy and numeracy on the one hand, and '21st-century skills' such as problem solving and collaboration on the other?
- What practical issues arise in implementing performance-based assessments?
- What differences arise in using performance-based assessments for AfL and AoL?
- How can technology support the effective implementation of performance-based assessments?
- How can I blend performance-based assessment with other forms of assessment into a broad, balanced approach to assessment?

Performance-based assessment and the shift to 21st-century skills

Few would argue that performance-based assessment has been around for some time. In secondary school, you may have completed oral examinations in French or Spanish, or maintained a portfolio of artwork that was submitted for grading at the end of a course. Earlier, at primary level you and your fellow-students may have been asked to complete a group project in history or geography, or to play a piece of music on an instrument. Many of you will remember completing and perhaps writing up experiments in science. You may be aware of the current debate around performance-based assessments at post-primary level, where teachers in some jurisdictions have been reluctant to mark their own students' work for certification purposes, preferring instead that marking be completed by anonymous examiners not familiar with the students who completed the work.

A performance-based assessment is the assessment of a student's ability to apply knowledge, skills and understanding, usually in authentic, real-life settings that are similar to those encountered in the world outside the classroom. Typically, students are required to create a product (such as a multi-media presentation) or demonstrate a process (such as solving a novel problem), or both. Performance-based assessment can be used to measure a broad range of learning outcomes, including more complex outcomes that cannot be assessed using indirect measures, such as multiple-choice tests and written examinations. Examples of performance-based assessments across primary and secondary education include:

- representing a character from a nursery rhyme in drama
- keeping a portfolio of artwork, including seasonal art
- demonstrating a routine, movement or dance in physical education or drama
- making a video to dramatise an historical theme
- editing a story, term paper or essay
- conducting a science experiment
- working with a group of students to design a student attitude survey
- using equipment such as a calculator to complete a task
- cooking a meal in the school kitchen
- reporting on a project by delivering a multi-media presentation.

Typically, assessing performance involves evaluating student learning. The evaluation (making a judgement about the quality of a performance) can be conducted by a teacher, an external marker or students themselves. Indeed, Klenowski and Wyatt-Smith (2014) point to student self-assessment, whereby students evaluate their own learning, and, most importantly, internalise assessment standards or criteria, as a major benefit of performance-based assessment. In conducting an assessment, the rater may use a scoring tool such as a checklist, a rating scale or a scoring rubric. The use of an appropriate scoring tool is essential to ensuring that relevant aspects of the performance are assessed (validity) and that the assessment is marked in a consistent manner (reliability). Evaluation can occur during a performance (for example, as a student delivers a presentation or solves a problem) or afterwards (for example, after an essay, a project or portfolio of work has been completed and submitted).

Performance assessments can vary in length from activities that take just a few minutes to complete, such as a solving a basic mathematics problem, to projects that may take several weeks and require students to present their findings to audiences inside and outside the school.

Various authors have identified aspects of knowledge and dispositions that can best be assessed using performance-based assessments, and some of these frameworks overlap:

- *Habits of mind* – according to Costa and Kallick (2008), these are problem-solving, life-related skills that are needed to operate effectively in society and include persisting, thinking flexibly, managing impulsivity, thinking about one's thinking (metacognition), applying past knowledge to new situations, taking responsible risks, thinking independently and remaining open to continuous learning.
- *Collaborative problem solving* – students are assessed as they work together to complete a project or another performance task (e.g. Von Davier and Halpin, 2013). In judging the outcomes of cooperative learning, there may be learning outcomes relating to the overall success of the project (for example, the development of a model or report), as well as outcomes specifying the expected contributions of individuals.
- *Twenty-first century skills* – these are skills that are deemed important for the world of work in the 21st century. Griffin and Care (2015) describe these as including: ways of thinking (creativity and innovation, critical problem solving, problem solving, megacognition); ways of working (communication, collaboration/teamwork); tools for working (information literacy, ICT literacy); and living in the world (citizenship, life and career, personal and social responsibility). Griffith and Care's work highlights the increasingly important role of ICTs in teaching, learning and assessment.
- *Higher-order thinking skills* – these comprise the more advanced skills on Bloom's revised taxonomy (Anderson and Krathwohl, 2001) and include: applying (using information in new situations); analysing (drawing connections among ideas); evaluating (justifying a stand or decision); and creating (producing new or original work). For illustrations of the application of assessment tasks using Anderson and Krathwohl's taxonomy, see Table 5.4 in Chapter 5.

Other sources that focus on the development and assessment of key skills across subject areas include the Curriculum for Excellence in Scotland (Scottish Government, 2008), the Junior Cycle framework in Ireland (DES, 2015a) and skills and capabilities (including cross-curricular skills) in Northern Ireland (CCEA, 2016a).

It is notable that many countries seeking to implement performance-based assessment, with a view to assessing 21st-century skills, also seek to ensure that students have acquired strong basic skills in literacy and numeracy. In Ireland, for example, there is currently an emphasis on literacy and numeracy across the curriculum, even as key skills such as self-management, working with others, being creative and managing information and thinking are being emphasised. Hence, assessment programmes at school level may need to include both basic skills and complex 21st-century skills.

A key rationale for using performance-based assessment is that it is possible to establish strong links between curriculum (expressed as goals or objectives), learning (expressed as performance standards or learning outcomes) and assessment (see Figure 7.1). In particular, aspects of the curriculum that cannot otherwise be assessed (such as collaborative problem solving) are emphasised and students can demonstrate their strengths in these areas. The outcomes of assessment can then feed into further teaching and learning activities, and gaps in student performance can be addressed. Some authors (for example, Klenowski and Wyatt-Smith, 2014) argue that performance-based assessment, if used effectively, has considerable potential as an instrument of educational reform and as a disincentive to teaching to the test (that is, preparing students to sit examinations that are often predictable in format and content). They also argue that it is consistent with social constructivist learning theories.

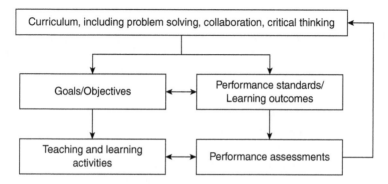

Figure 7.1   Teaching, learning and assessment cycle

Table 7.1   Examples of performance-based tasks

Learning outcomes (Standards)	Task	Source
Understand content knowledge in physics (e.g. flotation)	Given some clay, a drinking straw and paper, design a sailboat that will sail across a small body of water; students can test and retest their designs (Grade 8)	Darling-Hammond and Adamson (2010): from Illinois State Assessment
Demonstrate presentation skills in a formal setting; listen and respond appropriately to spoken language; use spoken and standard English effectively in speeches and presentations	Listen to a speech extract on television and represent its main points and biases; alternatively, listen to a school assembly and re-present its main points and explain its methods of presentation	Assessment and Qualifications Alliance (AQA, 2016): GCSE controlled assessment
Recognise questions that are appropriate for scientific investigation; design, plan and conduct investigations; organise and communicate research and investigative findings in a variety of ways, fit for purpose and audience, using relevant scientific terminology and representations	Over a three-week period, formulate a scientific hypothesis, plan and conduct an experimental investigation to test the hypothesis, generate and analyse primary data, and reflect on the process, with support or guidance from the teacher	National Council for Curriculum and Assessment (Ireland) (NCCA, 2016): Junior Certificate science extended experimental investigation

While it is clear that considerable progress is being made in broadening the range of skills that can be assessed using performance-based assessment (e.g. Griffin and Care, 2015), it has been pointed out that there is limited understanding of the constructs underpinning skills such as working collaboratively to solve a problem or thinking creatively (Von Davier and Halpin, 2013). Hence, it is important to specify as clearly as possible what outcomes are being assessed, and to distinguish between outcomes that can be described as cognitive and those that focus on other important 21st-century skills.

Table 7.1 provides further examples of performance-based assessments. It is notable that each assessment is designed to assess multiple learning outcomes, with some outcomes such as research and communication skills cutting across disciplines.

In the next section, we look at the process of implementing a performance-based assessment.

Implementing a performance-based assessment

A performance-based assessment task can be developed and scored by an individual teacher, a subject department, an external assessor or an examining board. A performance task seeks to assess learning targets or objectives that are specified in curriculum documents.

Such tasks may be carried out by individuals or groups. They can be scored as students work on the task and/or after it has been completed. Generally, scoring is done with one of the tools described in the next section. Often, curriculum objectives are expressed as standards or learning outcomes and these become the focus of a rating scale or a rubric.

A moderation process may be put in place, where a check on the quality of the grades assigned by the teacher is undertaken. This could involve a different rater taking a random sample of completed tasks and scoring them independently. Discrepancies between two or more raters can then be addressed in a marking or moderation conference. Sometimes, when moderation unearths a discrepancy, the assessor may need to review the standards (learning outcomes) to achieve a better understanding of them. This is not dissimilar to the moderation that occurs when exam papers are being corrected and a random sample is re-scored to ensure consistency (see Chapter 3).

Several sources (for example, Klenowsky and Wyatt-Smith, 2014; NCCA, 2016) advocate moderation meetings or 'subject learning and assessment review meetings', where teaching staff in a school can share examples of student work and share their judgements with other colleagues. The purpose of this activity is to develop a greater understanding of learning standards and to ensure a consistency of judgement about student performance. Klenowsky and Wyatt-Smith point to the value of technology for sharing and reviewing the scores or levels assigned to student tasks (ICT-moderated or e-moderated assessment). However, they also argue that, in the case of assessment for learning, the validity of judgements about individual pieces of work takes precedence over reliability, with diagnostic use of the outcomes taking precedence over the consistency in scoring.

Another form of moderation is to provide raters with samples of student work that exemplify each point on a rating scale or scoring rubric. This enables raters to achieve a better understanding of the required standards and to mark more reliably as a result.

A simple approach to assessing agreement across raters is to calculate the percentage agreement. Thus, if two raters assign the same overall scores to 80% of tasks (papers, projects), we would say that there is 80% agreement. An agreement rating below this level might signal a need to review the scoring guide and re-score the tasks.

The final stage in assessing performance on a task is to assign a grade or mark. This may take the form of a numerical score (for example, 1–5), a descriptor (for example, approaching mastery) or a grade. More extensive feedback may be provided to the student who completed the task – such as comments, an indication of areas in need of further improvement, or targets that the student should strive to reach in the future.

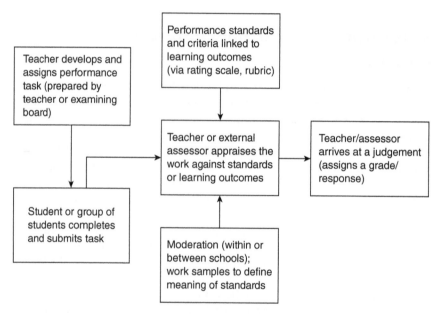

Figure 7.2   Process of performance-based assessment

Tools for assessing performance-based assessment

In this section, four tools that are used to assess how well students do on a performance-based task are described. These are: anecdotal records, observational checklists, rating scales and scoring rubrics.

Anecdotal records

Anecdotal records are notes based on teachers' observations about students as they perform an assessment task. They allow teachers to document student strengths and weaknesses as they edit a text, solve a problem or search for information. Data gleaned from anecdotal notes can be reviewed with other information (such as a finished product) to arrive at an overall judgement of a student's performance.

Observational checklists

A checklist consists of a list of behaviours, characteristics or activities and a place for marking whether each is present or absent. For example, a checklist designed to assess a student's ability to proofread a text might include:

- Read and re-read the text carefully.
- Check for and correct spelling errors.
- Check for and correct grammatical errors.
- Check and correct problems with punctuation (capital letters, full stops, question marks).
- Suggest how the readability of the text could be improved.

A checklist can focus on a procedure, a behaviour or a product. Students may use a self-evaluation checklist to review their own work. This may enable them to internalise the criteria for performing well on a task, and they can also build metacognitive knowledge as their understanding of their own learning processes increases. A potential disadvantage of a checklist is that it does not show degrees of quality – only whether a criterion has been met or not.

Rating scales

Rating scales are often used for aspects of a complex performance that do not lend themselves to a yes–no or present–absent judgement. A rating scale assesses the degree to which a student has attained the learning outcomes linked to a performance task (such as an oral presentation). A rating scale can be used as a teaching tool (to familiarise students with what is required to achieve a standard) as well as an assessment tool. The end points of a rating scale are usually anchored ('always', 'never'), with intermediate points defining levels of performance ('seldom', 'occasionally', 'frequently'). In general, the more points on the rating scale, the more reliable are the scores. An example of a rating scale is given in the section on project work below.

Scoring rubrics

Scoring rubrics, as highlighted in Chapter 6, are a type of rating scale on which each level has a complete description of performance and quality. Rubrics may be analytic, where each of several dimensions is assessed, or holistic, where either a judgement about overall quality or an overall judgement on performance is made. Rubrics may also be general (i.e. the same rubric can be applied to different tasks) or task-specific (where the rubric describes quality with respect to a particular task). An analytic rubric has the potential to generate specific feedback on strengths and weaknesses on each dimension of a task. For example, in the case of a written text, the rater might make judgements on the quality of organisation, content, conventions, structure and vocabulary. As with checklists and rating scales, scoring rubrics can be shared with students before they complete a task, to support them in internalising the standards or criteria associated with strong performance. Students can also participate in the construction of a rubric. An example of a scoring rubric is given in the section on oral presentations below.

A number of threats to the reliability of scores based on performance tasks have been identified. According to Nitko and Brookhart (2014), these include: leniency error (where the rater is too lenient and all students achieve high scores); severity error (where the rater is too extreme and marks all students at the low end of the scale); halo effect, where the rater lets general impressions of the student affect assigned scores; and rater drift, where initial interpretations of a rating scale or rubric are set aside and raters begin to redefine the rubric for themselves.

Strategies that can be deployed to guard against unreliable scores include moderation, where a fixed number of tasks is selected at random, and scored by additional raters; and the use of work samples to describe different points along a scale or rubric. In cases where a problem is identified, a rater may need to be retrained and tasks may need to be re-scored.

Performance-based assessments that are used for accountability purposes (such as an evaluation of the quality of learning at school level) or for certification (when the score that a student achieves contributes to the grade in an examination) must be both valid and reliable.

Performance-based assessments have been a subject of criticism. Koretz (2008) notes that they are difficult to design and can be subject to construct-irrelevance variance and under-representation, because they assess skills and knowledge that are not essential to a domain or that cover limited aspects of it (thereby threatening validity). Isaacs et al. (2013) note that they are time-consuming and may take time away from teaching. In England, performance-based assessments (controlled assessments or coursework contributing to examination grades) at GCSE have been a subject of concern.

A controlled assessment is a performance-based assessment that is carried out in a supervised environment such as a classroom. Controlled assessments were introduced in England in 2009 to address concerns about the reliability and authenticity of coursework (performance tasks), the way work was produced by students, and the marking and moderation of teachers and exam boards (Ofqual, 2013). High, medium or low levels of control are set for each of the controlled assessment stages – task setting, task taking and task marking. For each stage, the level of control is designed to ensure reliability and authenticity, and to make assessments more manageable for students.

For most GCSE subjects, up to 25% of marks are available for controlled assessments, usually for one task, with the balance (75%) based on a final examination. For others, such as practical or creative subjects, up to 60% of marks are available for up to three assessment units.

As GCSE subjects are revised for first examination from 2017 onwards, it is planned to eliminate controlled assessments, except in subjects in which they are seen as necessary, such as science. This arises from an inconsistency in GCSE results in the past (especially in 2012) and concerns about grade inflation linked to controlled assessments. In the case of English, performance on listening and speaking, based on controlled assessment, will be reported on GCSE certificates, even though it will not form part of the main (written) GCSE examination.

Range of performance-based assessments

In this section, a range of performance-based assessments is described including projects, portfolios, oral performances, experiments and investigations, and simulations. It should be noted that the tasks underpinning these assessments may overlap. For example, an oral performance might be assessed on its own merits, or it might be part of a project or an investigation.

Projects

Projects are long-term structured activities completed by individuals or groups that result in a product such as a model, a substantial report or a collection of artefacts. According to Nitko and Brookhart (2014), projects can call on a broad range of skills and knowledge, including creativity, communication skills, problem solving, critical thinking and subject matter knowledge. While individual projects focus on the work of one student, group projects focus on the activities of several students. In addition to evaluating the final product, assessment may look at whether students work together collaboratively. Indeed, collaboration is specified as a learning target in many curricula. As noted earlier, it is considered to be an essential 21st-century skill.

A scoring rubric for a group project may have several dimensions, each of which is rated on a three- or five-point scale. The dimensions, which relate to group and individual contributions can include:

- teamwork and collaboration
- content and creativity
- subject matter knowledge
- presentation of outcomes
- individual written reflection (allowing students an opportunity to outline their contributions to the completed project, and their understanding of the outcomes).

Examples of group projects include:

- creating a newsletter
- researching an historic figure on the internet
- implementing and reporting on an attitudinal survey
- researching a national issue (e.g. taking steps to manage climate change) or a local one (e.g. granting planning permission for a new shopping centre) and giving both sides of the argument
- designing a campaign to persuade teenagers to take more exercise.

The rating scale for scoring the *Heroes or Villains* project (see Figure 7.3) could include three components, corresponding to the three clusters of learning outcomes described in the project task – Working as a historian, Collaborative learning and Communication. The purpose of the rating scale in Table 7.2 is to assign scores to a group as a whole. Although a 5-point scale is given, only three points (5, 3, 1) are defined. However, scores of 2 or 4 can be awarded if the rater decides that a student's work falls between a 1 and a 3, or between a 3 and a 5 respectively.

Some educators may question the inclusion of collaborative learning and communication on a rating scale designed to assess an understanding of history. However, if the history curriculum includes these elements as goals or learning objectives, or expresses them as learning targets, they should be included in an assessment.

People in Ireland who took part in the 1916 Rising have been hailed as heroes by some and as villains by others. In cooperative groups, source at least two articles giving these contrasting viewpoints, summarise the information provided and prepare a PowerPoint presentation that seeks to explain these contrasting viewpoints. You have two weeks to complete the project.

Your work will be assessed on the following learning outcomes:

Working as a historian:

Asks questions about a piece of evidence
Compares accounts of a person from two or more sources
Appreciates that evidence can be interpreted in different ways
Selects and organises historical information
Discusses how an event in the past may have been perceived by those who participated in it

Collaborative learning:

Works with other students to complete the project
Contributes ideas and resources to the group

Communication:

Prepares for a presentation in advance
Communicates understanding using multi-media applications
Demonstrates an understanding of the audience

Figure 7.3   Example of a history project (Grades 6–8): Heroes or villains?

Table 7.2   Rating scale for group history project on heroes or villains

	5 points 4 points	3 points 2 points	1 point
Working as a historian	• Students provide a detailed description of the contrasting perspectives on rebels' actions, drawing on at least two reputable sources • Students provide clear reasons for differing interpretations	• Students indicate a general understanding of differing perspectives, but explanations are weak or unclear, and show limited understanding • Reasons for differing interpretations are moderately well organised	• Students do not provide two contrasting perspectives; presentation is poorly researched • Reasons for differing interpretations are weak and lack clarity
Collaborative learning	• Students collaborate well with each other in researching background information • Students consistently share ideas and information with each other	• Students engage in some collaboration • Students engage in research and share some information or ideas	• Students rarely collaborate with one another • Students do not engage in research or share information or ideas with one another

	5 points	4 points	3 points	2 points	1 point
Communication	• Students prepare a detailed and appropriate presentation in advance, drawing on relevant resources • Students show an awareness of the audience and respond to audience questions		• Students prepare a moderately appropriate presentation that includes some relevant resources • Students show some audience awareness and deal satisfactorily with some audience questions		• Students prepare a weak presentation, drawing on resources that are not really relevant to the presentation • Students show a limited awareness of the audience and do not respond satisfactorily to questions

Personalities in educational assessment: Patrick Griffin

Patrick Griffin, chair of educational assessment at the University of Melbourne and director of the Assessment Research Centre, is one of just a handful of Australians admitted to the International Academy of Education. He has been heavily involved in ground-breaking initiatives in assessment in Australia and internationally for over 30 years. His work has been in the areas of language proficiency, industrial literacy, and literacy and numeracy in school settings. Other areas of activity include the development of curriculum profiles, professional standards, portfolio assessment and online assessment. Professor Griffin has pioneered the computer-based assessment of 21st-century skills. He has spearheaded the work of the Partnership for 21st Century Skills, a major international effort supported by companies such as CISCO and Microsoft, investigating how such skills can be defined and measured. He has also been involved in the assessment of problem solving, through work with PISA.

Oral presentations

Many performance-based assessments involve an oral presentation. Such presentations allow students to demonstrate their knowledge and skills through interviews, speeches and presentations, including those that are multi-modal. An oral presentation may be a stand-alone activity or may be part of a larger project which culminates in the communication of key findings by participants.

While sharing checklists and scoring rubrics with students can heighten their awareness of the criteria associated with effective oral presentations, teachers can also model effective presentations and draw attention to important strategies, such as opening with one or more key questions, making eye contact with listeners and using signalling terms such as 'in summary' and 'in conclusion'.

The following are some topics that could be addressed in student presentations:

- Explain why iPads and other tablets are excellent tools for learning.
- Does frequent use of social media lead to lower levels of concentration and focus?
- Should recycling be compulsory and why?
- Do advertisements on social media influence what we eat and drink?

- Is a sugar tax a good idea for tackling obesity?
- Should cars with large engines be banned?

Oral presentations can be evaluated with a variety of tools, including scoring rubrics. Table 7.3 shows a rubric for evaluating oral presentations. It focuses on three main aspects – delivery, content and organisation, and enthusiasm and audience awareness – while provision is also made for adding comments (an important element of assessment for learning).

Portfolios

A portfolio is a collection of material designed to showcase a student's best work or to show the student's growth and development over time (for example, over a term or school year). Entries to the portfolio may be linked to learning targets and may include self-reflections on the student's own work. Portfolio entries may be annotated by the student, allowing the teacher to track student thinking and explanations as well as progress over time. Portfolios may also be used as a basis for diagnosing a student's learning difficulties in a subject area.

Examples of tasks for which portfolios might be appropriate are given below. Each is accompanied by specific or implied learning targets:

- Visual Arts, where the student is facilitated in putting together a personal assessment portfolio to demonstrate their growth and learning. This may be linked to learning targets such as:

  o gathering samples (assembling completed pieces before making a final selection)
  o selecting and supporting (providing a rationale for selecting specific pieces)
  o reflecting (thinking about what has been learned and looking ahead)
  o applying and extending (indicating how new learning can be applied in the future).

- Physical Education, where the student is asked to assemble a portfolio that demonstrates:

  o understanding of factors that impact on student performance
  o planning, developing and implementing of approaches to enhance personal performance
  o monitoring, recording and evaluating performance development. (see Scottish Qualifications Authority, 2015)

- English Literature and Creative Writing, where the student completes a portfolio that includes pieces drawn from a range of genres:

  o Responding to literature: Relating events to illustrations
  o Group discussion: Comparing texts in different genres
  o Imaginative verse: People of the future (students compose poetry)
  o Written narrative: What a mess
  o Oral presentation: Words or pictures?
  o Biographical letter: News from the goldfields
  o Group discussion: Literary mood. (see ACARA, 2014)

Table 7.3 Rubric for assessing an oral presentation

Component	Excellent	Good	Fair	Needs improvement
Delivery	• Holds attention of the entire audience with the use of direct eye contact, seldom looking at notes • Speaks with fluctuation in volume and inflection to maintain audience interest and emphasise key points	• Consistent use of direct eye contact with the audience, but still returns to notes • Speaks with satisfactory variation of volume and inflection	• Displays minimal eye contact with the audience, while reading mostly from notes • Speaks in uneven volume with little or no inflection	• Holds no eye contact with the audience, as the entire report is read from notes • Speaks in low volume and/ or monotonous tone, which causes audience to disengage
Content/ Organisation	• Demonstrates full knowledge by answering all class questions with explanations and elaboration • Provides clear purpose and subject; pertinent examples, facts, and/or statistics; supports conclusions/ideas with evidence	• Is at ease with expected answers to all questions, without elaboration • Has a somewhat clear purpose and subject; has some examples, facts and/ or statistics that support the subject; includes some data or evidence that supports conclusions	• Is uncomfortable with the information and is able to answer only rudimentary questions • Attempts to define the subject and purpose; provides weak examples, facts and/ or statistics, which do not adequately support the subject; includes very thin data or evidence	• Does not have a grasp of the information and cannot answer questions about the subject • Does not clearly define the subject and purpose; provides weak or no support of subject; gives insufficient support for ideas or conclusions
Enthusiasm/ audience awareness	• Demonstrates strong enthusiasm about the topic during entire presentation • Significantly increases audience understanding and knowledge of topic; convinces an audience to recognise the validity and importance of the subject	• Shows some enthusiastic feelings about the topic • Raises audience understanding and awareness of most points	• Shows few or mixed feelings about the topic being presented • Raises audience understanding and knowledge of some points	• Shows no interest in the topic presented • Fails to increase audience understanding and knowledge of topic

Comments:

Source: International Reading Association and NCTE (2013)

The English literature portfolio includes printed texts and multi-media artefacts such as video or audio recordings.

In setting up a portfolio assessment, it is important to outline what learning outcomes are to be assessed, what proportion of marks is available for each section and when the portfolio should be submitted. The teacher will also need to decide what level of support or scaffolding should be provided to the student.

Portfolios can be assessed using checklists, rating scales or scoring rubrics. They also allow for self-assessment, as students review their own work and comment on it, drawing on a rubric developed by the teacher. Where possible, a rubric can be co-developed by teacher and students.

An electronic portfolio or e-portfolio is a collection of student work, usually saved on the Web. Evidence of learning may include texts, electronic files, images and multi-media. Such a portfolio allows students to share their work with teachers, parents, administrators and other students. In addition to contributing to the development of target skills linked to the learning targets for a course, the e-portfolio builds a student's digital skills. As well as providing students with a chance to reflect on their learning processes and progress, an e-portfolio facilitates the participation of the student's teacher, peers and parents in the learning process as feedback and comment can be provided. Perhaps the key advantages of an e-portfolio are that it enables students to track their learning over a lengthy period of time, and to reflect on their learning at any time.

When introducing e-portfolios, issues such as whether the student's work can be made public, and whether students can view and comment on one another's work may need to be addressed.

Experiments and investigations

An experiment or investigation is a performance task in which a student (or students) prepares for, implements and interprets the results of a research study.

Experiments and investigations allow the teacher to assess whether students use the appropriate enquiry skills and methods.

With experiments and investigations, one or more of the following outcomes can be assessed:

- plans and carries out investigations
- forms a testable hypothesis or prediction with justification
- describes considerations related to reliability and fairness
- safely assembles and accurately uses appropriate equipment
- describes the method used to gather good quality data
- records a sufficient amount of good quality data
- describes relationships between variables
- presents data in an appropriate way
- develops alternative interpretations and looks at data in more than one way
- acknowledges the strengths and weaknesses of the investigation.

While experiments and investigations are appropriate for many content areas, the following are examples that are science-related:

- How does the air pressure of a soccer ball affect how far it travels when kicked?
- How does the temperature of water affect the time it takes to freeze into ice cubes?
- In a blind taste test, can you tell the difference between non-fat, low-fat and whole milk?
- Which can support more weight: paper or plastic grocery bags?
- How does the tension in a violin's strings affect its pitch?
- How does the time of day affect your body's temperature?
- What type of ground layer limits erosion the most: sand, gravel or soil?
- Which has a longer life: an LED or an incandescent light bulb?
- Does a person's weight vary throughout the day?

Figure 7.4 provides an example of a science investigation for students in Grade 7 (Year 7). The level of support or scaffolding that is provided in the description of the activity will depend on your expectations of the students and what they can attempt without help.

This investigation can be assessed using a scoring rubric, such as the one presented in Figure 7.5.

Making and testing an electrical circuit

Learning outcomes to be assessed:

Set up a simple electric circuit

Test for electrical conduction in a variety of materials and classify each material as a conductor or an insulator

---

Task:

1. Make an electrical current using a battery, wire, a light bulb and switch
2. Make a simple drawing of your circuit, labelling all parts
3. Use the circuit to test which of the following conduct electricity: plastic spoon, steel washer, string, nail, 5-pence/cent coin, rubber band
4. Describe what the objects that conduct electricity have in common
5. What have the objects that don't conduct electricity in common?
6. What broad conclusions can you draw?

Figure 7.4 Science investigation: Making and testing a simple electric circuit

---

Making and testing a simple electrical circuit

---

4 points: Draws a complete and accurate diagram of a circuit with supporting evidence; demonstrates a strong understanding of the concepts of electricity and conductivity; may use descriptive terms (conductor, insulator, flow, current, etc.); draws appropriate conclusions

3 points: Includes a complete diagram of a circuit; demonstrates good understanding of the concepts of electricity and conductivity; identifies most of the objects that conduct electricity; conclusions generally correct, if not always stated in scientific terms

2 points: Draws diagram of a circuit where some components are missing or incomplete; shows some understanding of the concept of electricity but not conductivity; conclusions partially correct

1 point: Does not include a diagram of a circuit; most answers incorrect; does not draw appropriate conclusions

---

Figure 7.5 Scoring rubric for science experiment

Simulations

While teachers have used technology as part of the assessment process for a long time (for example, by asking students to respond orally or in writing to a segment from a film on DVD, and to compare it with the novel on which the film is based), in recent years there has been an extensive use of simulations in science, mathematics and other subjects that are designed to assess students' ability to manipulate a number of variables simultaneously, and to draw conclusions about what they have found. For example, in the OECD Programme for International Study Assessment (PISA) in 2015 (see Chapter 3), 15-year-olds in most participating countries encountered a combination of traditional science items (multiple-choice and short answer) and 'interactive' or simulation-based items, all delivered on computer (OECD, 2016a). The simulation-based items described scenarios such as running in hot weather. Here, the student can manipulate air temperature, air humidity and whether the runner drinks water or not, to draw conclusions about the conditions in which heat-stroke or dehydration are likely to occur. In addition to manipulating variables, students are asked to draw on the relevant science knowledge (for example, sweating cools the body, helping to regulate body temperature). Students are also asked to answer questions where the answer cannot be found in the simulation, but can be inferred (they were asked whether it was safe to run without water at 40° C and 50% air humidity, when the slider for air humidity could only be set at either 40% and 60%). Another simulation asks students about the effects of varying outdoor temperature and roof colour on energy consumption (defined as maintaining room temperature at a constant 23 degrees celsius).

Simulations such as these have the potential to tap into aspects of knowledge and understanding that are less assessable with more traditional stimuli and questions. They may be categorised as performance-based assessments since students interact with stimuli that represent real-world situations, and are required to communicate their reasoning. Equally, simulations can be useful as teaching and learning tools as they allow students to access real-life situations that would not otherwise be accessible, and to engage in reasoning as they consider how variables are related to one another and change over time.

Join the debate: Addressing issues in performance-based assessments

It is generally acknowledged that, when used to assess students' learning in classroom settings, performance-based assessment can provide teachers with valuable information about students' ability to implement a broad range of skills that cannot be assessed using more traditional assessment tools. Hence, performance-based assessment has tremendous potential in the context of AfL classrooms. In a similar vein, students can assess their own performance and draw conclusions on how their learning has progressed. However, there is divided opinion on the use of performance assessments for certification purposes (AoL or assessment of learning). Based on their experience in Australia, Klenowski and Wyatt-Smith (2014) have argued that teachers can be supported through systemic moderation to interpret standards (learning outcomes) and provide reliable data from performance-based assessments that can then be used for accountability purposes. Others, such as the Office of Qualifications and Examinations Regulation (Ofqual) in England, have raised questions about the fairness of performance-based assessments at GCSE level, even when they are administered and scored under controlled conditions, and have taken steps to decouple them from examination grades, beginning with English language and English literature. Do you think that performance-based assessments should contribute to examination grades? Draw on your own experience, the information provided in this chapter and the relevant literature to make your case. The companion website includes further resources useful in this debate.

Now, for each of the statements about performance-based assessment below indicate your agreement, or disagreement, and provide at least one reason for each response:

Statement	Agree	Disagree	Reason
Performance-based assessments allow teachers to assess students' processes as well as the products they produce			
Performance-based assessments, especially more complex ones which extend over several weeks, can eat into valuable teaching time			
High-quality performance-based assessment tasks can only be created by assessment professionals			
Performance-based assessments are especially suited to students with special educational needs, or those who speak a language at home that is different to the language of instruction in school			
The key drawback of performance tasks is the lack of reliability between raters			

Visit the companion website at: https://study.sagepub.com/murchanshiel

Chapter summary

The focus of this chapter was on performance-based assessment and how it can be deployed to assess a range of 21st-century skills that cannot be assessed using other methods such as written tests and exams.

A distinction was drawn between the use of performance-based assessment for AfL and for AoL, and the strengths and weaknesses of performance-based assessment were outlined. It was noted that the use of performance-based assessments, particularly in classroom contexts is consistent with constructivist learning theory.

Broad approaches to performance-based assessment that were outlined include projects, oral presentations, portfolios, experiments and investigations, and simulations. Tools that could be used to assess performance on these measures, including rating scales and rubrics, were described.

The value of performance-based assessments in developing students' metacognitive knowledge was stressed. It was noted that students could internalise performance standards by evaluating their own work, using an appropriate rubric in which outcomes and criteria are clearly specified (for example, self-evaluation).

Throughout the chapter, the key concepts of validity and reliability were stressed, and it was noted that, in the context of using performance-based assessment for AfL, reliability may be less important than validity, as teachers use the outcomes of performance tasks to identify students' strengths and weaknesses, and modify instruction accordingly.

Questions for discussion

1. What are the possibilities and applications for the use of performance assessment with very young children and primary school students? To what extent can young students engage with the self-assessment aspects of performance assessment?
2. The essay format is sometimes characterised as a performance assessment, as we do in this chapter, yet it is one of the oldest and most traditional approaches to assessment. Do you believe that essays should be considered performance assessments? Does the not-uncommon practice of rote learning for examinations compromise the claim of the essay to be a performance assessment?
3. Two challenges in implementing performance assessments are time constraints and workload management for teachers and students. Think of a subject in which you could introduce a performance assessment such as a portfolio or project. What steps could you take to make it more manageable?

Further reading

Brookhart, S.M. (2011). *The use of teacher judgement for summative assessment in the United States: Weighed in the balance and (often) found wanting*. Paper presented at the invited research seminar on teachers' judgments within systems of summative assessment: Strategies for enhancing consistency. Oxford University Centre for Educational Assessment. Available at: http://oucea.education.ox.ac.uk/wordpress/wp-content/uploads/2011/07/Brookhart-FINAL.pdf

Harlen, W. (2005). Trusting teachers' judgment: research evidence of the reliability and validity of teachers' assessment used for summative purposes. *Research Papers in Education, 20* (3), 297–313.

These articles review research on the reliability of teachers' judgements about student performance. What overall view do they convey about the use of teacher judgements to evaluate student learning and what research evidence is provided to support that view?

8

Interpreting and using scores from standardised tests and examinations

What you will learn in this chapter

In Chapter 3, we looked at several tools that are typically associated with assessment of learning (AoL). Two of these tools – standardised tests and public examinations – feature again in this chapter. You will be familiar with the outcomes of these assessments from your own schooling. Indeed, it is unlikely that you have reached this stage in the education system without achieving test scores and/or examination grades that were in the above-average range or higher. In the context of standardised tests, we consider ways in which outcomes are interpreted, referring specifically to norm-referenced and criterion-referenced interpretative frameworks, how test scores can be interpreted (and misinterpreted), and how standardised tests can inform both assessment of learning and assessment for learning. In the case of examinations, we consider strategies for combining results from external tests and coursework (projects, e-portfolios and work samples), potential sources of error in students' examination grades and the potential effects of examinations on teaching and learning. Throughout the chapter, recent changes to tests and examinations in the UK and Ireland are considered. By the end of the chapter, you should have a good understanding of the strengths and weaknesses of a range of approaches to scoring and grading tests.

When you finish the chapter, you should be able to answer these questions:

- What are the benchmarks against which I can interpret a student's performance on an assessment?
- How is students' achievement on formal tests reported?
- How confident can I be that the results I report are accurate?

This and subsequent chapters in the book focus on using assessment information drawn from a variety of assessments, for a range of stakeholders and for a variety of purposes. Figure 8.1 illustrates the relationships between the remaining five chapters.

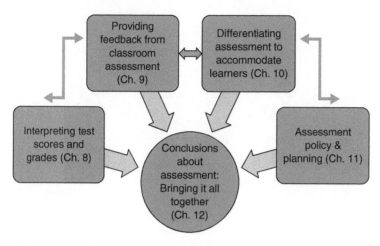

Figure 8.1   Content of chapters on using assessment information

Interpreting and using standardised test results

Purposes for which standardised tests are used

You may remember from Chapter 3 that standardised tests assess the abilities, knowledge and skills of individuals (or groups) under carefully controlled conditions relating to administration and scoring, and that the interpretation of scores is based on an 'interpretative framework' provided with the test (and usually specified in the test manual). Standardised tests scores are typically interpreted with respect to a norm-referenced framework. A student's performance (score) is interpreted by comparing it with the scores of a specified group of students who have taken the same test. This might be a nationally representative sample of students at the same grade level as the student taking the test, or it could be a local norm group, such as students in Year (Grade) 3 in a local education authority. Normative information can be used to describe the strengths, weaknesses and progress of students.

The second broad framework that is used to interpret performance is a criterion-referenced one. This framework interprets a student's performance according to the skills and processes they are likely to demonstrate in a domain. These might comprise discrete learning outcomes (such as solving word problems involving the addition and subtraction of four-digit numbers) or attainment of proficiency levels (statements of the skills that students at a particular level of performance on a test are likely to succeed on). In effect, the student is measured against their ability to perform tasks, rather than on how they do relative to other students. Some standardised test scores may be interpreted with reference to both norm-referenced and criterion-referenced interpretative frameworks.

Norm-referenced interpretative framework

A norm-referenced interpretative framework provides an interpretation of a student's performance by comparing it to the performance of other students on the same assessment in a well-defined norm group of students with similar characteristics who have taken the same test. Thus, the performance of students on a test of reading taken at the end of Sixth Class (Ireland) or at the end of Key Stage 2 (England) might be compared with the performance of other students nationally at the end of those stages of education. Aggregated scores (for example, the average score of all students in a school on reading or mathematics) can also be compared with the average scores of other schools.

Until recently, students taking National Curriculum Assessment tests (SATs – Standardised Assessment Tests) at the end of Key Stages 1 and 2 (KS1 and KS2) were awarded levels of achievement. For example, at KS1 (end of Year 2 or age 7), students who performed 'below expectation' achieved Level 1, those who performed 'at the expected level' achieved Level 2 (which was further subdivided into 2a, 2b and 2c) and those who performed 'above expectation' achieved Level 3 ('exceeding expectation') or Level 4 ('exceptional'). The 'level scores' effectively ranked students according to how well they performed compared with other students nationally at the end of the same key stage, without referring directly to the underlying numerical scores. Nevertheless, the scoring system can be viewed as norm-referenced, since the level awarded to an individual student was referenced against the levels awarded to other students (DfE, 2014b).

Since 2016, the SATs have been based on revised curricula (introduced from 2014 onwards) and the system of awarding levels has been replaced by raw scores (number of correct items answered), derived scaled (standard) scores and an indication as to whether the national average was reached, using descriptors. These descriptors are: *working towards the national standard, working at the national standard* and *working at a greater depth within the national standard.* A provisional report of national average scores for 2016 (September) indicated the following average scaled scores for all schools in England: Reading, 103; Grammar, 104; Mathematics, 103, all slightly above the expected average of 100 (DfE, 2016). Since different tests will be used from year to year, it is likely that the raw score corresponding to the national standard score of 100 will vary somewhat each year.

At the time of writing, it is expected that, from 2016, students at KS1 will be assessed by their teachers in mathematics, reading and writing, and speaking, listening and science, using either tasks or externally set but internally scored tests, at a time decided on by the school. At KS2, students will be assessed on externally set and externally marked tests in reading, grammar, spelling and punctuation, and maths (including arithmetic and reasoning). Testing will typically take place in May each year. Teachers of students at KS2 will assess their own students on reading, writing, mathematics and science and performance on writing (which will be moderated) will be used, alongside performance on formal tests, to evaluate school-level performance, an accountability function for the results.

It is intended to administer a separate and secure 'anchor test' to representative samples of students from time to time. Unlike the annual SATs, the questions on this test will not change. Hence, results can be used to adjust SAT scores, if necessary, and guard against score inflation.

School-level progress between lower- and upper-primary grades will, in general, be assessed by comparing performance at the end of KS1 with performance at the end of KS2.

To allow for valid norm-referenced interpretations, a test must be administered in the same way to students in your class or school as it was administered to students in the norm group when the test was being standardised. This means that the same instructions must be provided and the amount of time allocated must be the same. It is very important to gain an understanding of who was in the norm group. A clear understanding leads to a more valid norm-referenced interpretation. In particular, it is useful to know if certain students were excluded from testing, and, by extension, from the norm group, such as those with special educational needs. Administering a standardised test to students with special educational or other needs, where the norm group did not contain students with similar characteristics, may constitute a threat to the validity of conclusions drawn from the scores. This and further related issues about the assessment of special populations of students are discussed in Chapter 10.

While raw scores (the number of correct answers) and percentage correct scores (the percentage of items answered correctly) can be generated for most tests, these are difficult to interpret in isolation, and additional, derived scores are required. A number of derived scores may be available for students who complete a standardised test. Some of the most common types are presented below:

- *Normalised standard score* – this score tells where a student's raw score is located in relation to a normal distribution fitted to the norm group. For many tests, the mean score is set at 100 and the standard deviation at 15. As shown in Figure 8.2, this means that 68% of students in the norm group performed between one standard deviation below the mean and one standard deviation above the mean (85–115), while 95% performed between two standard deviations above the mean and two standard deviations below the mean (70–130). Scores below 70 and scores above 130 are relatively rare (they are achieved by fewer than 5% of students).[1]
- *Percentile rank* – this is the percentage of students in a norm group scoring lower than a particular raw score. If a student achieves a percentile rank of 70, it means that he or she performed as well as or better than 70% of students in the norm group. Percentile ranks should not be confused with percentage correct scores. Percentile scores cannot be averaged to derive a mean percentile rank.
- *Sten score* – this is a score on an equal-interval scale ranging from 1 (low) to 10 (high) (see Figure 8.2). Sten scores are transformations of standard scores, with a mean of 5.5 and a standard deviation of 2. Parents and others may find these somewhat easier to interpret than standard scores or percentile ranks.
- *Age-equivalent score* – an age-equivalent score gives an estimated age level in an attribute (such as reading) based on the average score of learners of that age. Thus, a child who achieves a reading age of 7 years and 6 months can be said to perform at the same level as the average child of that age in the norm group. A child aged 8 years and 6 months, who has a reading age of 7 years

---

[1] Raw scores can also be transformed into a non-normalised scale. This typically involves transforming raw scores into standard scores (with, for example, a mean of 100 and a standard deviation of 15). However, a simple raw score transformation may lead to a spread of scores that does not match that found in a normalised distribution, such as the one shown in Figure 8.2.

and 6 months, can be said to be about a year behind in the aspect of reading assessed by the test. Particular care needs to be exercised in interpreting reading ages at the extremes of a distribution, as these are often extrapolated or estimated, based on what the reading ages would be if a sufficient number of high or low achievers had been assessed. Another problem is that growth slows as children become older, meaning that reading ages are less useful for reporting on the performance and development of older children.

- *Test-wide scale score* – these scores may be provided when a test assesses students at a range of grade levels (Year 1, Year 2, Year 3, and so on) in the same subject area. Typically, one grade level is identified as an anchor level, and scores are distributed across grade levels, with common items included in tests administered at adjacent grade levels. A test-wide scale can be set to have any mean and standard deviation (for example, 250/50 or 500/100). Test-wide scores can be used to check progress from year to year and to provide an alternative to using a child's percentile rank for this purpose. Thus, if a child progresses by 70 score points, and the average progress for his/her grade level is 50 points, we can say that the child made greater-than-average progress. Rates of progress may vary by grade level, with, for example, greater average progress in the lower grade levels and less progress later on.

Standard error of measurement

As noted in Chapter 2, in the context of discussing the reliability of test scores, a student's performance on a standardised test is likely to vary from one occasion to the next. A statistic termed the Standard Error of Measurement (SEM) estimates the size of the error associated with test scores. It estimates how repeated measures of the same person on the same test are distributed around his or her 'true' score. If the same student took a test multiple times (with no additional learning occurring between test administrations and no memory effects coming into play), the SEM would be the standard deviation of their repeated test scores. In practice, the SEM is calculated using an estimate of test reliability (such as the KR_{20} or Cronbach's Alpha reliability coefficients).

Because of measurement error, we need to exercise care in comparing two scores that are adjacent to one another. For example, let us suppose that the 95% confidence intervals associated with standard scores of 90 and 95 (based on a SEM of 3) are 84–96 and 89–101 respectively.[2] Because these intervals overlap, the true scores of students achieving scores of 90 and 95 may in fact be the same. Hence, we cannot claim that one student outperformed the other. For this to happen, the gap between scores would need to be at least 12 score points.

The use of sten scores for reporting purposes addresses measurement error to some extent. A sten score represents an interval into which a student's standard score falls and there is a built-in margin of error. However, a student scoring just below the cut-off point for a sten score interval may miss out on the higher interval by just one

---

[2] The 95% confidence interval around a score, x, is x ± 1.96SEM. Hence, the 95% confidence interval around a score of 90 with a SEM of 3 is 84–96 (after rounding).

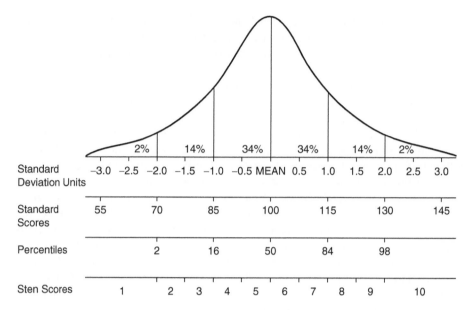

Figure 8.2   Normal distribution, normalised standard scores, percentile ranks and sten scores

standard score point (and vice versa). A similar issue arises with examination grades (see below), where a student may miss out on a higher grade by just one or two points. Conversely, a student may avoid a lower grade by the same narrow margin.

Conversion tables

If a standardised test is administered in paper-based format, the accompanying test manual will include a conversion table that enables test users to transform raw scores (such as the number of questions answered correctly) into derived scores (such as normalised standard scores or percentile ranks). Table 8.1 provides a table from a mathematics test that converts raw scores into standard scores, percentile ranks and sten scores when the test is administered in the spring (a different table of norms is available for autumn administrations of the same test). An interesting feature of the table (on the left-hand side) is that raw scores of 70 or higher convert into percentile scores of 98 or 99. This suggests that relatively few students cluster at the top of the distribution and that the test discriminates reasonably well among higher-achieving students (that is, very high scores on the test are relatively rare). Nowadays, conversions from raw scores into derived scores are often done by computer software. This allows for the generation of comprehensive reports in a short time frame, but the same underlying tables as those used with paper-based tests underpin the software algorithms used.

In Table 8.1, a raw score of 71 converts into a standard score of 132, a percentile rank of 98 (indicating that just 2% of students achieved higher scores) and a sten score of 10. Very few students achieve scores that are this high. A raw score of 35 converts into a standard score of 97, a percentile rank of 42 (indicating that 58% did better) and a sten score of 5. Qualitative descriptions of what these scores mean can be found in Table 8.2. These descriptors may be useful in communicating what scores mean to parents and indeed to students themselves.

Table 8.1 Partial conversion table for a mathematics test (spring administration)

TOTAL SCORE				TOTAL SCORE (contd.)			
Raw score	Stand. score	Percent. rank	Sten score	Raw score	Stand. score	Percent. rank	Sten score
75	139	99	10	37	98	45	5
74	137	99	10	36	98	45	5
73	136	99	10	35	97	42	5
72	134	99	10	34	96	39	5
71	132	98	10	33	95	37	5
70	131	98	10	32	95	37	5
69	129	97	9	31	94	35	5
68	128	97	9	30	93	32	5
67	126	96	9	29	92	30	4
66	125	95	9	28	92	30	4

Source: ERC (2007)

Table 8.2 Qualitative descriptors corresponding to standard score and sten score ranges

Standard score range	Sten score	Descriptor	Coverage
115 and above	8–10	Well above average	Top one-sixth of pupils
108–114	7	High average	One-sixth of pupils
93–107	5–6	Average	Middle one-third of pupils
85–92	4	Low average	One-sixth of pupils
84 and below	1–3	Well below average	Bottom one-sixth of pupils

Based on this, a student who achieves a standard score of 132 or a sten score of 10 can be considered to have scores in the 'well above average' range, and their scores are in the top one-sixth of the normalised distribution. A student who achieves a standard score of 97 (corresponding to a sten score of 5) can be considered to have a score that is in the average range or the middle third of the distribution. The use of descriptors (instead of numerical scores) can perhaps reduce the competitive atmosphere that is sometimes associated with standardised testing programmes. Some standardised tests may have more than one form, including some computer-based tests. Approaches to scaling tests allow psychometricians (those who scale tests) to place multiple forms of the same test on a common scale.

How scores are reported

Test scores can be reported in a variety of ways. Earlier, we indicated that, since 2016, performance on Key Stage 2 tests in English reading and mathematics in England is reported with reference to raw scores and nationally referenced scaled scores (with a mean of 100 and, we assume, a standard deviation of 15), and a statement on whether the student has attained the required national standard. In Ireland, performance on English reading and mathematics in grades 2, 4 and 6 is reported to parents and (in aggregated form) to national educational authorities with reference to sten scores, though schools may choose to report standard scores to parents instead, if they wish. In Northern Ireland, schools may report performance on computer-based tests of literacy to parents using standard scores (mean = 100 and standard deviation = 15) and/or age-related outcome ranges (where raw scores are converted into age-related score intervals, such as between 9 years 3 months and 9 years 6 months). In both England and Ireland, parents may also be provided with scores based on teacher judgements of performance as well as scores based on standardised tests. Teacher assessments may focus on aspects of learning that cannot be captured by current tests, such as oral expression, aspects of writing and some of the key skills highlighted in our discussion of 21st-century skills in Chapter 7.

Criterion-referenced framework

As noted earlier, some standardised tests allow for both norm-referenced and criterion-referenced interpretations of performance. Such tests report on performance with reference to:

- standard scores, percentile ranks and other derived scores that allow for a comparison between a student's performance and that of other students in the norm group
- proficiency levels, performance bands or other indicators of the content or processes that a student is likely to have mastered.

Figure 8.3 shows the skills that students performing at Band 3 on a standardised mathematics test are likely to demonstrate. These skills are based on the most difficult items that students in Grade 4 performing at Band 3 are likely to answer correctly.[3] In planning instruction for these students, teachers may wish to reinforce the skills associated with Band 3 and provide instruction on the skills associated with the next highest level, Band 4.

Readers may come across the term 'criterion-referenced assessment' outside the context of standardised tests. Many teacher assessments, where teachers assess their students against specific standards, learning outcomes or levels of attainment, based on the available assessment information, can be described as criterion-referenced (for example, teacher assessments under National Curriculum Assessment in England or teacher assessments based on the progression continua in the new language curriculum for junior primary classes in Ireland (NCCA, 2015). Criterion-referenced assessment is also common in vocational training programmes where students may be asked to demonstrate their competency on

---

[3] The use of Item Response Theory (IRT) scaling allows test developers to place students and test items on the same underlying scale. This facilitates the specification of the tasks that students at each proficiency band are expected to accomplish.

Band 3: Average level of achievement (95–104) (Grade 4)

Number/Algebra – pupils at Band 3 can complete multiplication number sentences involving the associative property, express tenths in decimal form and identify place value in decimal numbers. They can multiply two-digit numbers by one-digit numbers, and divide two-digit numbers by one-digit numbers with remainders. They can order decimals on the number line. They can solve word problems involving place value in three-digit numbers, multi-digit subtraction and fractions as sets.

Shape and space – they can identify the use of 2-D shapes in the environment, describe properties of 3-D shapes, construct 3-D shapes from 2-D shapes and recognise an angle as a rotation.

Measures – they can compare lengths (m, cm), rename units of length and compare areas of irregular shapes. They can solve word problems on subtraction of dates on a calendar, addition of money and addition of weights (kg and g).

They can also do the tasks described in Bands 1 and 2 (not shown).

Figure 8.3 Skills associated with Band 3 on a standardised test of mathematics

Source: ERC (2010)

a range of job-related skills. As noted in the next section, examinations may sometimes be described as criterion-referenced.

Teacher assessment under National Curriculum Assessment in England requires teachers to rate student performance as 'working towards expected standards', 'working at the expected standard' and 'working at greater depth within the expected standard'. According to a recent clarification statement (Standards and Testing Agency, 2016a), students 'working at greater depth' in handwriting at the end of Key Stage 1 'must demonstrate joined up handwriting, using diagonal and horizontal strokes needed to join letters in most of their writing, as well as all of the statements relating to handwriting in the preceding standards' (p. 2). These are the assessment criteria against which students' work is judged. A somewhat similar approach to deriving criteria is envisaged for interpretations of student work by teachers as part of Junior Cycle reform in Ireland. This is illustrated in the case study of the Junior Certificate towards the end of this chapter.

Interpretation of grades in public examinations

In Chapter 3, we reviewed the purposes and approaches associated with examinations. In Chapter 2, we considered strategies that can be used to ensure that examinations are marked reliably. In this section, we focus on the interpretation of examination grades, the phenomenon of grade inflation and the effects of examinations on teaching, learning and student motivation. Where relevant, we highlight the proposed changes to grading systems.

Criterion- or norm-referenced interpretation?

It is often unclear whether examination grades, such as those achieved by students taking GCSEs in England, Wales and Northern Ireland or the Junior Certificate in Ireland, are mainly based on norm-referenced or criterion-referenced frameworks, or some combination of the two. On the one hand, marking schemes may provide a detailed description of the competencies that must be observed if a particular grade is to be awarded (a criterion-referenced approach). On the other hand, examining bodies often adhere to a distribution of grades that was similar to the distribution obtained in previous years (a norm-referenced approach). When the GCSE was introduced in 1988, it was intended to represent a criterion-referenced approach to the marking and awarding of grades, meaning that the proportion achieving each grade would be based on how well or how poorly students performed in a particular year. However, over time, there has been increasing attention paid to the distribution of grades, with the distribution for a particular year often very similar to the previous year's distribution. For example, the Joint Council for Qualifications website (http://www.jcq.org.uk/examination-results/) shows that the proportion achieving grade A* or grade A on English GCE A Levels in the UK ranged from 20.7% in 2013 to 19.1% in 2016, while the proportion achieving these grades in mathematics ranged from 43% in 2013 to 41.8% in 2016. Efforts by examination boards to ensure that the proportions of grades within a subject are similar from year to year are likely to arise because of concerns in the media and among the general public about grade inflation. Small differences are usually attributed to natural variation in performance.

As noted in the description of ongoing changes to the GCSE exam, the proportions of students achieving scores at each grade point (level) will be carefully controlled from the outset, and specific steps will be taken to ensure that grade distributions remain stable from year to year (that is, grade inflation will be kept to a minimum, unless there is clear corroborating evidence that standards in a subject have risen). This points to a norm-referenced interpretation of performance.

Ongoing proposals to reform the Junior Certificate in Ireland (see Junior Certificate case study later in the chapter), where students may sit classroom assessments (scored at school level) and assessment tasks and exams (scored externally), represent a hybrid system. The outcomes of the classroom assessments are intended to be largely criterion-referenced, with students provided with feedback on their performance, well before sitting their final exams. On the other hand, it is likely that the final exam scores will be interpreted with respect to criterion-referenced and norm-referenced frameworks. The criteria for each grade or descriptor are likely to be clearly specified and linked to learning outcomes (a criterion-referenced perspective), while it is also likely that the proportion of students achieving each descriptor will be carefully monitored from year to year (a norm-referenced perspective).

Case study   Forthcoming changes to GCSE examinations

The General Certificate of Secondary Education (GCSE) is taken by students in England, Wales and Northern Ireland at the end of compulsory schooling. Reform of the GCSE was, in part, motivated by concerns that the proportion of candidates awarded the highest grades had increased over time, while the proportion achieving the lowest grades had decreased (i.e. possible grade inflation).

In the past, the most common measure of success was 5 A–C grades, including English and mathematics. A new grading scale will use the numbers 1–9 only (with 9 being the top level). Those who fail to meet the minimum standard will be graded with a U (ungraded or unclassified), as before. The wider 1–9 scale is intended to provide greater differentiation between students achieving the middle and high grades.

Three subjects were introduced in 2015 (for first examination in 2017): English language, English literature and mathematics.

The transition to the new scoring system will be achieved through the use of 'anchor points'. Hence, about the same proportion of students will achieve a grade 7 and above as currently achieve a grade A and above, while the top 20% of these (the highest performers) will be awarded a grade 9. The bottom of grade 1 will be aligned with the bottom of the old grade G.

Broadly the same proportion of students will achieve a grade 4 and above as currently achieve a grade C and above. Grade 5 will be positioned in the top third of marks for a current grade C and the bottom third for grade B. It is also intended to align grade 5 with average performance in high-scoring countries in the international PISA assessment (described in Chapter 3), though it is not clear how this will be accomplished.

The new mathematics assessment will be tiered (i.e. available at two levels), with grades 4 and 5 available through both tiers.

In the years following 2017, it is intended to maintain the standards set in the first year of the new regime. Statistical evidence will be used to support examiners in establishing boundaries between grades. National reference tests will be used to monitor standards (and, presumably, also inform the setting of boundaries between grades).

Error around examination grades

We saw earlier how important it is to take measurement error into account when interpreting standardised test scores (for example, by reporting scores with reference to confidence intervals or bands). In general, error margins are not constructed around examination grades, though a number of approaches have been used to reduce error levels, while at the same time ensuring that there is some differentiation among students within a grade range. For example, until recently the Leaving Certificate in Ireland employed a 14-point grade band system (A1, A2, B1, B2, B3, and so on, with a difference of around 5% between each grade). These operated much like sten scores on standardised tests in that they described bands of achievement. However, from 2017 a modification resulted in the introduction of eight (wider) grade bands (H1 to H8 on Higher level papers, O1 to O8 on Ordinary level papers). As entry to university and other higher education institutions is normally based on the grades that a student achieves on the best six subjects, the new system is likely to spread students out more in terms of their aggregate scores (converted to points) across six subjects. However, the new system will penalise a student to a greater extent if he/she misses the cut-off point for a particular grade by just one or two percentage points.

In some examinations, there is a clustering of scores at cut-off points, where examinees are given the benefit of the doubt if they are on the borderline between two grades (for example, if a cut-off point for a pass grade is 50%, markers may be encouraged to look for additional evidence in the scripts of students achieving 48 or 49%, with a view to raising their scores to 50%). Sometimes students may believe that their exam papers have been scored too harshly, and may apply for re-grading. This practice is consistent with criterion-referenced approaches to assessment and generally follows the release of marking schemes to teachers and students, as well as examination scripts, so that a case for re-grading can be made.

Reform of examination systems

The current wave of reform in examination systems across countries reflects a number of concerns on the part of national education authorities:

- *Grade inflation* – greater proportions of students achieve the highest exam grades nowadays, compared with previous generations, even though it is not always clear that standards have risen.
- *Pressure on students* – some examinations place considerable pressure on teenagers, leading to high levels of anxiety, though some of this can be controlled (Putwain, 2008).
- *High levels of predictability* – examination questions can be highly predictable in terms of content as well as format and layout, leading to memorisation, rote learning and 'teaching to the test' (Baird et al., 2015).
- *Narrow range of learning outcomes assessed* – exams may not capture the full range of learning outcomes, including '21st-century skills' such as critical thinking and collaborative problem solving (Griffin and Care, 2015).
- *Inadequate preparation for higher education* – current examinations may not adequately prepare students for higher education (e.g. Eve, 2011; Murchan, 2014).
- *Strategic subject choice* – students can do better by selecting subjects in which it is easier to achieve higher grades, and avoid more challenging mathematics or science subjects (Mac Aogáin, 2005).

Efforts to address some of these issues are apparent in current reform efforts in England and Ireland described in this chapter. A noticeable feature of the reformed GCSE is the shift from modular to linear testing (where grades will almost always be based on a final examination result, rather than on scores achieved on tests and tasks administered at different points during lower-secondary schooling). If we compare the current reforms in England and Ireland, we see a stronger focus on the final examination in the new GCSE and a reduction in the weighting given to the final examination in Junior Certificate subjects. We see the abandonment of letter grades in both examinations, though these are replaced by numbers in GCSE and by descriptors in the Junior Certificate.

The different approaches to reform, even in two adjacent jurisdictions, clearly suggest that there is no universally agreed approach to examining student performance at lower-secondary schooling, or indeed at any level. Moreover, the form that assessment in general, and examinations in particular, take may be influenced by the prevailing political narrative (for example, the view espoused by some politicians and media outlets that the pre-reform GCSE exams were 'dumbed down' and 'not fit for purpose') and hence needed to become more challenging.

Combining marks from formal tests and school-based tasks to determine exam grades

Most examinations consist of several components, such as exam questions and practical work. A specific number of points may be associated with each component. The following is the breakdown for an Art examination currently available to Leaving Certificate students in Ireland (www.examinations.ie):

- Imaginative Composition or Still Life (based on practical activities completed before the exam) (100 points)
- Design or Craftwork (based on practical activities completed before the exam) (100)
- Life Sketching (based on practical activities completed before the exam) (50)
- Art History and Appreciation (written exam) (150).

Here, we see that the exam is weighted towards practical activities (250 out of 400 marks, or 62.5%), with the balance being allocated to the written component (150 out of 400, 37.5%). Language examinations often include a practical component. For example, GCSE French in Wales allocates 25% of the marks to an oral test that includes role play, a photo card discussion and a conversation, while 25% each are allocated to listening (non-verbal and written responses), reading and writing (WJEC/CBAC, 2016). Where practical and written components contribute to a final grade, it is important that both components make a balanced contribution. A practical component in which most or all students achieve maximum marks would mean that students' grades are mainly based on the written component. This would raise issues about the valid interpretation of exam scores, as parents and employers might assume that a grade represents a broad indication of proficiency in all aspects of the subject. Chapter 9 discusses this issue further and offers useful additional readings.

Using the outcome of examinations to inform teaching and learning

For the most part, this section has focused on examinations that students sit at the end of lower- or upper-secondary schooling. Of course, students take examinations throughout their schooling and these can contribute to improved teaching and learning.

In general, the type of feedback that arises from standardised tests and end-of-cycle exams is summative and such measures are designed to assess the outcomes of learning (that is, assessment of learning) rather than the process. Nevertheless, while individual candidates receive one grade or score for each subject, schools and teachers may receive several hundred grades, and these can be analysed to identify strengths and weaknesses at school level and to modify teaching and learning based on such analyses. Examiners' reports, which are issued by examining bodies and summarise students' strengths and weaknesses at the system level, can also be a useful source of information for teachers.

Teachers within secondary school may be involved in marking classroom assessments that are linked to public examinations or certification. Teachers' engagement in moderating marks assigned to student work can lead to a greater shared understanding of what is meant by standards or learning outcomes, and thus can lead to more effective teaching and learning (see Klenowski and Wyatt-Smith, 2014).

In-house exams, including the 'mock exams' taken by students in many education systems several months before they sit end-of-cycle exams, can provide useful feedback on strengths and weaknesses both to teachers and students. The outcomes of such exams, and indeed any other in-house exams administered by schools, can be used to inform planning for teaching and learning. However, there is a point beyond which taking practice exams is counterproductive. In some contexts, the content of teaching and learning may be defined by past examination papers, and this can lead to a focus on only those aspects of a subject that are likely to be examined, to the neglect of other important elements of the subject.

Case study   Changes to assessment at Junior Cycle in Ireland

A new framework for the Junior Cycle (First to Third Year or Grades 7–9) (DES, 2015a) has been proposed for implementation on a phased basis in Irish secondary schools. The framework provides 24 over-arching statements of learning and identifies eight key skills that should permeate teaching and learning across all subjects. Students can study (and receive certification for) traditional full-length subjects, short courses (for example, well-being, coding) and priority learning units (targeted at students with special educational needs).

A key innovation is the use of both classroom assessments and traditional end-of-cycle examinations. Most full-length subjects with new specifications will be assessed through two classroom-based assessments (CBAs) (one in Grade 8 and one in Grade 9), the outcomes of which will be reported to parents/guardians by the school. An additional assessment task, which will be externally marked, will also be administered to students. In addition, an examination will be administered at the end of Grade 9.

When assessing the level of student achievement in a classroom-based assessment against learning outcomes, teachers will use 'on-balance' judgement in relation to the features of quality, which are set out in four level descriptors – *exceptional, above expectations, in line with expectations and yet to meet expectations* (NCCA, 2015). Teachers are expected to share and discuss representative samples of students' work at Subject Learning and Assessment Review meetings (SLARs). This is expected to lead to a common understanding among teachers of the quality of their students' learning. For English in 2014–17, the focus on classroom-based assessments is on oral language performance and on the interpretation of text genres.

In addition to the two classroom-based assessments, it is anticipated that students will also complete an assessment task in school before the end of Junior Cycle. This will be externally set and externally scored, and performance on this task will be combined with performance on an exam offered at the end of Junior Cycle, with combined performance on the task and the exam contributing to a student's final grade. Letter grades will no longer be awarded. Instead, students will be given a descriptor that reflects their performance in each subject: Distinction (91% to 100%), Higher Merit (75–89), Merit (55–74), Achieved (40–54), Partially Achieved (20–39) and Not Graded (under 20%) (DES, 2016a). This system of grading is different to that used for the Leaving Certificate.

Certification at the end of Grade 9 will comprise a Junior Certificate Profile of Achievement that will include the outcomes of classroom-based assessments, examination results (where performance on the externally scored assessment task is combined with performance on an exam), the outcomes of short courses and, where relevant, Priority Units.

Finally, whereas in the past, all subjects were offered at two levels (higher and ordinary) at Junior Cycle, and at three levels for English, Irish and maths (higher, ordinary and foundation), the reform envisages two levels (higher and ordinary) for English, Irish and maths, and a common level for all other subjects.

The changes in assessment, though not universally welcomed by teachers in Ireland, are intended to place a stronger focus on assessment for learning (formative assessment) and to reduce the pressure on students associated with a single final exam in each subject. Moreover, it is intended that the Junior Certificate Profile of Achievement will recognise a wider range of learning, while reducing the focus on a final examination. It should be noted that the proposed reform of junior cycle assessment arrangements has been controversial and, at the time of writing, it remains to be seen what the final outcome of the reform will be.

Join the debate: How should student performance on public examinations be graded and reported?

1. As is evident from the case studies presented, the GCSE has introduced numbers instead of letter grades, while the Junior Certificate has introduced descriptors of achievement instead of letter grades. Which of these models is likely to lead to (a) more accurate (reliable) results, and (b) more interpretable outcomes for students? Give reasons for your answers. Should these exams have retained letter grades? Why? Why not?

2. There are two broad approaches to ensuring that roughly the same proportions of students achieve the same grades from year to year. One is to change grade boundaries (such that 85% correct or higher might convert to an A grade in one year, and 83% the next year). This is the approach used for GCSEs in England, Wales and Northern Ireland, and for Standard and Higher Still exams in Scotland (Baird et al., 2015). The other is to modify the current marking schemes (for example, by changing the criterion for achieving a particular score on a particular question until the expected grade distribution is achieved). Which of these is most transparent for students and their parents/teachers? Why?

(Continued)

(Continued)

3. Some examination systems publish the marking schemes (or criteria) that have been used to mark exam papers, so a student can find out what answers were required to achieve different point scores for each question, and, perhaps, mount an appeal. What is an advantage of making marking schemes available? What is a disadvantage?

Chapter summary

This chapter, one of several that looks at how assessment information can be used, extended several of the ideas introduced in Chapter 3 relating to standardised tests and examinations. In particular, a distinction was made between norm-referenced and criterion-referenced interpretative frameworks, though it was acknowledged that test scores and grades can sometimes be interpreted using both frameworks. In the case of standardised tests, a range of derived scores was described including standard scores, percentile ranks and sten scores. In the case of examinations, different schemes for reporting on performance were outlined including letter grades, number grades and descriptors of achievement. Some of these schemes were presented in the context of current reforms to examination systems in the UK and Ireland.

Sources of error associated with test scores and examination marks were also considered. The need to take measurement error into account in interpreting standardised test scores was emphasised. Issues unique to examinations, such as the weighting of practical tasks and tests in contributing to grades and the use of exam results to improve teaching and learning, were considered. It was concluded that the differing directions in which reforms to examinations in the UK and Ireland have gone in the last few years, indicates that there is no unique internationally agreed on blueprint for developing the perfect examination system.

Questions for discussion

1. The chapter discusses two interpretative frameworks for assessments – norm referencing and criterion referencing – that can be quite technical in nature. Can you identify examples when teachers in class use such frameworks in their work with students?

2. Report cards sent home to parents sometimes provide information about students' performance summarised as percentile ranks or standard scores. Consider the parent who approaches you, firmly believing that the score (say a low percentile in reading) is a precise description of the student's ability. With a colleague, role-play the conversation that you, as teacher, would have with the parent.

3. Think about the approach to student assessment at the end of compulsory education in your education system (typically around age 16 in most systems). Draw up a list of the strengths and weaknesses of the assessment arrangements. Which list is longer? Suggest recommendations to improve the system. Repeat the exercise for assessment arrangements presently in place at the end of upper-secondary education (typically age 18).

Further reading

Baird, J.-A., Hopfenbeck, T.N., Elwood, J., Caro, D., & Ahmed, A. (2015). *Predictability in the Irish Leaving Certificate*. Oxford: Oxford Centre for Educational Assessment. Available at: http://pure.qub.ac.uk/portal/en/publications/predictability-in-the-irish-leaving-certificate(8385b46c-826d-4801-9921-d9fd3bbd2259).html

This report addresses aspects of the predictability of examinations, including positive and negative aspects of predictability. Conclusions are situated in the context of examination practices in the UK.

Simpson, L., & Baird, J. (2013). Perceptions of trust in public examinations. *Oxford Review of Education, 39* (1), 17–35.

This article looks at the perceptions (expectations and requirements) of different stakeholders regarding the credibility of A level examinations in England, and the multiplicity of factors that contribute to credibility. The article highlights the complexity of ensuring that public exams are trustworthy.

9

Record-keeping, feedback and reporting from classroom assessment

What you will learn in this chapter

The previous chapter described the processes of gathering and using information derived from standardised tests and high-stakes certification examinations. In this chapter, we focus more on the collation, interpretation and communication of information generated by assessments undertaken as part of normal classroom practice. First, we consider the nature of feedback and the distinction between feedback for student learning and feedback for other purposes. Then, the chapter explores a number of contexts in which feedback is offered, largely within the classroom, through discussion, conferences and illustrations of student work. The final sections emphasise recording and look at approaches to reporting feedback at individual, in-class and school levels.

When you finish the chapter, you should be able to answer these questions:

- What useful information can be communicated to students, parents and other interested parties?
- What are the different approaches and methods available to teachers to communicate assessment information most effectively to different stakeholders for different purposes?
- How can I identify and record assessment information in a meaningful and manageable way for immediate and future use?

Overview of feedback

A key feature of assessment for learning is the provision of information about student learning to guide subsequent teaching and learning (Wiliam, 2011). Kulhavy and Stock (1989) suggest that feedback takes two possible forms for students: (i) verification of the standard of performance reached; and (ii) elaboration of what is required to reach a desired standard. Without elaboration, information from an assessment leaves it up to the student to work out how to proceed. Elaboration empowers students to motivate themselves and enables them to regulate their own learning.

Effective feedback can be characterised as being:

- based on accurate assessment
- descriptive rather than judgemental
- focused on the quality of the work or the process of learning in relation to specific goals
- clear and understandable to the student; consistent with their prior knowledge
- accepted by the student, prompting an appropriate cognitive response
- sufficient in quantity – not too little or too much
- timed appropriately in relation to the learning under way
- designed to help students regulate their own learning
- respectful of student effort and non-threatening to their self-esteem
- a positive experience. (Brookhart, 2007; Hattie and Timperley, 2007; Ruiz-Primo and Li, 2013; Faragher, 2014)

The use of feedback is informed by the general principles of assessment, introduced in Chapter 1. For feedback to be accurate, teachers need appropriate assessment competencies (Principle 7). Similarly, if feedback is to focus on the process of learning, then varied and evolving methods are required (Principle 4).

Oral approaches to providing feedback

Chapter 5 highlighted questioning techniques as part of formative assessment activities. By engaging in genuine dialogue through questioning, teachers can ascertain students' achievement and thus direct subsequent learning. Providing feedback orally to students as part of questioning strategies offers immediate verification of their learning and the opportunity to address any student conceptions and misconceptions.

Oral conferencing

Given the demands on teachers' time in class, they can spend surprisingly little time with any one student. Similarly, contact with parents can be sporadic, even in situations where technology offers the prospect of enabling greater contact between home and school. In your own teaching, it is worth exploring how time can be arranged to briefly discuss progress with individual students or groups of students. Group conferences might focus on a group's progress on a portfolio or other task. Providing feedback orally offers natural interactive dialogue between the key partners in education: teachers, students and parents. Conferences can be formal, semi-formal or informal and as frequent as is manageable for the teacher. Informal conferences can occur, for example, when parents of primary children drop off or collect their children at school. As fleeting and unstructured as these contacts are, they are nevertheless highly valuable in building relationships between home and school.

Parent–teacher conferences

These formal encounters help provide feedback to parents about the progress of their children, also fostering productive cooperation between home and school. The format, frequency and duration of parent–teacher conferences will vary but they share a focus on ensuring clear communication. Sometimes such meetings may be teachers' only direct point of contact with parents in the year. Some schools structure meetings as three-way discussions where the teacher, parent(s) and student meet together to discuss progress, necessitating careful preparation by teachers and students.

Guidelines for conducting effective parent–teacher meetings include the following:

1. Create a welcoming meeting environment, recognising that parents can be apprehensive.
2. Decide in advance what you wish to say, preferably with brief notes, prioritising what will make the most difference to the student.
3. Seek parents' perspectives on their child.
4. Be positive about the student's progress while also being honest in your assessment.
5. Provide illustrations of students' work, if possible, for parents to take away (samples of work, portfolio). Students might help decide on work to be included.
6. Be cautious about giving advice to parents, being mindful of any evidence to suggest that the advice will work.
7. Where relevant, seek the support of parents for any course of action with the student.
8. Stick to the allotted meeting duration, scheduling a follow-up meeting where further discussion is needed.
9. Make a brief record of key decisions, recommendations or proposed actions, possibly only in relation to a few students.
10. Recognise the confidentiality of matters discussed. It may not be appropriate to share certain information with your colleagues.

During a parent–teacher meeting in a primary school, the first author encountered a simple but unexpected question from the father of a child in 2nd Class: 'has he any friends?' This inquiry prompted careful monitoring that revealed interesting social patterns and brought ultimate benefit for the child, thus illustrating the value of sharing parent insights during meetings.

Teacher–student conferences and peer conferences

Regular semi-formal meetings between teacher and students can help foster a positive culture of review and planning in the classroom. This might be achieved by setting aside a period within specific lessons when students have the opportunity to discuss their work and progress with the teacher. Much planning and preparation for the conference can be undertaken by students who, with scaffolding over time, can learn to collate some examples of their work to discuss. This facilitates students in looking for evidence of growth in their own work, while the conference can help them to identify barriers and enablers to future growth.

Student feedback and reporting in peer and self-assessment

In Chapter 5, we discussed formative peer assessment. This provides a rich opportunity for students to share work with each other and offer suggestions for development. Peer conferencing reflects socio-cultural perspectives on learning and assessment. Self-assessment, also described in Chapter 5, helps students regulate their own learning, thus providing more learner autonomy. While peer and self-assessment represent valuable educational experiences for students, it is also essential that they yield actionable information or feedback to shape learning. Checklists, rating scales and scoring rubrics (see Chapter 7 for more information on these) can be used to scaffold students in assessing their own or other students' work, increasing the reliability of judgements and the validity of any inferences to be drawn.

A teacher of geography in secondary education whom we worked with reported that students swapped copies with homework partners, marked each other's maps with the marking scheme provided and wrote two things they liked and two things they could improve on. This feedback helped students improve for the next assignment. Another teacher set work for groups of 3–4 students: they worked on this together; then instead of the teacher correcting the work a set of written directions was given to the groups and they corrected it themselves. In the context of wider feedback, students' self-assessment data are now incorporated into formal reporting by schools to parents in Ireland, as part of the 'education passport' that accompanies students transferring from primary to secondary school (DES, 2015b). Students are encouraged to profile and evaluate their strengths and challenges on the passport. In Scotland, student profiles at P7 and S3 offer students the opportunity to reflect on their achievement in school across a range of areas and to communicate this directly to their parents (Scottish Government, 2012).

Communicating students' growth through work samples and portfolios

Portfolios, discussed in Chapter 7, reflect many assessment principles espoused in this book. They can be used for formative or summative purposes; can reflect a wide diversity of student experience and learning; offer possibilities for digital learning and assessment; and provide a repository for evidence to support judgements and feedback. It is advisable that portfolios move beyond merely offering an enjoyable classroom activity for students to also providing opportunities for effective assessment – opportunities that do not come without challenges for the teacher. Students should have a central role in selecting what to include in a portfolio and judging the quality of the work. Scaffolding such student reflection using checklists, prompts and rubrics helps make judgements more valid and reliable. Use of even broad criteria, such as having students identify and justify entries as *best work, most creative, most difficult, most effort, most fun, most improved*, and so on, promotes meta-cognitive reflection (McMillan, 2011). Portfolios may be scored by rating individual elements within the portfolio (each essay, science sheet, test, presentation) or the portfolio as a whole. In either case, use of clear scoring rubrics is advisable.

Activity 9.1

Try this out – Creating a rubric for a portfolio

Mid-way through secondary school in Ireland, many students enrol in a 'transition year' during which alternative curricula are followed. Some weeks are spent on work experience with local employers, community groups and other agencies, and students are required to keep a record of their experience. A portfolio could be used by students to document their experience. Table 9.1 presents a partly completed holistic rubric that could be used to assess the portfolio. Work with a partner to expand the rubric to assess student portfolios at the end of the work placement (say three weeks). What evidence would you expect to see in the portfolio submitted by a student placed with a local supermarket, community group or other provider? What entries could the student include? How could they be assessed?

Table 9.1   Portfolio rubric: Evaluating students' report on work experience

Rating	Evaluative criteria
Exceptional (4 points)	
Strong (3)	
Acceptable (2)	
Needs further development (1)	Portfolio exhibits little or no evidence that learning outcomes associated with the placement have been reached; little evidence of self-reflection; several required elements are missing from the portfolio

Join the debate: How reliable is assessment information from portfolios?

Portfolios are often seen as a way to promote the acquisition and assessment of 21st-century skills by students. They hold out the promise of engaging students in selecting, organising, evaluating and communicating their learning in a wide variety of areas, with positive effects on goal setting, self-regulation, motivation and achievement. Enthusiastic supporters of portfolios are aplenty. Yet, one large-scale evaluation of portfolios raised significant reservations. Policy-makers in Vermont trialled portfolios for state-wide monitoring of student achievement in writing and mathematics at Grades 4 and 8. An evaluation by Koretz et al. (1994a) identified positive impacts on teacher motivation, instructional practices and professional development opportunities for teachers. However, the researchers found wide variation in what teachers were actually doing with portfolios, making a comparison of schools difficult, along with low levels of inter-rater reliability. Overall, they noted that the 'positive effects of the programme have come at a steep price in time, money and stress' (1994a: 13).

Review what is written in Chapter 7 and in some other textbooks about portfolios. If possible, talk to a teacher who uses them in class. You might like to access another report by Koretz et al. (1994b), listed in the further reading at the end of the chapter. How trustworthy is evidence from portfolios (i) for formative feedback to students and teachers in class and (ii) for summative reporting to parents or other stakeholders such as education ministries? The companion website provides some useful resources to help you engage with this debate.

Visit the companion website at: https://study.sagepub.com/murchanshiel

Scoring, grading and feedback

Grading

A recurring theme of this book recognises the different stakeholder needs in relation to assessment, one of which is accurate, concise information about students' learning. Frequently, this involves grading – the summation of information from one or more assessments and relating this a value judgement about the level of achievement. Grades take many forms, such as percentages, letters, achievement levels and proficiency levels. Within schools, use of grades includes summary feedback to students and parents, administrative record keeping, an estimation of students' learning profiles' strengths and weaknesses, and the identification of students with special educational needs. Grades have other uses and impacts in relation to student motivation, informing other teachers in a school about student progress, data-led instruction and school evaluation. Notwithstanding the literature critical of grading (Black and Wiliam, 1998; Hattie and Timperley, 2007), grades are intrinsic to most school systems. Some grading needs are external to the school: informing parents and other schools about students' learning and their use as 'currency' in certification systems at key points of progress and transfer. Many national assessment competencies and standards expected of teachers assume that teachers will regularly provide some form of grades to relevant stakeholders. For example, the following list highlights expectations on teachers wishing to attain full registration with the General Teaching Council for Scotland (2012).

Teachers should:

- know and understand how to apply the principles of assessment, recording and reporting as an integral part of the teaching process
- have extensive knowledge and a secure understanding of the principles of assessment, of methods of recording assessment information, of the use of assessment in reviewing progress, in improving teaching and learning and in identifying next steps, and of the need to produce clear, informed and sensitive reports
- record assessment information in a systematic and meaningful way in order to enhance teaching and learning and fulfil the requirements of the curriculum and awarding bodies
- produce clear and informed reports for parents and other agencies which discuss learners' progress and matters related to personal, social and emotional development in a sensitive and constructive way.

Teachers need to consider how different aspects of achievement are to be weighted and combined (tests, daily assignments, homework, lab work or responses to oral questioning) in the formation of an overall composite grade. We might also need to consider whether the achievement should be judged in relation to other students (norm-referenced interpretation), some absolute standard (criterion-referenced interpretation) or the individual's learning potential and previous levels of achievement (self- or ipsative-referenced). Teachers in secondary schools sometimes draw on grading and marking systems in examinations set by external awarding bodies when framing their own grading and reporting practice. For example, many teachers in upper-secondary education in Ireland make significant use of past examination papers and rubrics, and base their own personal grading practices on the grade and mark schemes used in the Leaving Certificate examination, especially as the exams come closer (Smyth and Banks, 2012; MacNeela and Boland, 2013; Elwood et al., 2015).

Thomas Guskey (2006) characterises 'hodgepodge grading', whereby teachers combine students' attributes such as achievement, work habits, behaviour and punctuality into one aggregate grade that is difficult for parents and other teachers to interpret. Instead, he suggests rewarding different student characteristics with separate grades in a multiple-grading system.

Activity 9.2

Try this out – Formulating a grading plan for your class

Review a time in your school placement or teaching when you sought to provide summative grades for all or some students in your class. Draw up a retrospective 'grading plan' for that occasion by answering the questions below:

- What is the purpose to which the grades will be put?
- What learning outcomes are being assessed?
- What type of information and activities will you draw on in formulating the grade?
- What specific assessment approaches and tools will you use?
- To what extent have you sufficient assessment *events* or information?
- How will you combine the relevant assessment information into one grade?
- What form of grades will you use (letter grade, numerical grade, level descriptor or other)? Why?
- What additional feedback, if any, will be provided with the grades?
- How should the user of the grade interpret its meaning? Write out a simple explanation of the specific meaning you intend for (i) the highest grade achieved in the class, (ii) the lowest, and (iii) one in the middle.
- What follow-up will you initiate in relation to these grades?
- How can you be sure that the grades assigned to students are trustworthy?
- What are the strengths of your grading plan? What are its weaknesses?

Detailed treatment of how to combine marks from different assessments (exams, portfolio, coursework) can be found in Nitko and Brookhart (2014) and Miller et al. (2013).

Comment-only marking

Concerns about the limited and even negative effect of grading have led to an investigation of alternatives such as comment-only marking. Though grades can motivate some students, for others grades can have the opposite effect. Bangert-Drowns et al. (1991) undertook a meta-analysis of various forms of feedback provided to students in primary, secondary and college settings. They concluded that of four possible types of feedback (right–wrong, correct answer, repeat until correct and explanation), the least effective form was simply indicating to the student that the response was correct or incorrect.

Rather, grades need to be framed carefully within an overall feedback system if they are to have the motivating effects that many teachers and parents believe they have.

Case study   Questioning the assumption that grades are good for all students

Alli Klapp (2015) investigated the educational outcomes of a cohort of 8,558 secondary school students in Sweden. Due to regional differences in educational policy, half of the students received grades at the end of primary school (Grade 6) and half received no grades. Klapp's study looked at how these two groups of students fared academically as they progressed through secondary school. The results were interesting and confirmed the outcomes of some smaller-scale studies. Low-ability students who were not graded at Grade 6 did better in secondary school than low-ability students who had been graded. Amongst high-ability students, there was a slight additional gain if they had been graded in primary school, especially for girls, but the effect was very modest. The conclusions of this large study seem to support those advocating for more comment-only grading in schools, designed to provide informative feedback to students.

Formative use of summative data

Harlen (2007: 127) identifies two interesting questions in relation to formative and summative assessment:

- Can evidence used in summative assessment be used to help learning?
- Can evidence collected for formative purposes be used for summative assessment?

For the former, timing is crucial, as is structuring the process so that teaching to the test is avoided. When a teacher or student draws insights from students' (summative) assessment outcomes and uses this information to adjust and enhance learning, this is formative use of the assessment. The time lag between receiving the feedback (information from a test) and using it productively in class or with the student must be short. The case study below illustrates teachers using information from a test to address some underlying challenges for students.

Case study   Using summative tests formatively

One of the authors was involved in a project designed to provide advice to teachers about the types of errors being made by students in primary mathematics. Short written 'testlets' were administered to students in different topics soon after the topics were completed. Student responses were analysed by the researchers and the most common errors underlying poor performance were identified. In one Third Class, a common difficulty was quickly identified amongst students – children had difficulty recognising and recording patterns in number, from 0 to 999. A brief intervention was developed and implemented with the class and a retesting of students a few days later showed a significant increase in students' performance on this topic. A development of this project using computerised testlets instead of paper resulted in immediate analysis and feedback to the teachers, allowing teachers to address errors and misconceptions while the topic was still being taught (Murchan, Oldham and O'Sullivan, 2013).

In relation to Harlen's second question, portfolio assessment provides an example of drawing on data collected for formative purposes for subsequent summative use. Development portfolios help illustrate students' progress as they develop competency, for example through drafting in writing. Students can select pieces for inclusion, reflect on them and further refine their work based on self- and peer reflection and insights from the teacher – all classic elements of formative assessment. The teacher and/or student might subsequently review the best evidence in the portfolios to match the quality of the best work with clearly established criteria. Where these criteria are, for example, common across all students in a class or cohort, the judgements offer summative evaluation of the quality of the work in comparison to set criteria or others in the cohort, thus providing a possible summative appraisal of work gathered as part of a formative process, subject to caveats about fairness and ethics highlighted in Chapter 12.

Record keeping at school and class levels

Why keep records?

Appropriate, accurate and manageable record keeping in relation to student progress is an essential requirement at school and classroom levels. The responsibilities placed on school administrators, leaders and teachers may be different, but all must ensure that appropriate records are maintained in a form consistent with purposes and in keeping with local and national guidelines. For example, legislation in England (DfE, 2012) requires schools to publish specific aggregated information about student achievement and progress on their websites. Without accurate record keeping by teachers, this information would not be available to school authorities. In Ireland, requirements on primary schools to upload aggregated assessment data to the Department of Education and Skills (DES, 2011a) presuppose the initial gathering, collation and storage of such information at the class and school levels.

Even when assessment is more formative, teachers need to maintain effective recording and storage systems. Teachers encounter a myriad of events and pressures in class every day. It is not possible to retain all information about students in your head. Rather, you need to judiciously select the most salient information that needs to be retained for further use and record this in an appropriate manner. Finding the correct balance between record keeping and the many other pressing tasks is something that comes with time, and can even prove challenging to experienced teachers!

We need to consider both professional and statutory reasons why teachers need to keep records and make reports. Statutory or other required obligations stem from government legislation or guidelines issued periodically by education ministries or local education agencies. In the main, these often relate more to summative purposes of assessment and reporting outcomes. Professional obligations also inform and determine teachers' recording practices. Meeting the expectations of professional bodies, such as teaching councils and accreditation boards, generally requires teachers to adopt systematic record keeping and reporting. For example, 27 teacher competencies are identified by the General Teaching Council for Northern Ireland (2011), four of which specifically relate to assessment. Consider the two examples below:

- Teachers will focus on assessment for learning by monitoring pupils' progress, giving constructive feedback to help pupils reflect on and improve their learning (Competence 24, p. 40).
- Teachers will liaise orally and in written reports in an effective manner with parents or carers on their child's progress and achievements (Competence 27, p. 43).

Implicit in these competencies is the need to maintain appropriate records to monitor progress, provide feedback and help students reflect on and improve their learning. Meeting such expectations would be very challenging if teachers didn't have access to structured information on students' development, regularly maintained throughout the year.

Resources for recording and reporting

Teachers vary in what they record and how they record relevant student information. What is important is that a teacher puts in place suitable, manageable systems. Teachers should maintain a structured file for each student and record progress and any other relevant information based on the full range of assessment approaches available. Teachers will also have access to a more formal student file maintained within the school. Such files are central repositories providing information for teachers when preparing summative reports for parents and are helpful for teachers who will have subsequent responsibility for the students. These files are frequently in digital format and updated regularly. The format of the files is typically decided by the schools, many of whom purchase database software from commercial companies. Where data are held on students, teachers and schools need to be mindful of relevant legislation, such as the Data Protection Acts 1988 and 2003 in Ireland and the Privacy Act 1993 in New Zealand. One implication of the Irish legislation, for example, is that schools need to benchmark their data-gathering and storage policies against eight rules: fairness in obtaining data; purpose for the data; use and disclosure of information; security safeguards; appropriateness of data; accuracy; duration for which data are retained; and rights of access to these data (www.dataprotectionschools.ie/en/).

Generating student reports

Teachers communicate with parents using a variety of approaches – informal, semi-formal and formal. As mentioned earlier, informal contact includes that which occurs when parents come into school to drop off and pick up their children – this characterises much of the contact in the early years of schooling. Teachers also use more semi-formal continuous approaches such as notes in student diaries, journals, phone calls, texts and emails. For many teachers and parents, the parent–teacher meeting and the periodic report card represent the formal aspect of the parent–teacher engagement. Formal written reports to parents generally follow a school-developed template, itself frequently informed by regional or national guidelines. The frequency of formal written reporting varies from every few weeks to more typical termly or annual reporting. The purpose of report cards is to summarise students' learning, progress and achievement, and some summary symbol is generally used to convey information concisely. Three basic types of information are typically contained in the reports (Table 9.2).

Table 9.2   Information contained in school reports

Information in report	Illustrations of data or information
Student achievement in curriculum areas	Benchmarks, proficiency levels, grades, numerals, letter grades, numerical scales, percentages, written descriptors
Test results	Percentages, percentile ranks, standard scores, sten scores, grade-equivalent scores or other derived scores
Behavioural and study traits	Comments on attendance, punctuality, behaviour, class interaction and attitude

Activity 9.3

Try this out – Review the student report template from one school

Request access to the report card template for a school you know. Use the questions below to analyse the report card. Compare your card and report with a colleague who worked with a different report.

1. How many times per year is the report issued to parents?
2. What information is provided in relation to:

    i.   Student achievement?
    ii. Specific test results?
    iii. Other student attributes?

3. Identify the benchmarks or reference points against which the information provided should be compared (for example, other students in the class or education system).

4. Identify any words, phrases, symbols or educational jargon that parents may have difficulty understanding; and any that students would not understand.
5. What information would you like to see added to the report?
6. How clear and attractive is the report card? How would you improve it?
7. If possible, discuss the report card with a parent and compare your own evaluation of the card with the parent's view.

Increasingly, schools use electronic report cards that enable schools to automate some of the entries. Whereas electronic report cards can make the compilation and distribution of reports more efficient, teachers need to ensure that comments selected from 'comment banks' do not lose the individuality and impact that come with traditional narrative approaches. Some teachers make use of free online report card writers such as www.schoolreportwriter.com/

Reporting to other stakeholders

As highlighted in Chapter 1, a range of stakeholders has an interest in the activity of schools and teachers. The specific type of information required by each stakeholder will vary. For example, whereas detailed diagnostic analysis of errors made by students might be of assistance to teachers in planning interventions in mathematics, such detail would be unsuited to policy-makers charged with allocating resources at national level. Frequently, schools and teachers have obligations to provide specific information to students, parents and regional/national educational authorities. In Ireland, primary schools must report to parents on the progress of their children at least twice per year, including the provision of standardised test results at least once for selected classes. They must also annually provide aggregated information from standardised tests of mathematics and reading to both the school's Board of Management and to the national ministry. In England at KS2, results of teacher assessments in English reading, writing, mathematics and science must be submitted to the Standards and Testing Agency (2016a). Schools are also required to submit the results of statutory national curriculum tests in aspects of English and mathematics. These two national examples illustrate a feature of modern education systems. Technology has reduced the distance between national supervisory agencies and the schools within the system. Increasingly, schools are required to provide student outcome data online to education ministries who use this data for a range of monitoring, planning and accountability purposes.

Chapter summary

Management of information about student learning is crucial for the implementation of effective assessment systems. Elaborate assessment approaches are of limited use if the resultant information is not recorded, distilled and communicated effectively to the relevant parties. Information or feedback can take a variety of forms – traditional and non-traditional. Appropriate use of digital technology facilitates the storage, retrieval and communication of complex illustrations of learning, for example in the availability of students' digital portfolios for review by parents. Traditional requirements on schools in relation to grading and reporting student progress continue to exist and influence educational processes and outcomes. The distinction frequently made between formative and summative purposes of assessment can create artificial boundaries between the two functions of assessment. Particular challenges include: how assessment conducted for one purpose (formative) can simultaneously serve the other (summative) and vice versa, and how schools can meet the needs of various stakeholders for information about student learning.

Questions for discussion

1. A teacher notes that a Key Stage 2 student who received a low *scale score* on the national curriculum test in reading had, in fact, worked very hard during the school year and did her best. How can the teacher (and school) acknowledge the effort that the student put in, without undermining the interpretation of the score, which is benchmarked against national standards? Identify the challenges and possible solutions in this scenario.
2. Teachers sometimes feel that too much time is spent maintaining records in school, at the expense of teaching. Are teachers unique in this? Talk to two people who work in other professions. Identify the types of records they are required to keep, who requires this and the purposes to which the records are put. What conclusions do you draw?
3. Review the characteristics of effective feedback highlighted in the chapter. With a colleague, evaluate the feedback you have received to date in a current or previous college module in relation to this list. How would you improve the feedback? What resource implications are there in relation to implementing your suggestions?

Further reading

Brooks, V. (2002). *Assessment in secondary schools*. Maidenhead: Open University Press.

Two chapters by Val Brooks provide useful additional information to complement the topic of the present chapter: Chapter 6 on record keeping and reporting; Chapter 7 on assessment, accountability and standards.

Gardner, J. (2012). *Assessment and learning* (2nd edition). London: Sage.

Chapter 6 by Wynne Harlen in this edited volume explores the relationship between formative and summative assessment purposes.

Koretz, D., Stecher, B., Klein, S., & McCaffrey, D. (1994b). *The evolution of a portfolio program: The impact and quality of the Vermont program in its second year (1992–93)*. CSE Technical Report No. 385. Los Angeles, CA: University of California. Available at: http://eric.ed. gov/?id=ED379301

This report draws on data collected from teachers and principals involved in implementing Vermont's large-scale portfolio programme in the period 1988–93. Findings reflect issues of manageability, the impact on teaching and the reliability of scoring writing portfolios.

Shute, V.J. (2007). *Focus on formative feedback*. ETS Research Report No. RR-07-11. Princeton, NJ: Educational Testing Service. Available at: www.ets.org/Media/Research/pdf/RR-07-11.pdf

This report provides an overview of literature exploring various aspects of feedback, especially for formative purposes. Advice on ways to enhance feedback, along with tips on what to avoid, is provided.

10

Differentiating assessment to accommodate learners' needs

What you will learn in this chapter

The principles of assessment first explored in Chapter 1 and revisited throughout the book come together especially when we work with students from diverse contexts and presenting with atypical personal characteristics. The fundamental aims of education generally emphasise both personal and societal development and well-being. Assessment should contribute to this development while supporting students' acquisition and use of a broad range of knowledge, skills and competencies. In Chapter 4, we saw how our concept of learning continues to evolve and broaden. Similarly, the profile of students enrolling in school has evolved significantly in recent years. Policies promoting the inclusion of as many students as possible within 'regular' or 'mainstream' schooling has altered classroom dynamics and required teachers to be more eclectic and innovative educators.

Teachers need to teach and assess fairly and ethically, responding to student diversity so that everybody is provided with learning suited to and taking account of individual needs. Alex's disruptive behaviour in class may simply be because he finds the pace of lessons too slow and the content lacking in challenge, something that ongoing monitoring should identify. Sandra's diagnosis on the autistic spectrum may explain why unexpected changes in lesson content or teaching (for example, a surprise test) leave her agitated and uncomfortable in class. Concluding that Lara, recently arrived from another country, is weak at mathematics based on her score on a standardised test may be a misjudged and invalid inference when using a test that was not normed with students whose second language is English. To realise the promise and potential of formative and summative assessment, primarily helping students to learn, teachers need to gather relevant and credible evidence using appropriate methods. They need to ensure that each student's educational experience is framed around the most appropriate expectations, content and pedagogical approaches so that assessment works for rather than against the student. This chapter reflects calls for what is termed universal design in learning and in assessment, requiring that learning spaces, curricula, classroom management, pedagogy and assessment be optimised for all learners, not only for those who already have little difficulty in school.

When you finish the chapter, you should be able to answer these questions:

* What assessment opportunities and challenges are presented by student diversity in my class?
* Where can I find out about my legal and professional obligations in relation to meeting the needs of all learners?
* How can I make my teaching and assessment practices more inclusive for students with diverse personal/educational needs and from diverse backgrounds?
* How can digital approaches assist me in providing an inclusive environment in my classroom?

Educational inclusion: Policy context

What is a typical mix of students in a class? The answer to this question is very different in the 21st century than at any time previously. Teachers today work with student cohorts characterised by a wide range of differences in cognitive, social, emotional, physical, cultural and linguistic traits and contexts. This change is due to a combination of national legislation and policies around inclusion, the increased monitoring and identification of special educational needs and the mobility of families and students internationally.

Quantifying special educational needs in school

Historically, some schools and classes were quite diverse, especially where multi-grade teaching was practised. More recently, however, with better means to identify children with special needs at an early stage, the school-going population diagnosed with special educational needs has increased substantially and schools are therefore required to be well-attuned to individual student need. Estimates of the number of persons with disabilities vary. The World Health Organization (2016) estimates that over 1 billion (15%) of the world's population live with some sort of a disability. In the USA, almost 1 in 10 students attending school are identified as having a disability, with almost half of these having a learning disability (Brigham and Bakken, 2013). We can provide a lower-bound estimate that the number of students in Ireland either receiving resource teaching support in mainstream schools or attending special schools during the 2014–15 year was over 56,000 students, representing over 6% of the primary and secondary school population (DES, 2015d; NCSE, 2016). Rose et al. (2015) highlight the difficulty in quantifying from available statistics the total number of children receiving support in school, so the real figure is likely to be significantly higher than 6%.

Policy response

International treaties

Increasingly, in policy at least, education systems seek to provide inclusive learning environments for almost all students within regular or mainstream school structures. One driver for this trend has been binding United Nations treaties such as the UN Convention on the Rights of the Child (1989), ratified by 195 countries, that have focused national governments' attention on ensuring that children are educated in the most inclusive environment possible. Perhaps more significantly in an assessment context, the Convention on the Rights of Persons with Disabilities (UN, 2006), ratified by 172 countries, sets out the legal obligations on states to promote, protect and ensure the human rights of persons with disabilities. Article 24 deals specifically with education and Section 1 of that article is presented in Figure 10.1:

States Parties recognize the right of persons with disabilities to education. With a view to realizing this right without discrimination and on the basis of equal opportunity, States Parties shall ensure an inclusive education system at all levels and lifelong learning directed to:

(a) The full development of human potential and sense of dignity and self-worth, and the strengthening of respect for human rights, fundamental freedoms and human diversity
(b) The development by persons with disabilities of their personality, talents and creativity, as well as their mental and physical abilities, to their fullest potential
(c) Enabling persons with disabilities to participate effectively in a free society.

Figure 10.1   UN Convention on the Rights of Persons with Disabilities, Article 24.1

Four subsequent sections to Article 24 (2–5) reinforce the types of initiatives required of signatories to ensure that children are provided with the education most appropriate to their needs. This includes, for example, providing reasonable accommodations for learners, ensuring that effective individualised support is provided, as well as education in braille, sign language and the use of alternative modes of communication, educational techniques and materials to support persons with disabilities.

National policies

In framing national policy and guidelines in relation to inclusion, national governments and state agencies draw on elements of the UN and other, earlier international agreements. For example, guidelines for the inclusion of students with special educational needs in Irish secondary education (DES, 2007a) acknowledge the importance of meeting international obligations when implementing the provisions of relevant national legislation in the form of the Education for Persons with Special Educational Needs (EPSEN) Act 2004. This act defines special educational needs as 'a restriction in the capacity of the person to participate in and benefit from education on account of an enduring physical, sensory, mental health or learning disability, or any other condition which results in a person learning differently from a person without that condition' (Government of Ireland, 2004: Section 1 [1]). Legislation and codes of practice in England recognise that children presenting with a special educational need may also have a disability as defined by the English Equality Act 2010. This provides a broader interpretation of children's rights to support from schools, covering long-term health conditions such as asthma, diabetes, epilepsy and cancer (DfE, 2015).

Equivalent federal legislation in the USA is the Individuals with Disabilities Education (IDEA) Act 2004, covering some 6.5 million young people. This legislation explicitly recognises a number of forms of disability, including deafness, hearing impairment, visual impairment, deaf-blindness, intellectual disability, multiple disability, emotional disturbance, orthopaedic impairment, other health impairment (for example, ADHD) and specific learning disability. Given the breadth of legislation, policy and practice internationally, there is understandable confusion with regard to the terms disability and special educational need. Cumming and Maxwell (2014) make an interesting distinction between impairment and disability. Impairment represents a 'state of being', whereas disability is a result of the barriers set before persons with impairment in relation to mobility, work opportunities, learning practices and social exclusion. For educational policy-makers and teachers, the emphasis needs to focus on facilitating and including students with impairments by removing the disabling barriers to their learning potential.

Teachers also need to plan around a more comprehensive range of students presenting with atypical contexts and characteristics. Contexts and needs identified by Education Scotland include: attention deficit disorder, autistic spectrum disorder, complex needs, visual impairment, deaf and hearing impaired, dyslexia, English as an additional language, healthcare needs, highly able children, looked after children, refugees and asylum seekers, service families, travelling communities and young carers. Other atypical contexts also exist. Having one student in your class presenting with one of the above contexts would be challenging. In reality, classrooms can contain many children with exceptional needs and sometimes students with multiple needs, such as those with English as a second language who also present with a learning disability such as dyslexia.

Teachers' response

A clear challenge for teachers is how to meet the needs of such a diverse set of learners. Assessment, in its broadest sense, clearly has a role in helping to identify the specific context and/or impairment underpinning students' needs. Often, when teachers and parents think of assessment in relation to special educational needs, the focus is on the more formal processes involved in obtaining a diagnosis for a child. Under Section 8 (7) of the Disability Act in Ireland (Government of Ireland, 2005), children are entitled to an assessment of need if the parents feel that their child has a disability. The result of this assessment is often the first official confirmation and recognition by the state authorities that the child has a disability. The assessment report typically identifies the following:

- whether the child has a disability and the nature and extent of the disability
- the health and education needs arising from the disability

- appropriate services to meet those needs (though delivery of these are not guaranteed in the legislation)
- when a review of the assessment should be carried out.

Whereas the assessment may highlight the services that *should* be provided to the child, this is tempered significantly in the statutory *service plan* that is developed in response to the assessment. Section 11 (7) (d) of the Act notes that the service plan should be framed, in part, by taking into account the financial 'practicability of providing the services identified in the assessment report', thus removing any statutory entitlement for the child and parents to service to address the needs identified in the assessment.

As children enter and progress through the school system, the term assessment in relation to students with SEN is often also perceived in relation to obtaining support for students. Results of psychological, emotional, speech therapy, occupational therapy or other assessments can form the evidential basis for requests for support and services, such as a special assistant, a specialist referral or assistive technology. Many authors focus significantly on specific aspects of special needs and the range of associated assessments, for example Meyen and Skrtic (1995), Groth-Marnat (2009) and Taylor (2008). The scope of this book is, however, focused more on tapping the affordances of formative and summative assessment to inform teaching and learning in relation to all students, including those with a range of special needs and characteristics. One way to do this is to frame assessment as a key element of differentiated teaching and learning. This is the focus of the next section.

Role of assessment in differentiated learning

In Chapter 4, we explored the challenges for teachers in providing appropriate educational experiences and opportunities for each student. Increasingly, curriculum planners address this challenge through the principles and practices of differentiation. Tomlinson's (1999, 2000) approach focuses on adaptations to *content* (varying the learning outcomes for different students), *process* (tasks, activities, grouping and pedagogical approaches), *product* (how the students demonstrate and represent their learning) and *learning environment*. In a study of teachers' use of differentiated reading strategies involving 330 primary teachers, Heneghan and Murchan (2014) found that process variations, such as the grouping together of students of similar ability, were the most understood form of differentiation, and the prioritisation of differentiation in the school's policy was the greatest driver of its use. The study also showed that a majority of the teachers indicated that careful goal setting, including individual education plans and different assessments for different students, were key factors that teachers thought could facilitate the implementation of differentiated reading. The role of school policy in encouraging differentiation illustrated the value and influence of school-wide policies, planning and collaboration on teachers' pedagogical practice. Such adaptations, or combinations of them, granted, make teaching more challenging for teachers, but also make learning more accessible to students. The identification of student needs must precede any instructional strategies that aim to support individual students' learning difficulties and contexts that impact on learning. Thus, formative and diagnostic approaches help establish baseline information about learners so that teachers can tailor experiences to specific students.

It is important that the forms of assessment used are sufficiently sensitive to enable an accurate identification of needs so that teachers can tailor appropriate educational experiences to all students. For example, questions accompanying mathematics textbooks at primary level frequently use colour illustrations in representing data via histograms. Caution needs to be taken in interpreting responses to such material by students with any degree of visual impairment. Similarly at secondary level, using cloze-type question paragraphs (where students supply missing words or phrases) to assess the geography knowledge of students with English as a second language, can lead to invalid inferences about students' understanding of geography.

Individual education plans (IEPs)

For most students in special education settings and increasingly for students with specific disabilities in the regular classroom, an individual education plan (IEP) or individual education programme is used to foster a collaborative differentiated approach to meeting students' needs. The basic concept underpinning IEPs is intuitively sensible: teachers, parents and other relevant professionals agree a set of learning outcomes, taking into account the student's prior performance and current needs, and then implement approaches to help the child realise the outcomes. It is essential to involve parents fully in the process and gain their support in reinforcing the school programme at home. The IEP helps frame the expected learning outcomes against which progress and performance can be measured. In Ireland, IEPs are used in cases where more graduated classroom and school support plans and interventions are not adequate to meet the needs identified by school staff and parents (DES, 2007b). Where IEPs are used, schools may draw on external expertise such as psychologists, speech and language therapists, occupational therapists and others. Items typically incorporated in IEPs include:

- the names of individuals contributing to the plan (e.g. teacher, parent, support worker)
- a summary of the student's abilities and needs (educational and other)
- long-term educational aims for the student
- short-term targets for the student
- instructional approaches and other supports (e.g. a special assistant, assistive technology) to help the student reach their targets
- approaches to evaluating student learning and progress and to reviewing the plan.

Formative approaches to assessment facilitate the continued monitoring of student progress and the re-calibration of support by personnel working most closely with the student on a day-to-day basis. Follow-up formal review after a longer period involving the school team and parents provides the necessary information to help re-frame the educational expectations and approaches for the next cycle of learning. Samples of IEPs can be found at www.sess.ie/resources/teaching-methods-and-organisation

Activity 10.1

Try this out – How has assessment informed development of policy on SEN

Review the video *Special education revisited*, produced by the Centre for Studies in Inclusive Education (CSIE) in the UK (available at: www.csie.org.uk/resources/free. shtml). This 15-minute animated video offers a short history of special education policy in the UK.

Use the resources on the companion website to explore the following questions: How has the understanding of disability changed over the past 150 years? Identify any forms of assessment that informed policy and practice in the UK over that period. To what extent has assessment been a feature in enabling or impeding appropriate educational provision for students with SEN? Reflect on the medical and the social models of disability: What are the assessment implications in relation to the two models? Which model do you agree with?

Visit the companion website at: https://study.sagepub.com/murchanshiel

Limitations of approaches used for general classroom assessment

The 'unthinking' use of regular assessment methods with atypical students is a threat to valid inferences about the learning and progress of those students. By unthinking, we mean not recognising that the content, form, administration or scoring of the assessment may obscure the view of student learning, leading to erroneous inferences, conclusions and actions. As explained in Chapter 2, incorrect inferences based on assessment performance constitute a significant threat to validity. For example, many approaches to assessment by teachers are predicated on the understanding that students speak English as their first language or, in a more globalised sense, speak the language of the school. Given population shifts across much of the world in recent years, this is a questionable assumption. One estimate, for example, indicates that there were approximately 65 million people forcibly displaced from their homes worldwide at the end of 2015, or one out of every 113 of the world's population (UNHCR, 2016). Many of these, we can assume, crossed borders and enrolled in education systems that work through a different language to their own. Such dramatic population shifts, combined with regular migration across borders, contributes to the multi-cultural and linguistic environment in many schools. In Ireland, just over 62,000 children born outside the country entered the Irish school system in the period 2009–14 (CSO, 2015). Some of these came from other English-speaking countries (the UK and the USA) and are likely to have had English as a first language. Just over 46,000 can be conservatively estimated to have had a first language other than English. In 20 schools in Dublin, two-thirds of students were recorded as having a non-Irish background (*Irish Times*, 2015). In Britain, there are 1.1 million children who speak 311 dialects, with English speakers comprising a minority in some schools

(*Daily Telegraph*, 2015). Patterns of migration ensure that similar student cultural and linguistic diversity is a feature of schools in cities, urban and even rural areas in many countries, signalling the need to take language experience and competency into account when framing assessments.

Students' language skills

Consider the performance assessment task where students in primary school are asked to orally present their history projects to the class. Unless the first language of students is taken into account, construct-irrelevant variance may be introduced into students' performance and subsequent interpretations (see Chapter 2). In addition to the focus on validity, how teachers and assessment systems deal with cultural diversity in schools and classrooms is also an issue of fairness. Is it fair to assess second-level students' knowledge of business principles using a test form that assumes high-level cognitive and academic fluency in the student's second language?

Jim Cummins (1991, 2000) identifies two forms of second language acquisition: Basic Interpersonal Communicative Skills (BICS) and Cognitive and Academic Language Proficiency (CALP). BICS includes the type of language and communication skills that enable people to converse and interact with a different-language society in a functional, effective way. CALP represents the more formal language required to follow instruction and succeed academically in school. Whereas conversational fluency (BICS) can be attained in a second language in about two years, it can take four or more years to reach grade norms in academic language and therefore the capacity to learn and demonstrate learning through the medium of a second language. This is an important validity and fairness consideration when planning assessments. A one-size-fits-all approach to assessment, where the task assumes that all students are equally fluent in cognitive and academic language, may not be appropriate, given the specific student population in your class or school. Such *one-sizing* may underestimate or misrepresent the learning of second-language learners, say in geography, science or mathematics.

Using traditional assessments

Cumming and Maxwell (2014) identify a number of problems associated with using traditional classroom tests and standardised assessments in classes where there is a wide range of student needs and contexts. These include the following:

- Tests may ignore important skills that some students have and others do not (e.g. highly detailed recall) in the desire to make the test the same for everyone.
- It may be difficult to reconcile the standardisation of procedures with the current emphasis on flexible and individual learning.
- The standards or criteria against which performance is judged may be inappropriate for some students.
- Some assessments may fail to detect small gains or changes in learning, often the type of gain crucial to some students' development.
- Traditional forms of reporting may not be appropriate for all students – reports suited to the majority of the class may fail to communicate the significant progress made by some students.

In relation to students with special educational needs in particular, Lysaght (2012) expresses reservations about the efficacy of inclusive school environments in the absence of more sensitive assessment approaches that better capture the learning of students with SEN. The use of standardised tests is clearly challenging in the context of inclusive classrooms, yet any assumption that teacher-designed tests and tasks are de facto more inclusive needs to be interrogated carefully. Unless teachers specifically build into the design of their own assessments the needs of SEN students, such approaches can be equally inappropriate for students with disabilities or with needs arising from a range of other issues such as a language other than English being spoken at home.

Making classroom assessment work for atypical and exceptional learners

In analysing Queensland's high-stakes certification at Year 12, Cumming and Maxwell (2014: 585) identify the form of assessment (for example, a written test) as a potentially disabling barrier that prevents some students from demonstrating their learning and progress. In other words, 'the secondary form of assessment gets in the way of the primary purpose'. Though this was noted in the context of high-stakes school-based certification in Australia, the same can be said of more formative and summative assessment where the stakes are lower or minimal. What if the assessment tells the wrong story for some individuals or groups? In earlier chapters in the book, we discussed a wide, fluid and interchangeable range of assessment approaches. These include teacher observation, written tasks, products, tests, orals, performance, group work and technology-assisted assessments. Particular care should be taken when evaluating the learning of students with atypical profiles. No one approach is sufficient, for example, to identify a specific learning disability impacting the progress of a student. Administration of a standardised objective test, use of miscue analysis and other approaches may be required. By marshalling a range of evidence to help draw inferences about student learning, teachers are in a better position to appraise the nature of the learning and plan appropriate strategies, and, in some cases, recommend additional assessment.

Given the focus of AfL on identifying what the learner knows, what they need to know and how to get there, many associated approaches are suited to use with atypical students. Regular assessment and feedback to students in the form of questioning, in-class tasks and self-assessment provide an evidential base for teachers to identify and describe the learning and development needs of students, plan learning opportunities to address them and evaluate the success of the approach.

Observation and questioning

As highlighted in Chapter 5, observation and questioning are two of the most widely used formative approaches reported by teachers. However, what teachers mean by both approaches and how effectively they implement them are less clear. Teachers can usefully focus observation on the learning of one or more students in class who may have a special educational need and use the findings from the observations to plan appropriate learning outcomes. The use of recording aids such as checklists or rating scales helps provide increased precision to the observations and can result in more informed and effective intervention strategies.

Feedback

Particular attention needs to be given to the role of feedback with students presenting with SEN. Used effectively, feedback can help highlight for students their current levels of learning and how targeted levels can be attained. For atypical students who may not be as well able to take in and process the feedback as other students in class, teachers need to provide more scaffolding, perhaps using alternative methods to communicate feedback and more sustained follow-up. The information may need to be communicated more concisely and be more explicitly stated than for students without such needs, for example through use of visual representations and short phrases. The teacher cannot assume that these students will recognise or strategise for themselves about how they can close the gap and bring about improved learning. Their metacognitive and self-regulation skills may be less well developed, thus requiring greater input from the teacher if policies of inclusion are to be realised and bring tangible benefits to students. The student may need to have learning broken down into more manageable chunks. For example, when preparing for a written activity in class, the teacher may guide a student with attention deficit hyperactivity disorder (ADHD) by emphasising discrete steps such as organising their materials (pen, paper), finding the relevant page/section in the workbook, giving directions when the time is nearly up, and helping with strategies to ignore distractions. Similar care and structure is needed in relation to any feedback offered to the student on performance on the task.

Assessment tasks

Differentiated teacher-developed tasks and assessments can also be used effectively with all learners. For example, the Key Stage 2 language and literacy curriculum in Northern Ireland requires teachers to ensure that pupils should be enabled to 'use the skills of planning, revising and redrafting to improve their writing, including that which they have composed digitally' (CCEA, n.d.). A learning outcome to support this objective might be:

> We will develop a creative story using a number of writing features such as plot, characterisation and setting.

Assessment for this could be through a short writing portfolio charting the development of three drafts to final completion. For students with a learning disability in relation to language, a greater number of drafts might be used, reflecting the additional scaffolding required by such learners.

Similarly, Unit AS 2 of the new Business Studies specification for GCE certification in Northern Ireland requires students to 'demonstrate and apply knowledge and understanding of the income statement and statement of financial position of a sole trader, including assets and liabilities and interpret the income statement and the statement of financial position' (CCEA, 2016b: 17). An in-class written test might be designed as a series of short paragraph-length responses to determine who has mastered initial principles underpinning financial statements before proceeding to more complex application using simulated figures for a company. For a student with motor-control difficulties, a discussion with the teacher while others in the class develop their written answers is more likely to capture levels of understanding accurately than asking the student to write the test. This is an example of providing *accommodations* within the classroom setting in response to the content matter, the purpose of the assessment and the teacher's knowledge of the student.

Accommodations and modifications

The term accommodation is a widely interpreted concept in assessment and education more generally. The *Standards for educational and psychological testing* (AERA et al., 2014: 190) interpret accommodations as:

> adaptations to test format or administration (such as changes in the way the test is presented, the setting for the test, or the way in which the student responds) that maintain the same construct and produce results that are comparable to those obtained by students who do not use accommodations.

A distinction is drawn between such accommodations (that don't change the construct of interest, for example reading comprehension) and modifications that do. Like accommodations, modifications are intended to make assessments accessible to as many students as possible, but they may change what is being assessed for those availing of the modification. Allowing a primary-level student with autism spectrum disorder (ASD) to provide evidence of oral communicative competency in a second language, using a series of email exchanges with the teacher instead of a face-to-face structured conversation like the rest of the class, would result in two different language constructs being measured and should, therefore, result in different interpretations about the student's facility with language. Had the child participated in the conversation, but with one or two short breaks (an accommodation), we could be more confident that similar constructs are being assessed.

Examples of other informal adaptations to formative assessments include:

- changing the look of the assessment (if the text of a test in the chapter is in small print, reproduce the questions in larger font with more space for students to record their responses)
- highlighting key words in an assessment prompt, either visually or by oral emphasis
- asking students to state the question or task in their own words and checking this interpretation for accuracy
- giving students some indication of the typical length of answer needed
- using a different form of assessment (a series of short questions instead of an expository essay on a topic – this may enable the student to demonstrate more comprehensively the extent of understanding)
- letting students determine the medium of response, for example an answer using a laptop, an annotated diagram or a concept map.

In much of your teaching, where the general purpose is to check on student learning to inform subsequent teaching and learning, accommodations and modifications are valuable in trying to provide as inclusive an educational environment as possible. Some teachers might be hesitant to offer alternative forms and routes to assessment for students of different abilities and characteristics. Yet, such an approach is simply another element of the broader concept of differentiation and is consistent with a socio-cultural interpretation of education. The fact that one or more students may show their understanding in a different way to many of the other students in the class simply reflects the diversity and need for inclusion in schools. It may become an issue where students' performance is being compared for certification or other reasons, but in the context of formative assessment there is immense value in differentiating the form, representation and demonstration of assessment to suit individual students, where practicable.

Atypical learners and summative high-stakes assessment

Need for reasonable accommodations

Tailoring assessments and examinations to student needs in high-stakes and large-scale assessment contexts is, in part, an illustration of the concept of *reasonable accommodations* promoted in the UN's Convention on the Rights of Persons with Disabilities (2006). Expressed in the context of a human right, accommodations are defined as:

> necessary and appropriate modification and adjustments not imposing a disproportionate or undue burden, where needed in a particular case, to ensure to persons with disabilities the enjoyment or exercise on an equal basis with others of all human rights and fundamental freedoms. (Section 24.2.c)

In applying this in more formal assessment contexts, for example in certification tests, teachers and assessment agencies often seek to offer accommodations to enable students to demonstrate their learning and achievement on a level playing field with other students (Tindal and Fuchs, cited in Thurlow, 2014). Typical accommodations in summative high-stakes tests include additional time, a different format of test (e.g. a braille version of an exam paper, test questions read to the examinee), a different location (e.g. in a small group in a separate room) and adaptations in computerised testing. As part of the examinations developed by Cambridge Assessment for administration worldwide, 'access arrangements' are provided to eliminate unnecessary obstacles and enable examinees to receive recognition for their attainment (Cambridge Assessment, 2015). In public examinations in Ireland, the State Examinations Commission (SEC) may provide 'reasonable accommodations' for examinees presenting with specific disabilities to help them take the examinations. For example, the SEC allows 10 minutes extra time per hour when a candidate needs the help of a scribe to complete an examination.

If a student avails of an accommodation such as access to a reader or a scribe, or a waiver from the assessment of grammar, spelling or punctuation, this may be noted on the student's certificate. While the Equality Authority in Ireland has argued that this is discriminatory, the courts have, up until now at least, upheld the practice. For example, in 2010, a High Court judge asserted that removing the annotation would 'tip the balance too far in favour [of the candidate] to the detriment of others with a legitimate interest in the fair and equitable administration of the Leaving Certificate' (*Irish Times*, 11 June 2010).

Types of accommodation in high-stakes exams

Accommodations can be grouped into a number of categories based on the obstacle to be overcome and these are illustrated in Table 10.1.

Table 10.1 Accommodations and modifications to help students access assessments and examinations

Obstacle addressed	Illustration
Content of assessment	Substitute text for diagrams
	Use of calculator (though this may be standard in some assessments)
Format of assessment	Human or digital reader
	Have directions clarified
	Large print or braille
	Tactile diagrams
	Coloured paper
	Visual cues
	Signed administration
	Digital/computer presentation
How students demonstrate learning	Use of a scribe
	Word processor
	Oral delivery; digital recording
	Pointing
Scheduling	Extra time for exam or coursework (minutes or % of test)
	Additional rest periods
	Alternative time of day
Exam environment	Separate room
	Small group/individual
	Alternative venue (hospital, home)
	Proximity to aural source (close to CD player)
	Personal recording of stimulus on induction loop
	Availability of medicine, food, drink
	Mobility facilitated during exam
	Appropriate furniture

Sources: Expert Advisory Group (2000); Thurlow (2014); Cambridge Assessment (2015); Rogers et al. (2016); SEC (2016)

Join the debate: Accommodations make sense, don't they?

Michelle is diagnosed with a learning disability and wishes to receive additional time in an examination as part of her secondary certification. This should 'remove any unnecessary barriers to the standard assessment, without compromising the standards being tested, so that [she] can receive recognition for [her] attainment' (Cambridge Assessment, 2015: 21). Or will it? There is appealing and intuitive logic in providing such accommodations and this is commonplace in large assessment programmes, yet research to support the practice is surprisingly inconclusive. For example, Christopher Rogers and colleagues reviewed the evidence for the effects of test accommodations for the National Center on Educational Outcomes in the USA, focusing largely on mathematics, reading, writing and science (see Rogers et al., 2016 in further reading). They found some positive effect for additional time and use of a calculator and also noted that a majority of both students and teachers perceived that accommodations are of assistance to performance and students' emotional state and self-esteem. However, the researchers concluded that the oral presentation of learning and the availability of low-distraction alternative accommodation had no effect on student performance. This is a troubling research finding for proponents of such accommodations.

For any school or testing programme you are familiar with, review the policy, if any, on assessment accommodations for students with special educational or other needs. Compare practice with the research findings from Rogers et al.'s study. What is surprising in the research? Why might research findings be in conflict with widespread policy and practice? How could the research be expanded or improved? How might assessment practice change?

Limitations of standardised tests in identifying learning difficulties

While group-administered standardised tests are generally constructed with great care to ensure appropriate content coverage, accurate scores, norms that are representative of the target population and a clear interpretative framework, they do have limitations. One such limitation is that it may not be possible to discern why a student has achieved a low score, and hence whether the student may have a learning difficulty. A low score on a standardised reading comprehension test in Primary Year 4, for example, might arise because a student has one or more of the following:

- decoding problem – the student is unable to read the words in the text at an appropriate rate
- vocabulary problem – the student does not understand the meaning of the words in the text

- lack of prior knowledge – the student does not have prior knowledge of the topic of the text and therefore cannot understand the information that has been presented
- comprehension problem – the student cannot make the inferences required to answer comprehension questions
- poor metacognitive skills – the student cannot manage their comprehension of the text, by, for example, re-reading a segment of text that is not understood, in relation to the purpose of reading
- low motivation – the student may have been poorly motivated and may not have exerted sufficient effort. In PISA 2009 in Ireland, it was concluded that secondary school students' level of engagement with the test had dropped compared with earlier cycles (Perkins et al., 2012)
- high levels of anxiety – a student's anxiety levels are related to performance in subjects like mathematics, with highly anxious students performing, on average, less well than students with low levels of anxiety (e.g. Perkins et al., 2013).

It is for this reason that a standardised test can only be viewed as providing a broad indication of whether a student may or may not have a learning difficulty. If a student achieves a low score, the teacher will need to reflect on the score and relate it to the broader context in which teaching and learning occur:

- Does the student's performance on the standardised test correlate with performance on similar classroom-based tasks?
- Does the student have a history of performing poorly on standardised tests and other assessments?
- Does the student perform less well in one curriculum area, compared with another (perhaps pointing to a learning difficulty in a particular subject)?
- What factors can be ruled out in explaining poor performance (e.g. can weak decoding skills be ruled out as an explanation for poor reading performance)?
- Does the student have the language skills necessary to perform well on the test?
- Does the student belong to a group who, on average, may perform less well on standardised tests (e.g. some students in socio-economically disadvantaged contexts may struggle to achieve their potential in the face of risk factors such as poverty, poor nutrition or health-related challenges)?
- Does one gender perform less well on the test than the other (e.g. male students often perform less well on average than females in language-based tests)?
- Does the student have one or more additional difficulties that might impact on performance, such as dyspraxia (sensory motor difficulties) or speech and language difficulties?

Hence, standardised tests may be useful in identifying that a student is performing poorly – but they cannot pinpoint why performance is poor. That is where follow-up diagnostic assessment plays a role in determining whether or not a student has a learning difficulty, and, if so, whether it is deep seated (i.e. whether it may represent a specific learning difficulty).

Using diagnostic assessment to help identify students' learning needs

As noted above, a low score on a standardised test of achievement may signal a learning difficulty. For example, a percentile rank of 15 on a nationally normed standardised test indicates that the student's score is in the bottom 15% nationally, and, hence, the student may have a learning difficulty. The selection of the 15th percentile is arbitrary. It may be appropriate to select the 20th percentile, or any other value as a cut-off, though a higher cut-off point means that more students will be identified as being at risk.

Although a student may perform poorly because of dispositional, socio-economic or language factors, we cannot rule out a learning difficulty in the presence of one or more of these, as any one of them can co-occur with a difficulty and compound its effects. A diagnostic assessment may need to be administered to find out more.

A diagnostic assessment identifies a student's strengths, weaknesses, knowledge, skills and abilities in a way that standardised tests cannot. Such an assessment typically leads to a plan to address the student's learning problems, and may result in additional support. A diagnostic assessment may be carried out by a student's class teacher, a specialist or resource teacher in the school, or an external specialist such as an educational psychologist. Often, it is individually administered, allowing the test administrator to reflect on how the student performs, and draw conclusions about his/her learning needs. Students who may struggle on a group-administered standardised test have a better chance of demonstrating their skills and abilities in a one-to-one situation.

Diagnosing reading difficulties

A diagnostic assessment of reading might involve administering tests in one or more subcomponents of reading, such as:

- phonological awareness – the ability to segment spoken words into syllables and/or sounds, which is a strong predictor of word reading
- alphabet knowledge – knowledge of letter names and/or their sounds, when letters are presented at random and in isolation
- listening comprehension – students with poor reading comprehension may also have poor listening comprehension, suggesting that their reading difficulty may be linked to more general language comprehension difficulties
- reading vocabulary – the understanding of word meanings, which can be assessed using an instrument that does not require students to read words, such as a picture vocabulary test, where a student selects a picture (from among four) corresponding to a concept called out by the test administrator
- phonics knowledge – the ability to read nonsense or pseudo words in isolation. The use of nonsense words means that students cannot draw on their memory of sight words and must apply phonics rules and generalisations
- word reading – the ability to read real words in isolation, thereby demonstrating knowledge of sight words and the ability to apply decoding rules flexibly, without the support of sentence or text context

- reading fluency – the ability to read with speed, accuracy and expression. This is often measured by computing the average number of words read per minute, while note is also taken of whether or not the student reads with expression, rather than in a word-by-word manner
- reading comprehension skills – the ability to respond correctly to a range of questions about a text that has just been read orally or silently. Skills assessed may include sequencing events, identifying causal relationships, relating pronouns to their references, capturing the main ideas (whether implicitly or explicitly stated) and making generalisations and drawing conclusions.

It is only after conducting a multi-faceted diagnostic assessment such as this, and taking background characteristics and performance on previous classroom assessments and standardised tests into account, that conclusions can be drawn about the nature and extent of a student's reading difficulty. The outcomes of a battery of diagnostic tests may lead to the development of an individual learning programme designed to address the child's learning difficulty. Such a programme may outline what measures need to be taken to address the child's difficulty in the classroom, in a learning support setting (if needed) and at home.

Despite targeted instruction designed to address their learning difficulties, a small proportion of children will continue to struggle with reading and may have a specific reading difficulty (sometimes referred to as a dyslexic difficulty). In order to identify whether such a difficulty is present or not, it may be necessary to conduct further diagnostic assessment into cognitive processes that are not usually assessed in classroom contexts, but which are based on a sound theory of learning difficulties in reading. These include working memory, rapid automatic naming and, on occasion, non-verbal intelligence. The outcomes of these tests may provide further insights into the nature of a child's learning difficulty and how it might be addressed (see, for example, Phillips et al., 2013).

Diagnosing difficulties in mathematics

If a child performs poorly on a standardised test of mathematics, it may also be necessary to implement a battery of diagnostic tests to pinpoint the extent and nature of the difficulty. According to Ketterlin-Geller and Yovanoff (2009), such an assessment might involve engaging in:

- cognitive diagnostic assessment, where the focus is on identifying a student's persistent misconceptions and misunderstandings relating to key mathematical concepts
- skills analysis, where sub-skills in mathematics that may be problematic are identified – for example, a difficulty with the space and shape content area, or a difficulty with a mathematical process, such as establishing connections between word problems and algorithms
- error analysis, where the errors students make on mathematics problems are examined, with a view to planning teaching sequences to address them.

Beyond this, and again, for a small proportion of students, there may be a need to investigate whether a specific learning difficulty in mathematics such as dyscalculia (a specific difficulty with arithmetical operations) is present.

Assessing second language learners

In general, the use of standardised tests of reading and other aspects of language normed on a general population may not be suitable for students for whom English is an additional language. The Educational Testing Service (2009b) notes three clusters of factors that can impact on the performance of EAL students (those with English as an additional language) in assessment contexts:

- linguistic factors (language background, proficiency in English, proficiency in the student's native language)
- educational background factors (the degree of formal schooling in the native language, the degree of formal schooling in English, the degree of exposure to and experience with standardised testing)
- cultural factors (varying degrees of acculturation in the host country).

In general, EAL students who have been learning English for a short period of time will not be expected to sit standardised tests. In PISA, for example, students who have received more than one year of instruction in the assessment language are expected to take part in testing (OECD, 2015b). However, it is arguable whether the test results of students who have such limited experience with the test language are valid, especially in light of the research on conversational fluency and academic language discussed earlier in the chapter. Certainly, such results are unlikely to provide a strong basis for making decisions about teaching and learning at the individual student level. This points to a need to employ a broader range of assessment tools in working with EAL students, including tools that will provide useful information for making informed instructional decisions.

Fortunately, there is a range of tools available for this purpose. These include:

- performance-based assessments such as those described in Chapter 7, but modified as needed (see, for example, Abedi (2010) where modified language is used)
- initial and ongoing assessment of language skills (speaking, listening, reading and writing) using schemes such as the Integrate Ireland Learning and Training primary and post-primary language toolkits (IILT, 2007a, 2007b) or the European Common Framework of Reference for Languages (Council of Europe, 2012) for pre-school, primary and post-primary levels. These toolkits result in the assignment of proficiency levels to students and can provide a basis for instructional decision making. Some of these measures include self-assessment components, where students can assess their own proficiency
- standardised measures of English as a second language, such as the Test of English Language Learning (TELL, Pearson Education, 2016) which comprises a standardised screening measure and a follow-up diagnostic test.

Identifying and addressing the needs of gifted and talented students

In general, tests of achievement standardised on a representative national sample may tell us relatively little about the performance or abilities of gifted and talented students. This is because such students quickly reach ceiling level (i.e. they answer many or most questions correctly). This means that it is difficult to define the upper limit of their performance, or to compare them with one another. Organisations that provide services for gifted and talented youth typically administer a battery of ability tests covering areas such as verbal reasoning, numerical ability and abstract reasoning. Often, it is necessary to administer ability tests that are designed for an older age group in order to discriminate effectively among students wishing to access services.

Classroom teachers wishing to assess their gifted and talented students, with a view to implementing enrichment programmes, may wish to administer out-of-level standardised tests. For example, a student in Grade 4 might be asked to complete a test designed for students in Grade 6. In interpreting the outcomes of such a test, the teacher will need to take into account the fact that the test norms, as well as the test content, were developed for students at a higher grade level. The performance-based assessments described in Chapter 7 are also relevant for gifted and talented students, though some adjustments may need to be made. For example, scoring rubrics may need to be modified to reflect the higher expectations held for gifted and talented students.

Chapter summary

The broad focus of this chapter was on differentiating assessment to address the needs of a broad range of learners who, for one reason or another, may struggle on formative and summative tasks designed for the general population of students, or may find them very easy. Among the groups considered were students with sensory, emotional or learning disabilities, including specific learning difficulties; students for whom English is an additional language; and gifted and talented students. The full range of disabilities and special educational needs likely to be encountered by you in your teaching is beyond the scope of this book, but more specialised sources are provided in the text and on the companion website as part of Activity 10.1. It was noted that, in many cases, tests designed for a general population may not be suitable for students in these specialised populations, as their needs were not taken into account in designing the assessments.

The provision of reasonable accommodation was identified as one approach to differentiating assessment for special populations of learners. However, it was noted that accommodations should not alter the underlying construct that is being assessed. For example, if a reading passage is read aloud to a student, the assessment is no longer one of reading comprehension for that student. Instead, modifications such as this were identified as changes to an assessment that alter the construct being assessed.

Two broad approaches to assessment that are more often associated with AfL than AoL are performance-based and diagnostic assessments. Both approaches also allow for differentiation. For example, performance-based assessments can be modified to accommodate students whose language proficiency may not be at the level of their peers. Diagnostic assessments can delve into aspects of a subject, or more general abilities, that may contribute to a student's learning difficulties.

Ultimately, differentiating assessment is about implementing approaches to assessment that accommodate the needs of atypical learners, while at the same time being fair to students who are not identified in this way.

Questions for discussion

1. Review the assessment policy of one school with which you are familiar or access the planning of one teacher. To what extent is formal identification of special educational or other needs incorporated into the planning? What are the steps employed in identifying such needs? How is the differentiation of formative and summative assessment evident in the plan in relation to atypical learners?
2. If possible, seek access to the individual education plan (IEP) for one student. Work openly with the school, parent and student so that your purpose in accessing the plan is clear and understood, and the confidentiality of the information is maintained. Identify the nature of the disability or other circumstances leading to the development of the IEP. What are the main targets for the student? For each target, identify (i) the approach to assessment and (ii) how the assessment information might be used to help the student.

Further reading

Cumming, J.J., & Maxwell, G.S. (2014). Expanding approaches to summative assessment for students with impairment. In L. Florian (ed.) *The Sage handbook of special education*, Vol. 2 (2nd edition, pp. 573–93). Los Angeles, CA: Sage.

This chapter offers an insight into the inclusion of students with SEN in the school system in Queensland. It advocates more equitable forms of assessment and critically analyses the provision of accommodations in assessment. The chapter also focuses on the role of moderated school-based assessments in providing appropriate differentiated assessments to students of different background and ability, even for high-stakes certification purposes.

Rogers, C.M., Lazarus, S.S., & Thurlow, M.L. (2016). *A summary of the effects of test accommodations: 2013–2014*. Research Report No. 402. Minneapolis: National Center on Educational Outcomes. Available at: https://nceo.umn.edu/docs/OnlinePubs/Report402/NCEOReport402.pdf

This report offers a snapshot synthesis of 53 research studies published during 2013–14 that explored the implementation and efficacy of test accommodations for students.

11

Assessment planning and policy at class, school and system levels

What you will learn in this chapter

As with your own academic or professional writing, whether college assignments or reports as part of your work, in developing this book we had to make choices about both the topics we would include (there are many others not included here) and the sequence of those topics. This penultimate chapter is a good illustration. Should we begin the book with a chapter on planning for assessment, or should we explore some practical and policy issues first and then look at planning? We opted for the latter, thus hopefully giving you greater insight into the reasons for assessment, the approaches available and how they can be used, before considering how assessment can be planned, both in your teaching and in education more generally. Thus, this chapter conceptualises assessment as a planned process that can be used to monitor, support and improve learning, yielding information of value to various stakeholders. Whereas spontaneity in teaching is valuable, for example where you might follow a line of discussion or inquiry that emerges during a lesson, much teaching, like assessment, is more effective if carefully planned. This attention to detail and preparation is evident in the use of assessment in a wide variety of contexts: classroom, school, local education authority, national and international. The chapter focuses first on the planned use of assessment at the macro level, highlighting the close interlinking of national and international assessment initiatives with system-wide education policy. Closer to classroom and school levels, we explore how assessment has become more regulated and systematised in school, requiring greater collaborative planning between teachers.

When you finish the chapter, you should be able to answer these questions:

* How is assessment planned and used to promote and prioritise key educational, social and economic aims?

- What approaches do teachers use to ensure that assessment practices and outcomes inform their teaching and the learning of students?
- How do teachers plan to incorporate assessment in their work?

Student certification and public examinations

Previously, in Chapters 3 and 8, we highlighted the use of standardised tests and public examinations as part of assessment of learning. One key role for assessment is its use in certifying the achievement of individual students. Awards, certification or, in some education systems, promotion from grade to grade have traditionally been on the basis of students' performance on examinations and assessment. Performance on public examinations generally has a significant bearing on students' educational or career opportunities, thus explaining the 'high-stakes' tag frequently applied to them (Stobart and Eggen, 2012). Therefore, certification assessments require high levels of validity and reliability and are typically developed by or in collaboration with state education agencies, examining boards or commercial testing companies. Legislation in Ireland defines a public examination as:

> an examination relating to post-primary, adult and vocational education and vocational training as may from time to time be conducted in accordance with procedures determined by the Minister or by a body of persons established by the Minister. (Government of Ireland, 1998: VIII, 49)

The central role of government in such exams suggests a level of importance above that of other forms of assessment not prescribed to the same extent.

A number of general characteristics of these exams can be identified. The development, administration and scoring of the exams is tightly regulated by government agencies or licensed providers. Exams are typically taken by students at terminal points of schooling: at the end of compulsory, the end of upper secondary and, in the case of some developing countries, at the end of primary school. The exams are highly aligned with specific subject areas and use a variety of item formats, including essay or constructed response, objective, aural, oral and practical demonstration, some of which may be undertaken as part of moderated coursework or assessment at school level. Performance is frequently expressed as grades or numerals that convey a clear meaning to stakeholders including students, parents, college admissions officers and employers. The prime functions of results include certifying student achievement and the selection of students for the next level of education. Additional uses involve motivating students, monitoring educational practice, directing learning and teaching in schools and facilitating individual and system accountability.

Two planning issues are noteworthy in relation to public examinations. The development, administration, scoring and reporting of such tests is a highly complex process subject to some of the most robust quality control practices in education. In addition, their importance to students, teachers and parents ensures that very significant efforts are expended by schools in terms of timetabling, planning and teaching, especially at secondary level.

Join the debate: What role should school-based assessment have in student certification at secondary level?

External state or public examinations such as A levels (England), the Leaving Certificate (Ireland) and the Baccalauréat (France) are sometimes lauded as a means to ensure fairness for all students. Everybody takes the same exam, on the same day, and student performance is generally evaluated anonymously by teachers who do not know the students. This process appears equitable for all students and is seen as serving a valuable quality-assurance function for the education system more broadly. An alternative perspective highlights what is perceived as the stifling grip of such exams on teaching and learning in schools where teachers and students combine to shape learning in a manner that maximises the likelihood of high grades on the examination. This is at the expense of a broader, more rounded education. In between are viewpoints and practices enabling student certification wholly through school-based assessments or a blend of external examinations and moderated internal assessments, as discussed in Chapter 8 in relation to some case studies of reforms of assessment in England and Ireland.

If you can, use your library's online journal service to access the article by Johnson (2013) in the further reading at the end of the chapter. Develop your own position in relation to this debate. What approach do you think is most appropriate at the end of upper-secondary education? What about at the end of compulsory education?

National assessments

Whereas assessments to certify student achievement offer some insight into patterns of achievement within a country, they miss many important dimensions of learning. Certification usually relates to terminal points in education, normally the end of compulsory or upper-secondary schooling, thus failing to capture achievement levels throughout primary schooling and at intermediate points in secondary schooling. Additionally, although across OECD countries, sizeable majorities of students complete upper-secondary education, some do not, with completion rates ranging from 45% (Mexico) to 98% (Korea). Therefore, policy-makers plan alternative national assessments to monitor and promote achievement at multiple time points during students' education. In this way, assessment is highly consequential to hundreds of millions of students and their teachers across the globe.

National assessments are frequently designed around a small number of 'core' subject areas to identify the overall levels of achievement in a population, such as a particular grade level. Inferences about population achievement are often based on samples of students and not all students are assessed. For example, the 2014 National Assessments of English Reading and Mathematics in Ireland tested approximately 4000 students at Second Class and 4000 students at Sixth Class (Shiel et al., 2014). Results are aggregated at national level to create a summary of achievement for the system as a whole. In contrast, census sampling in England, Wales and Northern Ireland, after the introduction of the national curriculum in 1988, meant that SATs or other assessments were administered to all students at particular grade levels (usually at the end of Key Stages 1, 2 and 3). In this case, results are communicated to parents and to schools, the latter of which are expected to draw on the results in planning subsequent teaching.

The types of questions that national assessments are designed to answer include the following:

- How well are students learning in a subject?
- What are achievement trends over time?
- How does the achievement of boys and girls compare?
- To what extent are system priorities and targets being met? How successful are system initiatives? (for example, literacy and numeracy strategies)
- What are strong and weak areas in learning?
- What factors are associated with learning?
- How well are schools meeting students' and system needs?
- What adjustments, if any, are required to curricula or teaching?
- What additional resources are needed?
- Which schools are performing well and why?

Planning assessments to answer such questions involves a careful analysis of the curriculum and matching of assessment tasks with curricular specifications. Typically, a state agency or contractor takes responsibility for developing the assessment, which is administered by the teachers of the students sampled. National language and mathematics are generally assessed, with other subjects such as science and second language included in some national assessments. Additional 'background' information is sometimes also gathered through surveys of teachers, students and parents, and this information is used to help interpret the achievement results. Following the scoring and analysis of student responses, findings are normally disseminated to the public, along with relevant recommendations for improving performance.

International assessments of achievement

Chapter 3 highlighted the role of international surveys and assessments of educational achievement in informing and shaping policy and practice in schools. Table 3.1 noted a selection of the main assessments such as PIRLS, TIMSS and PISA. Planning for these studies occurs largely at international and national levels, requiring cooperation between researchers, government education agencies and participating schools. In the case of PISA, for example, assessments are administered every three years with recent and planned surveys in 2012, 2015, 2018, 2021 and beyond. The scale of such studies is enormous, with over 70 education systems participating in 2015. Planning for the next PISA study is always well ahead of testing for the previous study; thus, preparation of content specifications, the development of items and consideration of analytic procedures for PISA 2018 were well under way before students were tested in 2015. Finding agreement across OECD and partner countries on definitions for constructs to be assessed requires discussion and negotiation at meetings of national coordinators who meet regularly between assessments to plan future events. This is evident in the subtle but important changes in definitions of mathematics assessed over the past decade, as indicated in Figure 11.1. A similar evolution has occurred in relation to reading and science, with a significant redefinition of the reading expected in the framework for PISA 2018 to reflect students' increasing engagement with digital text.

There is much policy and research support for the value of international assessments, for example Schleicher (2006) and Sahlberg (2015). Alongside this support are the contrasting voices of those who argue that a range of challenges complicates the interpretation of results, casting doubt on the appropriateness of using such surveys of achievement at all. Issues include translation difficulties and simplistic interpretations of scales (Goldstein, 2004; Arffman, 2013). Nonetheless, there can be little doubt about two points: first, enormous effort is associated with the planning, preparation, implementation, analysis and reporting of such assessments; and second, such assessments are likely to continue for the foreseeable future.

2006 and 2009	Mathematical literacy is an individual's capacity to identify and understand the role that mathematics plays in the world, to make well-founded judgements and to use and engage with mathematics in ways that meet the needs of that individual's life as a constructive, concerned and reflective citizen.
2012 and 2015	Mathematical literacy is an individual's capacity to formulate, employ and interpret mathematics in a variety of contexts. It includes reasoning mathematically and using mathematical concepts, procedures, facts and tools to describe, explain and predict phenomena. It assists individuals to recognise the role that mathematics plays in the world and to make the well-founded judgements and decisions needed by constructive, engaged and reflective citizens.

Figure 11.1 Evolving definitions of mathematics in PISA

Standards-based curricula and target-setting

The ebb and flow of curriculum development means that how curriculum is structured and presented varies over time and over education systems. Whereas curriculum frameworks were relatively light in the past, leaving much to the professional discretion of the teacher, many modern curricula include extensive specifications in relation to content, teaching approaches and resources. A particular feature has been the development of standards-based curricula, following on from models instituted in the USA, the UK and Australia. This involves developing granulated descriptions of learning to help students realise specific learning targets, with the curriculum sometimes expressed in terms of levels to be reached. Figure 11.2 provides some extracts from the recent language curriculum in Ireland (DES, 2015e).

This curriculum is structured around 94 specific learning outcomes covering the strands of Oral language, Reading and Writing across four grade levels. In addition, three essential *Elements* are further specified within each strand and learners are expected to develop their knowledge and skills in relation to each element for *each* strand. The arrows in Figure 11.2 highlight only one set of the many learning pathways within this curriculum. Within the *writing* strand, students are expected to *explore and use language* (in addition to engaging with the other two elements). Four learning outcomes have been identified for this 'relationship', one of which is further highlighted for this illustration (*Use the writing process when creating texts*

Strands	Elements
Oral language	Developing communication through language
Reading	Understanding the content and structure of language
Writing ⟶	*Exploring and using language*

Learning outcomes (for *exploring and using language in writing*)	**Progression steps** (for *use the writing process when creating texts collaboratively or independently*)
Draw and write with a sense of purpose and audience while creating texts in a range of genres, and develop an individual voice to share thoughts, knowledge and experiences.	Uses personal experiences and interests as stimulus for their texts.
Use the writing process when creating texts collaboratively or independently.	Begins to take part in collaborative writing with the teacher as scribe.
Elaborate on the meaning of own writing and discuss the texts of others, showing an emerging recognition of the author's intent.	Uses familiar topics as a stimulus for texts, while creating texts jointly with the teacher.
Write using cursive script.	Collaboratively plans texts orally; sequences and writes texts with other children; reads and talks about their writing.
	Independently plans, sequences and writes texts; reads and talks about their writing with the teacher to check if it makes sense and begins to suggest simple changes to improve it.
	Independently plans and gathers information to create texts with a beginning, middle and end; reads and discusses their writing, identifying changes to improve it.
	Draws on a range of text sources and begins to use graphic organisers to plan writing; composes proofs and edits to include feedback.
	Draws on a wider range of text sources and uses graphic organisers to plan independent writing; composes proofs and self-edits to improve texts.

Figure 11.2 Illustration of selected standards in the primary English curriculum: Ireland, Junior Infants to end Second Class

Source: DES (2015e)

collaboratively or independently). For that one outcome, the curriculum also specifies eight progressive steps to guide student learning (and assessment) up to the end of Second Class (midway through primary school). As you can imagine, planning assessment systems nationally and at school and class levels to capture the complexity of such a standards framework is a demanding and, as yet, unfinished challenge.

Curricula expressed in terms of standards have been around for some time, yet assessment and reporting approaches have been slow to adapt to reflect the changed emphases. Many schools, teachers and education systems continue to operate points or grade-based reporting systems that attempt to represent student achievement in a subject in a single numeral, grade or letter. This approach conflicts with standards-based approaches (Iamarino, 2014; Munoz and Guskey, 2015). In effect, the grade or numeral becomes the standard by which student achievement on the curriculum is judged. One's progress in relation to the standard (very broadly defined) is established using different grade points along the scale (A, B, C; or H1, H2, H3). A challenge with this approach is establishing the criteria associated with any particular grade. What does a B mean? What knowledge and skills does a student possess who earned a H3? Standards-referenced approaches try to link grades or assessment outcomes more overtly to the type of performance criteria illustrated in Figure 11.2. Thus, planning assessment and reporting systems that are compatible with standards-based curricula requires increased transparency about levels of student performance.

Incorporating assessment in school and classroom practice

Chapter 1 highlighted the professional expectations on teachers across a wide range of assessment-related standards and competencies. Teachers' capacity to embed assessment into teaching and learning, while also responding to external stakeholders' needs for assessment information, requires systematic and sophisticated planning, coordination and collaboration at school level. For example, the regulatory body in New Zealand identifies a number of criteria that must be met by teachers in relation to assessment, including issues around planning (Education Council New Zealand, 2015). Assessment planning features prominently in teacher standards in other jurisdictions. In England, for example, standards emphasise monitoring student progress, adapting teaching to the student needs identified and using assessment information to reflect on teaching approaches and effectiveness (DfE, 2011b). Teachers in Australia seeking national certification of exemplary teaching practice are required to demonstrate high accomplishment or lead teacher status across seven dimensions of practice. One of these, relating to assessment, includes assessing student learning, providing feedback, participating in moderation, using assessment data to modify teaching and reporting student progress to stakeholders (AITSL, 2014).

Planning at school level

At school level, the emphasis is often on complying with local or national requirements and on ensuring consistency across teachers. Most schools adopt curricular and pedagogical policies across a range of areas, including admissions and enrolment, teaching and learning, use of IT, behaviour management, special educational needs, student assessment and staff development, among many. Within such broad plans, specific assessment policies and protocols are normally described. The following suggestions, drawing on the work of a national professional development agency in Ireland, identify issues that might be contained in school assessment policies:

- the mechanism for developing assessment policy within the school
- the purpose and aims of assessment policy
- the relationship between assessment and the school mission
- the purpose of assessment in the school
- approaches to assessment for learning in the school
- the purpose, administration, communication and use of standardised tests

- the use of screening and diagnostic assessment to identify learning strengths and difficulties
- the role of psychological assessments
- the recording and storing of assessment outcomes
- the personnel involved in assessment and their responsibilities. (PPDS, 2007)

The work of schools is evaluated through a combination of external and internal review. Underpinning the School Self-Evaluation (SSE) process in Ireland are criteria for external and school self-evaluation developed by the DES (2016b). These criteria focus on two key dimensions of the work of schools, namely, teaching and learning and leadership and management. Within teaching and learning, four distinct domains are identified: learner outcomes; learner experiences; teachers' individual practice; and teachers' collective/collaborative practice. The appropriateness, quality, evidence and impact of assessment policy and practice are evaluated in the context of these domains, as presented in Figure 11.3.

Learner outcomes	Learner experiences
Students aware of learning outcomes	Students engage in goal-setting
Students adopt reflective approach	Self-assessment by students helps them plan and monitor their own learning, including development of key skills
Students' knowledge, skills and overall achievement are improving or at an appropriate standard	
	Students act on feedback received
Teachers' individual practice	**Teachers' collaborative practice**
Set learning objectives based on student needs	Develop a relevant whole-school policy on assessment including AoL and AfL and implement it
Employ data-led differentiated instruction	
Employ AoL and AfL focusing on knowledge, skills and dispositions	Frame assessment to support students' learning and to measure their attainment
Provide useful feedback to students	Adopt shared approaches to providing feedback, informed in part by collective review of students' work
Use success criteria, questioning, self- and peer assessment, and feedback	Communicate and collaborate with parents and other relevant parties in relation to student learning
Maintain appropriate records	Maintain appropriate records
Engage in relevant CPD	Engage in collaborative reflection and CPD

Figure 11.3 Indicators of quality in school provision for assessment

Source: Adapted from DES (2016b)

In England, inspectors draw on the Common Inspection Framework (Ofsted, 2015) to evaluate the work of schools and teachers in relation to a range of areas, including assessment. The evaluation of assessment competencies and policies within school include a focused consideration of:

- the *Teachers' Standards* (see Chapter 1, Table 1.3)
- the extent to which teachers gather relevant assessment information from students, their parents and other relevant stakeholders

- how assessment information is used to plan appropriate teaching and learning so that students can make good progress
- the extent to which students know how to improve as a result of feedback from teachers.

The focus by state inspectorates in a number of jurisdictions on assessment-related policies and practices highlights for schools the importance placed on assessment. This is, in turn, reflected in the planning of teaching and learning by the school as a unit and by individual teachers.

Activity 11.1

Try this out – Benchmark your assessment competencies against a school assessment policy

Seek access to the assessment policy of a school with which you are familiar. Note the elements or headings of the policy. How much of the policy focuses on formative purposes of assessment? How much on summative purposes of assessment? To work effectively as a teacher in this school, what do you need to know about assessment? Using a green highlighter, identify elements in the policy that you understand fully and feel confident about implementing. Use another colour to highlight elements about which you would need more information, advice or experience.

Planning by teachers

Long-term planning

At school level, local or nationally developed templates generally inform expectations about and approaches to planning. Readers with experience of teacher education programmes will be familiar with planning guidelines and formats promoted at programme level. This may take the form of long- and short-term planning processes, perhaps with individual lesson planning, in the early career stages at least. Long-term planning provides high-level direction to help ensure that learning is logically connected so that your teaching (and students' learning) is consistent with and builds on previous learning. This facilitates consolidation, continuity and progression over a defined period of time such as a year or a term. For teachers, long-term planning involves the consideration of a number of curricular and pedagogical dimensions. These might include learning aims for a subject, the specification of content and skills, the characteristics of learners, the teaching and learning methods to be employed, assessment approaches, resources, differentiation and personal reflection in relation to teaching.

Professional or regulatory agencies also offer suggestions to teachers about the expected content of planning documentation. However, it is understood that planning is highly individualistic and that teachers will vary in the scope and detail of planning, depending on their career stage and familiarity with the curriculum.

In Ireland, for example, novice primary teachers are encouraged to develop long-term plans for each subject, where each plan covers the expected teaching and learning over a term or half-year, resulting in perhaps two plans for each subject over the course of a year (NIPT, 2013). Whether in fact you refer to such planning as long-term or medium-term is not so important. Of more relevance is the use of such planning to think strategically in advance about the scope, sequence and resourcing of learning over an extended period so that students are provided with a coherent learning experience. As an integral element of teaching and learning, assessment requires careful consideration in such plans. In developing your personal plan, you will draw on the school plan along with your own resources suited to the subject and age or year group.

Whereas, traditionally, assessment might have focused on the conduct of school or statutory tests with associated reporting commitments, embedding AfL as discussed in Chapters 4 and 5 requires a deeper integration of assessment thinking and practices into your planning. Therefore, you could highlight in broad terms in the long-term plan where and how assessment purposes and approaches (formative and summative) will feature in each subject area across the period of the plan. Ideally, this should specify a combination and balance of formative approaches, such as the six dimensions highlighted in Chapter 5 – use of learning intentions, success criteria, providing feedback, questioning, peer assessment and self-assessment. Considering such approaches at the design or planning stage in advance of teaching will help ensure that the progress and learning of individual students will be at the heart of your teaching, including the needs of students with special educational needs, as discussed in Chapter 10.

Long-term planning also affords a crucial opportunity to specify a range of summative assessment approaches for each curriculum area alongside and complementary to the formative methods. You may find that many of the more summative approaches highlighted in Chapters 3, 6 and 7 are either required or advantageous in optimising learning experiences for your students. In the plan, you can specify the nature and timing of standardised tests or tasks and highlight the procedures and timing for periodic assessments of students' learning (for example, at the end of topics or end of term). You can also link specific assessment approaches to different curriculum areas or topics within areas. This might involve planning for use of a portfolio throughout the first term to highlight student development at mid-year parent–teacher meetings, or identifying opportunities for using digital media and/or digital approaches to assessment. Throughout this book, we have emphasised the value of enacting diverse assessment methods in your teaching, ensuring that the monitoring of and judgements about students' learning are undertaken on the basis of frequent assessment using multiple approaches and sources of evidence. The best way to ensure that such plurality of assessment purposes and approaches exists in your teaching is to build it in at the design stage from the outset, while allowing for flexibility and change as the year progresses. Through such long-term planning, you can clarify what you hope to achieve, strategise about how you will bring this about and thus teach with more confidence.

Short-term planning

The use of pro-forma templates is common within teacher education programmes or school systems to guide teachers in planning to short time frames. Cohen, Manion and

Morrison (2004: 126) characterise short-term planning as where teachers 'set out what they will be teaching on a week-by-week, day-by-day, and lesson-by-lesson basis'. They contrast strategic long-term planning with more tactical short-term planning, where teachers identify specific learning outcomes for students. Short-term planning may take the form of fortnightly or weekly plans where some detail is provided about what will be covered in each subject and, for student and novice teachers, lesson plans developed to a variety of suggested formats. In either case, the need to be flexible in the face of classroom reality is essential. With the best will, teachers can plan for every eventuality but should be sensitive to the opportunities provided by amending planned outcomes and learning experiences over the course of a week, day or lesson. This is not to suggest that careful planning is unnecessary; rather, through planning you will be emboldened with confidence to teach well, and through the experience of teaching you will have the confidence to modify that plan in real time in the classroom.

Incorporating assessment into short-term planning involves focusing on what to assess and how to use the information from that assessment for the intended purposes. Such tactical planning is hugely important as it is likely to influence the extent to which students benefit from teaching. Accordingly, the General Teaching Council for Scotland (2012) requires registered teachers to:

* 'have knowledge and understanding of planning coherent and progressive teaching programmes' (Standard 2.1.3), along with
* 'knowledge and understanding of the principles of assessment, recording and reporting' (Standard 2.1.5).

These two standards come together when teachers begin to consider how to incorporate assessment into their planning and teaching.

In framing a short-term plan, whether in weekly or lesson plan format, you need to draw on the detail or direction contained in the long-term plan and identify more specific learning outcomes and learning experiences for students. Monitoring students' progress vis-à-vis the intended outcomes is facilitated by the application of appropriate assessment methods that are directly calibrated with the learning outcomes. As indicated in Chapter 5, many teachers use learning intentions and success criteria to activate students' metacognitive awareness around lesson content. In choosing specific assessment approaches, care should be taken to ensure that the lesson outcomes or intentions are clear and relevant and that the assessment is the most direct or at least an appropriate means to ascertain if students have been successful in engaging with and achieving the intentions. Whether for a fortnightly/weekly plan or for a lesson plan, comprehensive use is made of assessments by posing, and acting on the answers to, three questions:

1. To what extent have individual students successfully attained the intended learning outcomes?
2. To what extent has the class or group as a whole successfully attained the intended learning outcomes?
3. How can I use the assessment information to plan the next learning experiences for individuals and for the group?

The last question in particular illustrates the power of assessment to facilitate reflection by teachers on their own practice and thus transform teaching. Teachers need constantly updated information about student learning if they are to cater to the different needs of individuals. This may involve modification to teachers' expectations of students, to the learning outcomes teachers specify, to teaching and learning strategies and to resources. It is this cyclical process of planning, teaching, assessing, reviewing and re-planning that offers the potential for real continuity and progression in student learning, as illustrated in Figure 11.4.

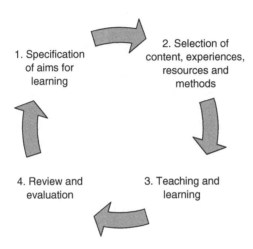

Figure 11.4   Role of assessment in planning and teaching

The power of assessment is embedded in all four stages in the model. In framing teaching and learning aims or outcomes (Stage 1), whether through long-term or short-term planning or lesson planning, aims need to be expressed in tangible form amenable to assessment through some of the varied approaches available. Adopting a combination of formative and summative approaches, assessment is inherently part of Stages 2 and 3. For example, a learning intention for an 11-year-old student might be to learn how to give a short speech persuading classmates of the benefits of school uniforms. In planning for this experience (Stage 2), the teacher can co-construct a simple rubric for students, enabling them to self-assess their own input, perhaps using digital capture with video or audio. Part of the implementation of the lesson could include self-analysis by students of their own performance using the rubric (Stage 3). After the lesson, review by the teacher in relation to the outcomes of the lesson (Stage 4) should help steer subsequent engagement with the topic or development from it, thus feeding into specification of the next learning outcomes. What is most significant in this model is that assessment does not come as a separate stage after Stage 3, nor is it contained solely in Stage 4. That stage uses the information provided by assessment that has been planned, designed and built into the lesson or learning sequence from the outset to help teachers understand more about the learning and teaching environment and processes in class.

Chapter summary

Figure 11.4 encapsulates the essence of the chapter, highlighting the message that assessment is a planned activity that runs in tandem with and is not subsequent to planning, teaching and learning. Assessment is a significant endeavour, whether at the macro international level or at the micro level of in-class monitoring. At every level, care should be taken to ensure that the instructional time spent on assessment yields learning and enactable information dividends for students, teachers, parents, policy-makers and wider society. Information from assessment can result in significant changes to educational policy – nationally and at school level. Information derived from assessment counts – ask the many education ministers whose systems were rocked or just reshaped by students' results on PISA. Or ask the student whose dyslexic difficulties were not identified until late in the primary education years. Assessment matters, so it is important to embed suitable approaches in teaching and learning from the outset. The scale of the task and the resources required may differ when planning for a national assessment or when an individual teacher undertakes short-term planning for a secondary school course in Art. This is different in scale, but the importance of assessment to the system or to the individual student is great. This book, overall, has illustrated many approaches to assessment and how they can be used. This chapter has focused on issues around planning so that the affordances of assessment can be harnassed for the benefit of the many stakeholders involved in education. As the old adage goes, *fail to prepare and prepare to fail.*

Questions for discussion

1. A criticism of statutory or national assessments is that they de-professionalise the teacher's discretion in relation to assessment and frequently assess the knowledge and skills of more importance to policy-makers than to students, parents and teachers. To what extent is there truth in this criticism? Put yourself in the place of the relevant policy-maker. What might his or her position be in relation to this criticism? Why are significant taxpayer funds put into planning and implementing system-wide assessments?

2. Teacher education and professional induction programmes emphasise planning by student teachers and early-career practitioners. Imagine a programme that eschewed planning, focusing more on 'getting on with the job'. Consider the implications of such an approach for teachers' use of assessment in their work.

Further reading

Cohen, L., Manion, L., & Morrison, K. (2004) *A guide to teaching practice* (5th edition). London: Routledge.

A well-established text that includes chapters on planning for teaching and on assessment.

Johnson, S. (2013). On the reliability of high-stakes teacher assessment. *Research Papers in Education*, *28* (1), 91–105.

This article explores the consistency with which teachers mark student performance on assessments where there are high-stakes implications. The author identifies the need for a greater investigation of the efficacy of consensus moderation across teachers.

12

Conclusions about assessment in education

What you will learn in this chapter

Throughout this book, we have advocated a balance between the needs of various stakeholders in relation to assessment, with one primary stakeholder, namely the learner. The learning, development and welfare of the individual student should be the fundamental focus of assessment efforts. In practice, that individual's development is largely set in and dependant on contexts such as family, peers, school, education system and wider society. Therefore, a comprehensive understanding of assessment of the individual requires acknowledgement of other forms and purposes of assessment that may focus on larger units such as schools and populations of students. A number of principles, summarised in Chapter 1, guided our discussion, analysis and suggestions in relation to formative and summative assessment. We pick these up again in this final chapter where we offer our interpretation of a range of opportunities, pressures and trends that are likely to shape educational and assessment practice in the coming years.

When you finish the chapter, you should be able to answer these questions:

- How can we ensure that the needs of the learner remain the focus of assessment?
- In what ways are those needs met by different individuals and groups?
- What are some of the issues relating to assessment that may come to the fore in the coming years?

The assessment paradigm wars

One of our aims in writing this book was to illustrate the possibilities, opportunities and challenges associated with assessment policy and practice across primary and secondary education. Indeed, many of the concepts covered also apply to other levels of educational practice – pre-school, third level, professional training and lifelong learning. Incorporating both formative and summative purposes of assessment was important in our conceptualisation of the book. As our task unfolded, we were mindful of the paradigm wars in relation to research methodology in the social sciences, where metaphorical battle lines have been drawn for decades between proponents of quantitative and of qualitative research, both with their own particular philosophical and epistemological underpinnings. Which is better, quantitative or qualitative? Which should I use for this study? For that study? The struggles focused on what was the better paradigm within which to conduct research: a numeric quantitative one or a more narrative and personal description of processes and contexts. Gradually, a third way emerged as many researchers embraced elements of both, creating a more mixed, eclectic way of thinking about research methods that draws on the strengths (and weaknesses) of both (see, for example, Johnson and Onwuegbuzie, 2004).

In assessment, we need to be careful that we avoid a fruitless re-run of those paradigm wars, with, on one side, standardised tests, alpha coefficients and grades, and on the other, portfolios, self-assessment and feedback. Nothing could be more unhelpful to teachers whose focus is on creating and maintaining nurturing, stimulating, challenging learning environments for students. It is difficult to argue that formative assessment is intrinsically better than summative assessment, or that summative approaches represent a gold standard in assessment. Both purposes have merit, contributing to teaching and learning as befits different contexts. The distinction is helpful in that it clarifies purpose but unhelpful if it leads to the contrived and unnecessary marginalisation of one or the other. Harlen's two questions, posed in Chapter 9, are relevant to this dichotomy: Can evidence used in summative assessment be used to help learning? Can evidence collected for formative purposes be used for summative assessment? In response, we can usefully focus on evidence of learning rather than on the particular form or type of assessment. Can evidence from a standardised test (summative assessment) be used to assist learning? Surely yes, with an *it depends* caveat attached. Can evidence collected for formative purposes be used for summative assessment? In theory, yes, but perhaps with some doubts about fairness. If you tell students that their portfolio won't be graded and then it is, that's a hard sell in ethical terms.

What forms of assessment should I use?

Those assessment paradigm wars (or, perhaps more accurately, sabre-rattling) lead to possible suggestions that teachers favour and should use only one form of assessment (formative, which is good), whereas the system (whatever that is) wants to use summative, which is bad. We highlighted in Chapter 6 Buck et al.'s finding (2010) that academic journal articles critical of testing outnumbered the favourable articles by a 9-to-1 ratio. We would be on the side of the nine if standardised tests were the only assessment tools used in school. But they are not; such tests are only one part of how students are assessed in a continuum of assessment methods (see, for example, in the Irish context, NCCA, 2007a: 13, reproduced in Figure 12.1). We must disclose our interest – we were both involved in drafting those assessment guidelines for schools – guidance for teachers that cherishes a plurality of assessment purposes and approaches.

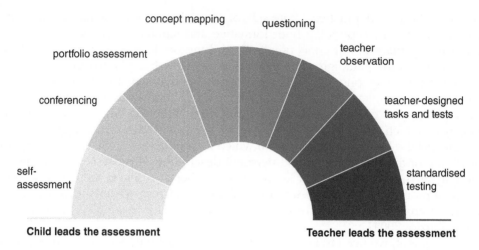

concept mapping   questioning

portfolio assessment

teacher observation

conferencing

teacher-designed tasks and tests

self-assessment

standardised testing

Child leads the assessment   **Teacher leads the assessment**

Figure 12.1   Continuum of assessment methods

Source: NCCA (2007a); reproduced with permission

As outlined in Chapters 3 and 11, great care is taken in the development, administration, scoring, reporting and review of standardised tests and other large-scale certification tests. Credit must be given for the seriousness with which they are planned and the quality controls established to provide a justifiable warrant for their use. When we think of the question: what forms of assessment should I use? it is useful to reflect on the aims of education, shared by most within society. We wish to develop the individual and individuals as a group that we call society; we want to push the boundaries of thinking so that individuals and society can flourish and prosper; we want to provide the opportunity for today's young people to develop their capacities for thinking, for invention, for feeling, for caring and for learning that will help them inherit, cherish, protect and enhance the world we leave behind. If these are some of the aspirations for education, then formative assessment can assist; so can summative assessment. Teachers need to know about both and be confident and competent in drawing on whatever is the most appropriate assessment at the right time for the right purpose. Generally, that purpose will have to do with the student, the individual. Sometimes it will relate to the group: class, school, LEA, national education system.

Diversity of stakeholders

It is increasingly rare that centralised authorities stay apart from education or from assessment. Governments get involved in education and, by and large, foot the bill at primary and secondary level. There are, of course, personal costs associated with education: in some instances, these are by choice where parents opt to purchase educational services outside the state system, or where parents must contribute towards their child's education even though it is nominally 'free', perhaps through book purchases, uniforms or trips. Exchequer funding for education is a major component of the state spend in many countries, with over 5% of GDP internationally channelled to education. Amongst other motivations, this is one reason why policy-makers seek information about the functioning of the education system. This is one summative purpose for assessment.

Advent of digital technologies in assessment

Lorrie Shepard (2000) highlighted the relative slowness of assessment practice to keep pace with changes in theory about how people learn, and with evolving curricula. Perhaps assessment is about to catch up or will need to, given the penetration of digital technology in many schools and into young people's lives. It may be difficult for individual teachers to enter this digital assessment space in relation to their own classroom assessments, given the technical issues involved, though programmes are increasingly available online offering the opportunity for teachers to create their own tests. Much development in digital assessment has occurred at the macro level. Significant development, trialling and implementation have occurred in relation to PISA, the Northern Ireland Numeracy and Literacy Assessments (NINA, NILA), standardised testing programmes in the USA and commercially available tests of reasoning and performance (for example, CAT4 and Drumcondra Reasoning Test). This opens up possibilities for more innovative and authentic assessment tasks, and more immediate, detailed and hopefully useful feedback to students, teachers, parents and others. At school level, the collation of student and class reports can usefully feed into schools' self-review and development processes. However, teachers need support in order to properly interpret the extensive reports from computerised assessments. Such needs should inform the content and direction of future initial teacher education and CPD programmes.

Promoting and assessing 21st-century skills

Another trend internationally is an emphasis on the acquisition of 21st-century skills such as creativity, problem solving, collaborative working and entrepreneurship. Aligning assessment approaches to these skills has not been straightforward to date. There are a number of reasons. The first is one of definition – deciding what such competencies mean. There is some evidence of the introduction of such broad skills in educational curricula and, to a lesser degree, in classroom practice (Partnership for 21st Century Skills, 2006; Davidson and Goldberg, 2010; Dede, 2010; Johnston et al., 2015). As discussed in Chapter 7, performance assessment is consistent with many of these competencies. The use of e-portfolios is one way that digital assessment can address challenges in assessing performance, possibly also solving one of the lingering practical difficulties with portfolios – physical space and manageability in classrooms. However, achieving the levels of reliability in marking portfolios required for high-stakes assessment remains a challenge.

We pose the question: where to for 21st-century skills? Efforts to embed these wholeheartedly in national curricula have had mixed success, with resistance sometimes on the basis that they are not assessed (if it's not assessed, it's not worth teaching!). Getting such competencies on the exam (or more generally as part of assessment) is, in reality, the ticket to having them enacted and emphasised in school. We will watch with interest the extent to which their inclusion in PISA will prompt action at national levels. PISA, like other international assessments, can nudge national policy towards novel approaches, providing additional impetus for initiatives that may well have been gestating locally. On the other hand, we wonder about the authenticity of some PISA tasks designed to assess 21st-century skills. Examples include collaborative problem solving in 2015, where collaboration means engagement with pre-set dialogue and the selection of pre-set responses rather than human-to-human problem solving (see OECD, 2016b and the illustration in Figure 12.2). The withdrawal of a number of OECD countries from a proposed assessment of global competencies in PISA 2018 also points to the tensions that can arise when new assessment domains are introduced.

Figure 12.2 presents an illustration of the type of digital interface and item presented to students when addressing collaborative problem-solving tasks on the PISA 2015 test. In this field-trial example, the task for the examinee is to engage in decision making with computer-simulated classmates and a teacher to plan a trip for a group of exchange students coming to visit the school. Each successive screen adds to the simulation, prompting the examinee to make decisions indicative of their capacity to work collaboratively with peers. Student 'decisions' are made by responding to multiple-choice items for each scenario, under the broad umbrella of planning for the exchange students' trip.

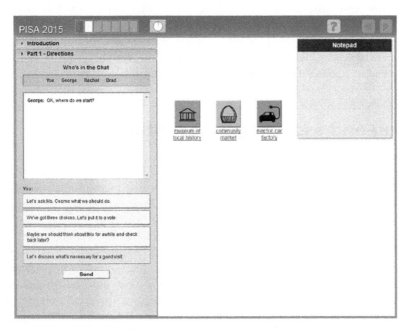

Figure 12.2   Example of digitally administered task assessing collaborative problem solving

Source: OECD (2016b); reproduced with permission

In the illustration in Figure 12.2, the automated scoring algorithm credits the fourth option (let's discuss what's necessary for a good visit) as it illustrates that the student can identify and describe the tasks to be completed. The other options are not credited in the scoring process as they do not illustrate sufficient levels of collaborative problem solving. Individual scoring rubrics are presented for each scenario presented to examinees and a total scaled score for the task is derived from the examinee's responses across all elements of the simulation.

Assessment captures people's interest

We chose to include in the book a substantial chapter (2) covering three key 'success criteria' in relation to assessment: validity, reliability and fairness. This represents a reminder that assessment is important to everybody, not least students themselves. If, as Dann (2014) and others argue, assessment *is* learning, then it is all the more important that assessments are framed and used appropriately. We have to get assessment right. We need to have confidence in the conclusions we derive from the results (validity), those findings need to be replicable (reliability) and the rights of students should not be eroded by administration of the assessments or use of the results (fairness). Caveats around both formative and summative assessment in Chapter 10 give food for thought in relation to present provision and hope for a more inclusive approach in the future.

Education planners and policy-makers need to be aware of the limitations facing teachers in school. We identify a number of challenges to implementing formative approaches to assessment in Chapter 5, including practical implementation issues such as the available time, teachers' own assessment literacy, parental pressures and system pressures arising from forms of assessment perceived to compete with rather than complement formative assessment. Any one of these represents a significant obstacle to progress whereas in reality more than one of them may be at issue. Research is clear on how teachers respond to accountability pressures in their work, especially where test results are the accountability measure. Some element of teaching to the test (or assessment or portfolio system) invariably follows. The accountability pressures are felt by teachers even in systems that have overtly prioritised AfL in national policy such as in New Zealand (Crooks, 2011).

Professional development and research-led teaching

Engaging with this book is another step on your journey to developing your assessment literacy. As exemplified in the teacher assessment competency frameworks in a number of countries (Northern Ireland and Scotland, for example), this will be a career-long journey as you and your colleagues encounter and address the evolving changes in assessment knowledge, approaches and policies in the future.

For readers who are practising teachers, or educational administrators, this book can contribute to your ongoing professional development. It offers some insights into new technologies and emphasises the dissemination of good practice based on evidence. Teachers need to become more comfortable in the online and blended space. Knowing more about how students learn has the potential to really transform teaching and learning. It's not that we are without evidence – more is being accumulated all the time – but perhaps the evidence is not used sufficiently. We see this problem linked as much to communication as to research per se. Principals, teachers and policy-makers need to know how students learn and how assessment can assist learning. The *What Works Clearinghouse* (http://ies.ed.gov/ncee/wwc/) is one illustration of how one education system has attempted to synthesise the results of research to facilitate policy and classroom practice, though caution is needed as methodological constraints may be in operation (for example, the prioritisation of studies that used random controlled trials). The modern digital environment offers fertile ground for sowing the seeds of research-led practice, in assessment as in all aspects of education. Books, academic and professional journals, digital journals, online repositories, alternative media such as blogs, video posts and illustrations all have a place in sharing not only good practice but evidence-led practice. Schools are busy places and teachers' time is increasingly stretched to fit across a myriad of responsibilities. We need to find ways to share high-quality research about assessment in a succinct manner compatible with teachers' lives and the reality of schools.

In addition to keeping apprised of research findings about assessment, we encourage teachers to actively investigate their own practice in class and at school. For example, you might wish to introduce learning logs as part of your assessment practice (see Chapter 5). Table 12.1 illustrates a few questions you could usefully consider.

Table 12.1 Exploring the evidence for assessment practices

Does it work?	What evidence can I draw on to say that it works?
How does it work?	Will it work for all students in my class?
How can I make it work better for my students?	How could I find out if it works, with my class?
Why doesn't it work?	What will I do if it doesn't work?

One way (but not the only way) this call to investigate your practice can be expressed is graphically using a logic model (see, for example, Kellogg Foundation, 2004; Kekahio et al., 2014). Such models assume that in any initiative (say, introducing learning logs into your class) the class context, certain inputs, activities, outputs and outcomes are all highly relevant. Figure 12.3 presents a simple logic model revealing a teacher's assumptions about what will happen when learning logs are introduced into the class as part of AfL (A in Figure 12.3). It is assumed that a three-month use of the logs (B) will provide an opportunity for students to describe and reflect on their learning, say in musical appreciation (C). This in turn can lead to analysis and consideration of the student data by teacher and students (D), further response and modification to teaching and learning by both (E), with noticeable changes in the quality of student learning outcomes as a result of the process (F). It is based on these assumptions about what might happen that a teacher may decide to try out learning logs. Many variations of this process exist but all provide the opportunity for teachers to conceptualise in advance how an assessment should work in class, and offer a structure for trialling the process.

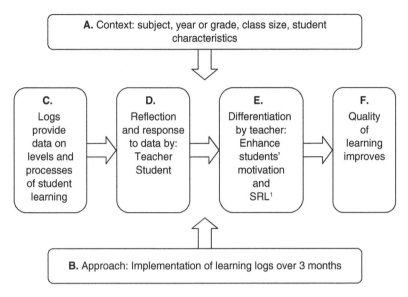

Figure 12.3   Possible logic model underpinning teacher's investigation of using learning logs in class

Note: 1. Self-regulated learning (see Chapter 4)

Present trends, future issues

As highlighted in Chapter 10, the number of students identified with disabilities and special educational needs is not insubstantial and is rising. There are many reasons for this, some of which have to do with more sophisticated identification and awareness on the part of parents, teachers and other professionals. Incorporating students with SEN into assessment processes devised by teachers or programmes will, increasingly, draw attention to issues of validity and fairness, especially in assessment. Most of the focus on accommodations has been on high-stakes examinations, yet more and more responsibility for assessment is actively devolved to teachers in classrooms. Similarly, it is important that the professional standards for assessment developed or in development in many education systems sharpen the focus on inclusivity in assessment so that the knowledge, skills, strengths and learning needs of *all* students can be identified and action taken, whether students have disabilities or other special educational needs, or are second language learners or children of exceptional ability.

Activity 12.1

Try this out – What are the implications of selected trends in assessment for AfL and AoL?

Table 12.2 presents a selection of key issues in relation to assessment now and in the coming years. We present these not necessarily as predictions of the future but as a

(Continued)

(Continued)

summary of possible needs, trends and directions. Some have implications largely in relation to AfL, some to AoL and some to both. As the final activity in this book, tick the boxes as you see fit and reflect on what the implications might be. Further prompts available on the companion website may be helpful.

Table 12.2   Selected assessment trends and issues

Assessment-related needs and trends	AfL	AoL
Growth in computerised testing and digitally-enhanced assessment		
Continued expansion of large-scale international assessments		
Need to assess cross-curricular and 21st-century competencies in assessments		
Retaining focus on the individual's development across a range of learning		
Drawing on school-based judgements of student achievement for certification purposes		
Priority given to literacy and numeracy		
Improving provision for the assessment of learners with special educational needs		
More extensive use of data on student learning to review and plan at teacher and school levels		

Visit the companion website at: https://study.sagepub.com/murchanshiel

Chapter summary

In today's education systems, helping hands abound, most notably those of the teacher who, in partnership with parents, plays the central role in helping learners to realise their potential. Therefore, the knowledge, disposition and skill set of the teacher determines to a great extent the benefit that will accrue to students from their attendance at school over the course of most of their first two decades of life. This is a tremendous responsibility on teachers, shared with parents, and therefore it is not surprising that codes of practice and expectations are increasingly the norm internationally, both in education generally and in assessment specifically. Other chapters in the book also reiterate that responsibility. This is evident in the planning, development, implementation and use of a variety of assessments discussed in Chapters 5, 6 and 7, following on from some context-setting about AoL and AfL in Chapters 3 and 4. Though part of school teams generally, teachers enjoy considerable autonomy in their interactions with students, so the competency of the teacher, in assessment and other dimensions of practice, has a profound influence on students' educational and, it can be argued, life chances. Teachers also need to be good communicators, in class with students and in how they mediate information about students' learning to students, parents and others. Chapters 8 and 9 touch on this theme, exploring how information derived from assessments can and should be shared.

Running alongside and through these chapters is also the recognition of those other helping hands supporting the learner. Though district officials, national planners and researchers don't stand in class, their responsibilities are ultimately to the student and students as a group. They cannot offer help without accurate information. Funding needs to be prioritised, curricula and pedagogy need to be relevant and updated from time to time, good practice needs to be identified and disseminated, and challenges that impede learning need to be addressed. Assessment provides information to aid such decisions, decisions that ultimately impact on groups and on individual students. Therefore, the needs of such stakeholders are legitimate and must be incorporated into principals' and teachers' planning and practice. Such issues are picked up throughout many of the chapters in the book, especially though not exclusively in relation to summative assessment, as in Chapters 1, 3, 8 and 11. Education is a large-scale complex process that increasingly requires collaboration between highly qualified individuals within and outside the teaching profession. What they share is the desire to further the best interests of the student, though they may come at this from different perspectives and using different approaches. For the individual student and their family, the stakes are high. It is the responsibility of the professional team – teachers, principals and educational support staff in school; along with curriculum developers, teacher educators, CPD providers, educational policy-makers, officials and the research community – to collaborate in the best interests of the student. Appropriate use of assessment represents an opportunity to have a real bearing on how successful that collaboration will be on behalf of the learner. It is an opportunity not to be missed.

References

Abedi, J. (2010). *Performance assessments for English language learners*. Stanford, CA: Stanford University, Stanford Center for Opportunity Policy in Education. Available at: https://scale. stanford.edu/system/files/performance-assessments-english-language-learners.pdf

Alderson, J.C., Clapham, C., & Wall, D. (1995). *Language test construction and evaluation*. Cambridge: Cambridge University Press.

American Educational Research Association (AERA), American Psychological Association (APA), & National Council on Measurement in Education (NCME). (2014). *Standards for educational and psychological testing*. Washington, DC: AERA.

American Federation of Teachers (AFT), National Council on Measurement in Education (NCME), & National Education Association (NEA). (1990). *Standards for teacher competence in educational assessment of students*. Available at: http://buros.org/standards-teacher-competence-educational-assessment-students

Anderson, L.W., & Krathwohl, D.R. (eds). (2001). *A taxonomy for learning, teaching and assessing: A revision of Bloom's taxonomy of educational objectives*. New York: Longman.

Arffman, I. (2013). Problems and issues in translating international educational achievement tests. *Educational Measurement: Issues and Practice, 32* (2), 2–14.

Armitage, A., Evershed, J., Hayes, D., Hudson, A., Kent, J., Lawes, S., et al. (2012). *Teaching and training in lifelong learning* (4th edition). Maidenhead: Open University Press.

ASG South Ayrshire. (n.d.). *Self- and peer assessment: Using rubrics for science and mentors of art*. Available at: www.educationscotland.gov.uk/resources/practice/s/self andpeerassessment/selfandpeerassessmentrubrics.asp?strReferringChannel=education scotland&strReferringPageID=tcm:4-615801-64

Assessment and Qualifications Alliance (AQA). (2016). *Unit 2: Speaking and listening. GSCE English language*. Available at: www.aqa.org.uk/subjects/english/gcse/english-language-4705/ subject-content/unit-2

Assessment Reform Group, The. (2006). *The role of teachers in the assessment of learning*. Cambridge: Cambridge University Faculty of Education.

Association of Educational Assessment (AEA) – Europe. (2012). *European framework of standards for educational assessment 1.0*. Rome: Edizioni Nuova Cultura. Available at: www. aea-europe.net/index.php/standards-for-educational-assessment

Australian Curriculum, Assessment and Reporting Authority (ACARA). (2014). *Australian curriculum: Work sample portfolio summary – Year 5 (Above satisfactory)*. Available at: www.acara.edu.au/curriculum/worksamples/Year_5_English_Portfolio_Above.pdf

Australian Institute for Teaching and School Leadership (AITSL). (2014). *Australian professional standards for teachers*. Melbourne: AITSL. Available at: www.aitsl.edu.au/australian-professional-standards-for-teachers

Ausubel, D.P. (1968). *Educational psychology: A cognitive view*. New York: Holt, Rinehart and Winston.

Baas, D., Castelijns, J., Vermeulen, M., Martens, R., & Segers, M. (2015). The relationship between assessment for learning and elementary students' cognitive and metacognitive strategy use. *British Journal of Educational Psychology*, *85*, 33–46.

Baird, J., & Black, P. (2013). The reliability of public examinations. *Research Papers in Education*, *28* (1), 1–4.

Baird, J., Hopfenbeck, T.N., Elwood, J., Caro, D., & Ahmed, A. (2015). *Predictability in the Irish Leaving Certificate*. Oxford and Belfast: University of Oxford and Queen's University Belfast.

Bandura, A. (1997). *Self-efficacy: The exercise of control*. New York: Freeman.

Bangert-Drowns, R.L., Kulik, C.C., Kulik, J.A., & Morgan, M.T. (1991). The instructional effect of feedback in test-like events. *Review of Educational Research*, *61* (2), 213–38.

BBC News. (2001, 19 June). *Should the exam have been cancelled?* Available at: http://news.bbc.co.uk/2/hi/talking_point/1388224.stm

Belfast Telegraph. (2012, 5 January). *Pupil evaluation test scrapped over scoring blunders* (by Lindsay Fergus). Available at: www.belfasttelegraph.co.uk/news/education/pupil-evaluation-test-scrapped-over-scoring-blunders-28699343.html

Bennett, R.E. (2011). Formative assessment: a critical review. *Assessment in Education: Principles, Policy and Practice*, *18* (1), 5–25.

Berry, R. (2011). Assessment trends in Hong Kong: seeking to establish formative assessment in an examination culture. *Assessment in Education: Principles, Policy and Practice*, *18* (2), 199–211.

Black, P. (1998). Testing: Friend or foe? In *The theory and practice of assessment and testing*. London: The Falmer Press.

Black, P., Harrison, C., Lee, C., Marshal, B., & Wiliam, D. (2003). *Assessment for learning: Putting it into practice*. Maidenhead: Open University Press.

Black, P., & Wiliam, D. (1998). Assessment and classroom learning. *Assessment in Education: Principles, Policy and Practice*, *5* (1), 7–74.

Black, P., & Wiliam, D. (2009). Developing the theory of formative assessment. *Educational Assessment, Evaluation and Accountability*, *21* (1), 5–31.

Bloom, B., Englehart, M.D., Furst, E.J., Hill, W.H., & Krathwohl, D.R. (1956). *Taxonomy of educational objectives: The classification of educational goals. Handbook I: Cognitive domain*. White Plains, NY: Longman.

Bloom, B.S., Hastings, J.T., & Madaus, G.F. (eds.) (1971). *Handbook on formative and summative evaluation of student learning*. New York: McGraw-Hill Book Company.

Breakspear, S. (2012). *The policy impact of PISA: An exploration of the normative effects of international benchmarking in school system performance*. OECD education working papers, number 71. Paris: OECD Publishing. Available at: http://dx.doi.org/10.1787/5k9fdfqffr28-en

Bridgeman, B. (2009). Experiences from large-scale computer-based testing in the USA. In F. Scheuermann & J. Bjornsson (eds) *The transition to computer-based assessment: New approaches to skills assessment and implications for large-scale testing* (pp. 39–44). Luxembourg: Office for Official Publications of the European Communities.

Brigham, F.J., & Bakken, J.P. (2013). Assessment and LD: determining eligibility, selecting services, and guiding instruction. In J.P. Bakken, F.E. Obiakor & A.F. Rotatori (eds) *Learning disabilities: Identification, assessment, and instruction of students with LD* (pp. 55–74). Bingley, UK: Emerald Publishing.

Brookhart, S.M. (2007). Feedback that fits. *Educational Leadership, 65* (4), 54–9.

Brookhart, S.M. (2011). Educational assessment knowledge and skills for teachers. *Educational Measurement: Issues and Practice, 30* (1), 3–12.

Brophy, J.E., & Good, T.L. (1986). Teacher behaviour and student achievement. In M.C. Wittrock (ed.) *Handbook of research on teaching* (3rd edition, pp. 328–75). New York: Macmillan.

Brown, G.T.L., & Harris, L.R. (2013). Student self-assessment. In J.H. McMillan (ed.) *Sage handbook of research on classroom assessment* (pp. 367–93). Thousand Oaks, CA: Sage.

Buck, S., Ritter, G.W., Jensen, N.C., & Rose, C.P. (2010). Teachers say the most interesting things: an alternative view of testing. *Phi Delta Kappan, 91* (6), 50–4.

Cambridge Assessment (2015). *Cambridge handbook 2015 (international): Regulations for conducting Cambridge examinations.* Cambridge: Author.

Council for the Curriculum Examinations and Assessment (CCEA). (2009). *Assessment for learning: A practical guide.* Belfast: CCEA.

CCEA. (2016a). *Skills and capabilities at Key Stages 1–2.* Belfast: CCEA. Available at: http://ccea.org.uk/curriculum/key_stage_1_2/skills_and_capabilities

CCEA. (2016b). *CCEA GCSE specification in business studies.* Belfast: CCEA.

CCEA. (n.d.). *Statutory requirements for language and literacy at Key Stage 2.* Available at: http://ccea.org.uk/curriculum/key_stage_1_2/areas_learning/language_and_literacy

Central Statistics Office (CSO). (2015). *Foreign nationals: PPSN allocations, employment and social welfare activity.* Dublin: CSO. Available at: www.cso.ie/en/releasesandpublications/er/fnaes/foreignnationalsppsnallocationsemployment andsocialwelfareactivity2014/

Clarke, S. (2005). *Formative assessment in action: Weaving the elements together.* London: Hodder Murray.

Clarke, S. (2008). *Active learning through formative assessment.* London: Hodder Murray.

Coe, R. (2010). Understanding comparability of examination standards. *Research Papers in Education, 25* (3), 271–84.

Cohen, L., Manion, L., & Morrison, K. (2004). *A guide to teaching practice* (5th edition). London: Routledge.

Collins, S., Reiss, M., & Stobart, G. (2010). What happens when high-stakes testing stops? Teachers' perceptions of the impact of compulsory national testing in science of 11-year-olds in England and its abolition in Wales. *Assessment in Education: Principles, Policy and Practice, 17* (3), 273–86.

Costa, A.L., & Kallick, B. (2008). *Learning and leading with habits of mind: 16 characteristics for success.* Alexandria, VA: Association for Supervision and Curriculum Development (ASCD).

Council of Europe. (2012). *European common framework of reference for languages.* Strasbourg: Council of Europe, Language Policy Unit. Available at: www.education-support.org.uk/teachers/ids/cefr/

Crooks, T. (2011). Assessment for learning in the accountability era: New Zealand. *Studies in Educational Evaluation, 37* (1), 71–7.

Crookes, A. (2007). The effects of topic choice on performance outcomes: an analysis of student selected third year essays. *Psychology learning & teaching, 6* (2), 85–90.

Cumming, J.J., & Maxwell, G.S. (2014). Expanding approaches to summative assessment for students with impairment. In L. Florian (ed.) *The Sage handbook of special education*, Vol. 2 (2nd edition, pp. 573–93). Los Angeles, CA: Sage.

Cummins, J. (1991). Interdependence of first- and second-language proficiency in bilingual children. In E. Bialystok (ed.) *Language processing in bilingual children* (pp. 70–89). Cambridge: Cambridge University Press.

Cummins, J. (2000). *Language, power and pedagogy: Bilingual children in the crossfire.* Clevedon, UK: Multilingual Matters.

Daily Telegraph, The. (2015, 24 July). *More than 300 languages spoken in British schools, report says.* Available at: www.telegraph.co.uk/education/education news/11761250/More-than-300-different-languages-spoken-in-British-schools-report-says.html

Dann, R. (2014). Assessment as learning: blurring the boundaries of assessment and learning for theory, policy and practice. *Assessment in Education: Principles, Policy and Practice, 21* (2), 149–66.

Darling-Hammond, L., & Adamson, F. (2010). *Beyond basic skills: The role of performance assessment in achieving 21st century standards of learning.* Stanford, CA: Stanford University, Standford Centre for Opportunity Policy in Education.

Darling-Hammond, L., & McCloskey, L. (2008). What would it mean to be internationally competitive? *Phi Delta Kappan, 90* (4), 263–72.

Davidson, C.N., & Goldberg, D.T. (2010). *The future of thinking: Learning institutions in a digital age.* The John D. and Catherine T. MacArthur Foundation Reports on Digital Media and Learning. Cambridge, MA: The MIT Press.

Dede, C. (2010). Comparing frameworks for 21st century skills. In J. Bellanca & R. Brandt (eds) *21st century skills: Rethinking how students learn* (pp. 51–75). Bloomington, IN: Solution Tree Press.

Department for Education (DfE). (2011a). *Teachers' standards.* London: Crown. Available at: www.gov.uk/government/publications/teachers-standard

Department for Education (DfE). (2011b). *Teachers' standards: Guidance for school leaders, school staff and governing bodies.* Available at: www.gov.uk/government/publications/teachers-standards

Department for Education (DfE). (2012). *School information (England) (Amendment) Regulations 2012.* Available at: www.legislation.gov.uk/uksi/2012/1124/pdfs/uksi_2012 1124_en.pdf

Department for Education (DfE). (2014a). *The national curriculum in England: Framework document.* London: Crown. Available at: www.gov.uk/government/uploads/system/ uploads/attachment_data/file/381344/Master_final_national_curriculum_28_Nov.pdf

Department for Education (DfE). (2014b). *Reforming assessment and accountability for primary schools: Government response to consultation on primary school assessment and accountability.* London: DfE. Available at: www.gov.uk/government/uploads/system/ uploads/attachment_data/file/297595/Primary_Accountability_and_Assessment_ Consultation_Response.pdf

Department for Education (DfE). (2015). *Special educational needs and disability code of practice: 0 to 25 years.* London: Crown. Available at: www.gov.uk/government/ publications

Department for Education (DfE). (2016). *National curriculum assessments at key stage 2 in England, 2016 (provisional).* London: Crown. Available at: www.gov.uk/government/ uploads/system/uploads/attachment_data/file/549432/SFR39_2016_text.pdf

Department for Education and Skills (DfES). (2006). *Primary national strategy: Primary framework for literacy and mathematics.* London: DfES. Available at: www.education england.org.uk/documents/pdfs/2006-primary-national-strategy.pdf

Department of Education and Skills (DES). (2007a). *Inclusion of students with special educational needs: Post primary guidelines.* Dublin: DES.

Department of Education and Skills (DES). (2007b). *Special educational needs: A continuum of support.* Dublin: DES.

Department of Education and Skills (DES). (2011a). *Circular 0056/11: Initial steps in the implementation of the national literacy and numeracy strategy.* Available at: www.education.ie/ en/Circulars-and-Forms/Active-Circulars/cl0056_2011.pdf

Department of Education and Skills (DES). (2011b). *Literacy and numeracy for learning and life: The national strategy to improve literacy and numeracy among children and young people 2011–2020.* Dublin: DES.

Department of Education and Skills (DES). (2015a). *Framework for Junior Cycle 2015.* Dublin: DES. Available at: www.education.ie/en/Publications/Policy-Reports/Framework-for-Junior-Cycle-2015.pdf

Department of Education and Skills (DES). (2015b). *Circular 0027/2015: Information in relation to actions under the literacy and numeracy strategy standardised testing, reporting, library support and other matters*. Available at: http://education.ie/en/Circulars-and-Forms/Active-Circulars/cl0027_2015.pdf

Department of Education and Skills (DES). (2015c). *Digital strategy for schools 2015–2020: Enhancing teaching, learning and assessment*. Dublin: DES. Available at: www.education.ie/en/Publications/Policy-Reports/Digital-Strategy-for-Schools-2015-2020.pdf

Department of Education and Skills (DES). (2015d). *Key statistics 2014/2015*. Available at: www.education.ie/en/Publications/Statistics/Key-Statistics/Key-Statistics-2014-2015.pdf

Department of Education and Skills (DES). (2015e). *Primary language curriculum: English-medium schools*. Dublin: DES & NCCA.

Department of Education and Skills (DES). (2016a). *Arrangements for the implementation of the framework for Junior Cycle, with particular reference to school years 2015/16 and 2016/17 (Circular Letter 0024/2016)*. Dublin: DES. Available at: www.education.ie/en/Circulars-and-Forms/Active-Circulars/cl0024_2016.pdf

Department of Education and Skills (DES). (2016b). *Looking at our school 2016. A quality framework for primary schools*. Dublin: DES.

Downing, S.M. (2006). Selected-response item formats in test development. In S.M. Downing & T.M. Haladyna (eds) *Handbook of test development* (pp. 287–301). New York: Routledge.

Du Bois, P.H. (1970). *A history of psychological testing*. Boston: Allyn & Bacon.

Dunn, K.E., & Mulvenon, S.W. (2009). A critical review of research on formative assessment: the limited scientific evidence of the impact of formative assessment in education. *Practical Assessment, Research & Evaluation, 14* (7). Available at: http://pareonline.net/getvn.asp?v=14&n=7

Earl, L.M. (2013). *Assessment as learning: Using classroom assessment to maximise student learning* (2nd edition). Thousand Oaks, CA: Corwin.

Ebel, R.L. (1980). *Practical problems in educational measurement*. Lexington, MA: D.C. Heath and Company.

Education Council New Zealand. (2015). *Practising teacher criteria*. Available at: https://educationcouncil.org.nz/content/review-of-standards-teaching-profession

Education Scotland (2015). *Literacy across learning in secondary schools 2015-16. Reading*. Available at: http://dera.ioe.ac.uk/25630/1/PDFReadingwithAppendices_tcm4-874285.pdf

Education Scotland (2016). *Benchmarks: Literacy and English*, Draft, August 2016. Available at: https://education.gov.scot/improvement/Pages/Curriculum-for-Excellence-Benchmarks-.aspx

Educational Research Centre (ERC). (2007). *Drumcondra Primary Mathematics Test – Revised – Levels 3–6*. Manual. Dublin: ERC.

Educational Research Centre (ERC). (2010). *Drumcondra Primary Mathematics Test – Revised. Progress in mathematics: Using class-level performance bands and monitoring progress over time. Supplement to the manuals for the DPRT-R, Levels 1, 2 and 3–6*. Dublin: ERC. Available at: www.erc.ie/documents/dpmt_combined_documents.pdf

Educational Research Centre (ERC). (2014a). *Sample maths items: Sixth Class – NA '14 released*. Available at: www.erc.ie/documents/na14_sample_items_maths6th.pdf

Educational Research Centre (ERC). (2014b). *Sample reading items: Sixth Class – NA '14 released*. Available at: www.erc.ie/documents/na14_sample_items_reading6th.pdf

Educational Testing Service (ETS). (2009a). *ETS international principles for fairness review of assessments: A manual for developing locally appropriate fairness review guidelines in various countries*. Princeton, NJ: ETS. Available at: www.ets.org/s/about/pdf/fairness_review_international.pdf

Educational Testing Service (ETS). (2009b). *Guidelines for the assessment of English language learners*. Princeton, NJ: ETS. Available at: www.ets.org/s/about/pdf/ell_guidelines.pdf

Eggen, T.J.H.M., & Lampe, T.T.M. (2011). Comparison of the reliability of scoring methods of multiple-response items, matching items and sequencing items. *CADMO, 19* (2), 85–104.

Elwood, J. (2013). Educational assessment policy and practice: a matter of ethics. *Assessment in Education: Principles, Policy and Practice, 20* (2), 205–20.

Elwood, J., Hopfenbeck, T., & Baird, J. (2015). Predictability in high stakes examinations: students' perspectives on a perennial assessment dilemma. *Research Papers in Education,* DOI: 10.1080/02671522.2015.1086015

Encyclopaedia Britannica. (n.d.). *Chinese examination system.* Available at: www.britannica.com/topic/Chinese-examination-system

European Union. (2006). Recommendation of the European Parliament and the Council of 18 December 2006 on Key Competences for Lifelong Learning. *Official Journal of the European Union* 31.12.2006. Available at: http://eur-lex.europa.eu/legal-content/EN/TXT/?uri=celex:32006H0962

Eve, M.P. (2011, 22 December). Secondary schools are not adequately preparing students for higher education. *Guardian Higher Education Network Blog.* Available at: www.theguardian.com/higher-education-network/blog/2011/dec/22/humanities-in-secondary-schools

Expert Advisory Group on Certificate Examinations. (2000). *Arrangements for the assessment of candidates with special educational needs in certificate examinations: Report to the Minister for Education and Science.* Dublin: Author. Available at: http://examinations.ie/schools/Expert_Advisory_Group_Report_ev.pdf

Faragher, S. (2014). *Understanding assessment in primary education.* London: Sage.

Flórez, M.T., & Sammons, P. (2013). *Assessment for learning: Effects and impacts.* Reading, UK: CfBT Education Trust.

Frey, B.B., Schmitt, V.L., & Allen, J.P. (2012). Defining authentic classroom assessment. *Practical Assessment, Research and Evaluation, 17* (2), 1–18.

Geisinger, K.F. (2016). Intended and unintended meanings of validity: some clarifying comments. *Assessment in Education: Principles, Policy and Practice, 23* (2), 287–9.

General Teaching Council (GTC) for Northern Ireland. (2011). *Teaching: The reflective profession.* Belfast: GTC.

General Teaching Council (GTC) for Scotland. (2012). *The standards for registration: Mandatory requirements for registration with the general teaching council for Scotland.* Edinburgh: GTC. Available at: www.gtcs.org.uk/web/files/the-standards/standards-for-registration-1212.pdf

Gillie, O. (1977). Did Sir Cyril Burt fake his research on heritability of intelligence? *Phi Delta Kappan, 58* (6), 469–71.

Gipps, C.V. (1994). *Beyond testing: Towards a theory of educational assessment.* London: Falmer.

Gipps, C.V., & Stobart, G. (2009). Fairness in assessment. In C. Wyatt-Smith and J. Cumming (eds) *Educational assessment in the 21st century* (pp. 105–19). Dordrecht: Springer.

Glaser, R. (1990). Toward new models for assessment. *International Journal of Educational Research, 14* (5), 475–83.

Goldstein, H. (2004). International comparisons of student attainment: some issues arising from the PISA study. *Assessment in Education: Principles, Policy and Practice, 11* (3), 319–30.

Government of Ireland. (1998). *Education act.* Dublin: Stationery Office.

Government of Ireland. (2004). *Education for persons with special educational needs act 2004.* Dublin: Stationery Office.

Government of Ireland. (2005). *Disability act.* Dublin: Stationery Office.

Griffin, P., & Care, E. (2015). The ATC21S method. In P. Griffin & E. Care (eds) *Assessment and teaching of 21st century skills: Methods and approach* (pp. 3–33). Dordrecht: Springer.

Groth-Marnat, G. (2009). *Handbook of psychological assessment* (5th edition). Hoboken, NJ: Wiley & Sons.

Guardian, The. (2014, 24 June). *English language tests inquiry declares thousands of test results invalid* (by Alan Travis). Available at: www.theguardian.com/uk-news/2014/jun/24/english-language-tests-cheating-results-invalid- overseas-students

Guardian, The. (2015, 20 August). *Take it from an examiner, your students' exam results could easily be wrong* (anonymous). Available at: www.theguardian.com/teacher-network/2015/aug/13/a-levels-gcses-examiner-exam-results-wrong

Guskey, T. (2006). Making high school grades meaningful. *Phi Delta Kappan, 87* (9), 670–5.

Haladyna, T.M. (2004). *Developing and validating multiple-choice test items*. Mahwah, NJ: Lawrence Erlbaum Associates.

Haladyna, T.M., & Rodriguez, M.C. (2013). *Developing and validating test items*. Abingdon, Oxon: Routledge.

Harlen, W. (2005). Trusting teachers' judgment: research evidence of the reliability and validity of teachers' assessment used for summative purposes. *Research Papers in Education, 20* (3), 297–313.

Harlen, W. (2007). *Assessment of learning*. London: Sage.

Harris, A. (1998). Effective teaching: a review of the literature. *School Leadership and Management, 18* (2), 169–83.

Hattie, J. (2009). *Visible learning: A synthesis of over 800 meta-analyses relating to achievement*. Abingdon, Oxon: Routledge.

Hattie, J. (2012). *Visible learning for teachers: Maximising impact on learning*. Abingdon, Oxon: Routledge.

Hattie, J., & Timperley, H. (2007). The power of feedback. *Review of Educational Research, 77* (1), 81–112.

Hayward, L. (2015). Assessment is learning: the preposition vanishes. *Assessment in Education: Principles, Policy and Practice, 22* (1), 27–43.

Heacox, D. (2002). *Differentiating instruction in the regular classroom: How to reach and teach all learners, Grades 3–12*. Minneapolis, MN: Free Spirit Publishing.

Heacox, D. (2012). *Differentiating instruction in the regular classroom: How to reach and teach all learners*. Updated anniversary edition. Minneapolis, MN: Free Spirit Publishing.

Heneghan, H., & Murchan, D. (2014). *Enhancing teachers' capacity to implement effective differentiated reading in Irish primary schools*. Paper presented at the annual meeting of the Educational Studies Association of Ireland, Athlone, April.

Henk, W.A. (1981). Effects of modified deletion strategies and scoring procedures on cloze test performance. *Journal of Reading Behavior, 13* (4), 347-357.

HM Inspectorate of Education (HMIE). (2007). *How good is our school?* Livingston: HMIE. Available at: www.educationscotland.gov.uk/Images/HowgoodisourschoolJtEpart3_tcm4-684258.pdf

House of Commons Children, Schools and Families Committee. (2008). *Testing and assessment: Government and Ofsted responses to the Committee's Third Report of Session 2007–08. Fifth special report of session 2007–08*. London: The Stationery Office. Available at: www.publications.parliament.uk/pa/cm200708/cmselect/cmchilsch/1003/1003.pdf

Husbands, C. (1996). *What is history teaching?* Buckingham: Open University Press.

Iamarino, D.L. (2014). The benefits of standards-based grading: a critical evaluation of modern grading practices. *Current Issues in Education, 17* (2), 1–11.

Integrate Ireland Language and Training (IILT). (2007a). *EAL primary schools assessment kit*. Dublin: NCCA. Available at: www.ncca.ie/en/Curriculum_and_Assessment/Inclusion/English_as_an_Additional_Language/IILT_Materials/Primary/

Integrate Ireland Language and Training (IILT). (2007b). *EAL post-primary assessment kit*. Dublin: NCCA. Available at: www.ncca.ie/en/Curriculum_and_Assessment/Inclusion/English_as_an_Additional_Language/IILT_Materials/Post-primary/EAL_Post_Primary_Assessment_Kit/EAL_Post-Primary_Assessment_Kit.html

International Reading Association and National Council for Teachers of English (IRA/NCTE). (2013). *Oral presentation rubric: Grades 3–12*. Newark, DE: IRA. Available at: www.readwritethink.org/classroom-resources/printouts/oral-presentation-rubric-30700.html

Irish Times. (2010, 11 June). *Leaving Cert dyslexia case dismissed* (by Mary Carolan). Available at: www.irishtimes.com/news/leaving-cert-dyslexia-case-dismissed-1.859452

Irish Times. (2010, 19 June). *The year Leaving Cert cheating stopped being a secret* (by Louise Holden). Available at: www.irishtimes.com/news/education/the-year-leaving-certificate-cheating-stopped-being-a-secret-1.680700

Irish Times (2015, 24 February). *Census figures raise concerns of ethnic segregation in schools* (by Pamela Duncan and Joe Humphreys). Available at: www. irishtimes.com/news/education/census-figures-raise-concerns-of-ethnic-segregation-in-schools-1.2114559

Isaacs, T., Zara, C., & Herbert, G., with Coombs, S.J., & Smith, C. (2013). *Key concepts in educational assessment*. London: Sage.

Jennings, J.M., & Bearak, J.M. (2014). Teaching to the test in the NCLB era: how test predictability affects our understanding of student performance. *Educational Researcher, 52*, 423–62.

Johnson, R.B., & Onwuegbuzie, A.J. (2004). Mixed methods research: a research paradigm whose time has come. *Educational Researcher, 33*, 14–26.

Johnson, S. (2013). On the reliability of high-stakes teacher assessment. *Research Papers in Education, 28* (1), 91–105.

Johnston, K., Conneely, C., Murchan, D., & Tangney, B. (2015). Enacting key skills-based curricula in secondary education: lessons from a technology-mediated, group-based learning initiative. *Technology, Pedagogy and Education, 24* (4), 423–42.

Joint Council for Qualifications. (2016). *Adjustments for candidates with disabilities and learning difficulties. Access arrangements and reasonable adjustments.* 1 September 2016 to 31 August 2017. London: Author. Available at: www.jcq.org.uk/exams-office/access-arrangements-and-special-consideration/regulations-and-guidance/access-arrangements-and-reasonable-adjustments-2016-2017

Joint Council for Qualifications. (Various Years). *Examination results: GCSEs.* Available at: www.jcq.org.uk/examination-results/gcse

Joyce, B.R., Weil, M., & Calhoun, E. (2000). *Models of teaching* (6th edition). Boston, MA: Pearson.

Kamin, L.J. (1974). *The science and politics of IQ.* Potomac, MD: Lawrence Erlbaum Associates.

Kekahio, W., Cicchinelli, L., Lawton, B., & Brandon, P.R. (2014). *Logic models: A tool for effective program planning, collaboration, and monitoring* (REL 2014–025). Washington, DC: US Department of Education, Institute of Education Sciences, National Center for Education Evaluation and Regional Assistance, Regional Educational Laboratory Pacific. Available at: http://ies.ed.gov/ncee/edlabs

Kellogg Foundation. (2004). *Logic model development guide.* Battle Creek, MI: Author. Available at: www.wkkf.org/resource-directory/resource/2006/02/wk-kellogg-foundation-logic-model-development-guide

Kentucky Department of Education. (2015). *Characteristics of highly effective teaching and learning.* Available at: http://education.ky.gov/curriculum/standards/teachtools/Pages/Characteristics-of-Highly-Effective-Teaching-and-Learning-(CHETL).aspx

Ketterlin-Geller, L.R., & Yovanoff, P. (2009). Diagnostic assessment in mathematics to support instructional decision making. *Practical Research, Assessment and Evaluation, 14* (16), 1–9. Available at: http://pareonline.net/getvn.asp?v=14&n=16

Kingston, N., & Nash, B. (2011). Formative assessment: a meta-analysis and a call for research. *Educational Measurement: Issues and Practice, 30* (4), 28–37.

Klapp, A. (2015). Does grading affect educational attainment? A longitudinal study. *Assessment in Education: Principles, Policy and Practice, 22* (3), 302–23.

Klenowski, V., & Wyatt-Smith, C. (2014). *Assessment for education: Standards, judgement and moderation.* London: Sage.

Ko, J., Sammons, P., & Bakkum, L. (2013). *Effective teaching: A review of research and evidence.* Reading, UK: CfBT Education Trust.

Koretz, D. (2008). *Measuring up: What educational testing really tells us.* Cambridge, MA: Harvard University Press.

Koretz, D., Stecher, B., Klein, S., & McCaffrey, D. (1994a). The Vermont portfolio assessment program: findings and implications. *Educational Measurement: Issues and Practice, 13* (3), 5–16.

Koretz, D., Stecher, B., Klein, S., & McCaffrey, D. (1994b). *The evolution of a portfolio program: The impact and quality of the Vermont program in its second year (1992–93).* CSE Technical Report No. 385. Los Angeles, CA: University of California. Available at: http://eric.ed.gov/?id=ED379301

Krathwohl, D.R. (2002). A revision of Bloom's taxonomy: an overview. *Theory into Practice, 41* (4), 212–18.

Kreiter, C.D., Haugen, T., Leaven, T., Goerdt, C., Rosenthal, N., McGaghie, W.C., & Dee, F. (2011). A report on the piloting of a novel computer-based medical case simulation for teaching and formative assessment of diagnostic laboratory testing. *Medical Education Online, 16.* Available at: http://doi.org/10.3402/meo.v16i0.5646

Kubiszyn, T., & Borich, G. (2013). *Educational testing and measurement* (10th edition). Hoboken, NJ: Wiley & Sons.

Kulhavy, R.W., & Stock, W. (1989). Feedback in written instruction: the place of response certitude. *Educational Psychology Review, 1* (4), 279–308.

Kyriacou, C. (2014). *Essential teaching skills* (4th edition). Oxford: Oxford University Press.

Lewis, H. (2012). *Written statement: PISA 2012.* Updated 3 December 2013. Welsh Government. Available at: http://gov.wales/about/cabinet/cabinetstatements/2013/pisa2012/?lang=en

Lukhele, R., Thissen, D., & Wainer, H. (1994). On the relative value of multiple-choice, constructed response, and examinee-selected items on two achievement tests. *Journal of Educational Measurement, 31* (3), 234–50.

Lynch, K., Grummell, B., & Devine, D. (2012). *New managerialism in education: Commercialization, carelessness and gender.* Basingstoke, UK: Palgrave Macmillan.

Lysaght, Z. (2012). Towards inclusive assessment. In T. Day & J. Travers (eds) *Special and inclusive education: A research perspective* (pp. 245–60). Oxford: Peter Lang.

Mac Aogáin, E. (2005). The points system and grading of the Leaving Certificate examination. *Irish Journal of Education, 36,* 3–24.

McCormack, O., Lynch, R., & Hennessy, J. (2015). Plastic people in pinstripe suits: an exploration of the views of Irish parents on the publication of school league tables. *Educational Studies, 41* (5), 513–33.

McMillan, J.H. (2011). *Classroom assessment: Principles and practice for effective standards-based instruction* (5th edition). Boston, MA: Pearson.

MacNeela, P., & Boland, J. (2013) *Leaving Certificate teachers' grading and marking practices: Report on the online consultation.* Dublin: NCCA.

Marzano, R.J. (2009). Setting the record straight on 'high-yield' strategies. *Phi Delta Kappan, 91* (1), 30–7.

Messick, S. (1989). Validity. In R. Linn (ed.) *Educational measurement* (3rd edition, pp. 13–100). Washington, DC: American Council on Education.

Meyen, E.L., & Skrtic, T.M. (eds) (1995). *Special education and student disability: An introduction* (4th edition). Denver, CO: Love Publishing Co.

Miller, M.D., Linn, R.L., & Gronlund, N. (2013). *Measurement and assessment in teaching* (11th edition/Pearson International Edition). Upper Saddle River, NJ: Pearson.

Morris, A. (2011). *Student standardised testing: Current practices in OECD countries and a literature review.* OECD Education Working Papers, No. 65. Paris: OECD Publishing. Available at: http://dx.doi.org/10.1787/5kg3rp 9qbnr6-en

Mortimore, P. (1993). *School effectiveness and the management of effective teaching and learning.* Paper presented at the annual meeting of the international congress for school effectiveness and improvement. Norrkoping, Sweden: Available as: ERIC document ED358560

Mullis, I.V.S., Martin, M.O., Foy, P., & Hooper, M. (2016). *TIMSS 2015 international results in mathematics*. Chestnut Hill, MA: International Association for the Evaluation of Educational Achievement. Available at: http://timssandpirls.bc.edu/timss2015/international-results/wp-content/uploads/filebase/full%20pdfs/T15-International-Results-in-Mathematics.pdf

Munoz, M.A., & Guskey, T.R. (2015). Standards-based grading and reporting will improve education. *Phi Delta Kappan, 96* (7), 64–8.

Murchan, D. (1993). The reliability and validity of essay-based examinations in secondary education. *Irish Educational Studies, 12*, 41–56.

Murchan, D. (2011). *The formative use of diagnostic assessments to support teaching and learning in mathematics*. Proceedings of the international conference Assessment for Learning in the 21st Century (pp. 147–56). Ohrid, Macedonia, 23 May. Skopje: USAID Macedonia.

Murchan, D. (2014). Changing curriculum and assessment mindsets in higher education. In A. Loxley, A. Seery & J. Walsh (eds) *Higher education in Ireland: Practices, policies and possibilities* (pp. 186–97). Basingstoke, UK: Palgrave Macmillan.

Murchan, D., Loxley, A., & Johnston, K. (2009). Teacher learning and policy intention: selected findings from an evaluation of a large-scale programme of professional development in the Republic of Ireland. *European Journal of Teacher Education, 32* (4), 455–71.

Murchan, D., Oldham, E., & O'Sullivan, C. (2013). *Applying CBA technology to traditional error analysis in elementary mathematics: Lessons from Maths Assist*. Paper presented at the annual meeting of the American Educational Research Association, San Francisco, April.

Murchan, D., Shiel, G., Vula, E., Gashi Bajgora, A., & Balidemaj, V. (2013). *Vlerësimi formative [Formative assessment guidebook]*. Pristina: Basic Education Program. Available at: http://bep-ks.org/wp-content/uploads/2013/10/BEP-Vleresimi-formativ_shq.pdf

National Board for Professional Teaching Standards. (1989). *What teachers should know and be able to do*. Available at: www.nbpts.org/sites/default/files/what_teachers_should_know.pdf

National Council for Curriculum and Assessment (NCCA). (2007a). *Assessment in the primary school curriculum: Guidelines for schools*. Dublin: NCCA.

National Council for Curriculum and Assessment (NCCA). (2007b). *Exceptionally able students: Draft guidelines for teachers*. Dublin: NCCA. Available at: www.ncca.ie/en/Publications/Syllabuses_and_Guidelines/Exceptionally_Able_Students_Draft_Guidelines_for_Teachers.pdf

National Council for Curriculum and Assessment (NCCA). (2014). *Key skills of Junior Cycle*. Dublin: NCCA.

National Council for Curriculum and Assessment (NCCA). (2015). *Junior Cycle English: Guidelines for the classroom-based assessments and assessment tasks* (1st edition). Dublin: NCCA. Available at: www.education.ie/en/Circulars-and-Forms/Active-Circulars/cl0024_2016.pdf

National Council for Curriculum and Assessment (NCCA). (2016). *Junior Cycle science: Guidelines for classroom-based assessments and assessment task* (1st edition). Dublin: NCCA. Available at: http://curriculumonline.ie/getmedia/153bc83f-9848-49f0-ad87-0a0d6b9b596c/Specification-for-Jr-Cycle-Science-EV_20160126-(1).pdf

National Council for Special Education (NCSE). (2016). *Annual report 2015*. Trim, Ireland: NCSE.

National Induction Programme for Teachers (NIPT). (2013). *Long-term planning: Draft guidelines*. Dublin: NIPT. Available at: www.nccaplanning.ie/support/pdf/long_term_planning.pdf

Newton, P.E. (2007). Clarifying the purposes of educational assessment. *Assessment in Education: Principles, Policy and Practice, 14* (2), 149–70.

Newton, P.E., & Baird, J. (2016). *Assessment in Education: Principles, Policy and Practice. Special Issue on Validity. 23* (2).

Newton, P.E., & Shaw, S.D. (2014). *Validity in educational and psychological measurement*. London: Sage.

Newton, P.E., & Shaw, S.D. (2016). Disagreement over the best way to use the word 'validity' and options for reaching consensus. *Assessment in Education: Principles, Policy and Practice, 23* (2), 178–97.

New Zealand Ministry of Education. (2011). *Position paper: Assessment.* Wellington: Learning Media.

Nitko, A.J., & Brookhart, S.M. (2014). *Educational assessment of students* (6th international electronic edition). Harlow: Pearson.

Northern Ireland Executive. (2013). *PISA highlights need for continued reform – O'Dowd,* 3 December. Available at: www.northernireland.gov.uk/index/media-centre/news-departments/news-de/news-de-december-2013/news-de-031213-pisa-highlights-need.htm

Nusche, D., Earl, L., Maxwell, W., & Shewbridge, C. (2011). *OECD reviews of evaluation and assessment in education: Norway.* Available at: www.oecd.org/ norway/48632032.pdf

OECD. (2001). *Definition and selection of competencies: Theoretical and conceptual foundations (DeSeCo).* Background paper, revised December. Neuchatel, Switzerland: OECD/DeSeCo Secretariat.

OECD. (2005). *Formative assessment: Improving learning in secondary classrooms.* Paris: OECD Publishing.

OECD. (2013). *Synergies for better learning: An international perspective on evaluation and assessment.* Paris: OECD Publishing.

OECD. (2014). *TALIS 2013 results. An international perspective on teaching and learning.* Paris: OECD Publishing. Available at: www.oecd-ilibrary.org/education/talis-2013-results_9789264196261-en

OECD. (2015a). *Education at a glance 2015: OECD indicators.* Paris: OECD Publishing. Available at: http://dx.doi.org/10.1787/eag-2015-en

OECD. (2015b). *PISA 2015 technical standards.* Paris: OECD Publishing. Available at: www.oecd.org/pisa/pisaproducts/PISA-2015-Technical-Standards.pdf

OECD. (2016a). *PISA 2015 results (volume I): Excellence and equity in education.* Paris: OECD Publishing. Available at: http://dx.doi.org/10.1787/9789264266490-en

OECD. (2016b). *PISA 2015 released field trial cognitive items.* Paris: OECD Publishing. Available at: www.oecd.org/pisa/pisaproducts/PISA2015-Released-FT-Cognitive-Items.pdf

Office of Qualifications and Examinations Regulation (Ofqual). (2013). *Review of controlled assessment in GCSEs.* Coventry: Ofqual. Available at: www.gov.uk/government/uploads/system/uploads/attachment_data/file/377903/2013-06-11-review-of-controlled-assessment-in-GCSEs.pdf

Ofsted. (1996). *The annual report of her majesty's chief inspector of schools.* London: HMSO.

Ofsted. (2015). *School inspection handbook.* Available at: www.gov.uk/government/uploads/system/uploads/attachment_data/file/391531/School_inspection_handbook.pdf

O'Leary, M. (2006). Towards a balanced assessment system for Irish primary and secondary schools. *Oideas, 52,* 7–24. Available at: www.education.ie/en/Publications/Education-Reports/Oideas/Oideas-52.pdf

Painter, D.D. (2009). Providing differentiated learning experiences through multigenre projects. *Intervention in School and Clinic, 44,* 288–93.

Partnership for 21st Century Skills. (2006). *A state leader's action guide to 21st century skills: A new vision for education.* Tucson, AZ: Author.

Partnership for 21st Century Skills. (2015). *P21 framework definitions.* Available at: www.p21.org/storage/documents/docs/P21_Framework_Definitions_New_Logo_2015.pdf

Pat-El, R.J., Tillema, H., Segers, M., & Vedder, P. (2011). Validation of assessment for learning questionnaires for teachers and students. *British Journal of Educational Psychology, 83,* 98–113.

Pearson Education. (2016). *Test of English language learning* (TELL). Menlo Park, CA: Pearson Education.

Perkins, R., Cosgrove, J., Moran, G., & Shiel, G. (2012). *PISA 2009: Results for Ireland and changes since 2000.* Dublin: Educational Research Centre.

Perkins, R., Shiel, G., Merriman, B., Cosgrove, J., & Moran, G. (2013). *Learning for life: The achievements of 15-year-olds in Ireland on mathematics, reading literacy and science in PISA 2012.* Dublin: Educational Research Centre.

Phillips, S., Kelly, K., & Symes, L. (2013). *Assessment of learners with dyslexic-type difficulties*. London: Sage.

Pintrich, P.R. (2000). The role of goal orientation in self-regulated learning. In M. Boekaerts, P.R. Pintrich & M. Zeidner (eds) *Handbook of self-regulation* (pp. 451–502). San Diego, CA: Academic Press.

Pollitt, A. (2012). The method of adaptive comparative judgement. *Assessment in Education: Principles, Policy & Practice, 19* (3), 281–300.

Popham, W.J. (2011). *Classroom assessment: What teachers need to know* (6th edition). Boston: Pearson.

Popham, W.J. (2012). *Assessment bias: How to banish it* (2nd edition). Boston: Pearson. Available at: ati.pearson.com/downloads/chapters/Popham_Bias_BK04.pdf

Primary Professional Development Service (PPDS). (2007). *Prompt questions towards drafting an assessment policy*. Available at: http://www.educatetogether.ie/wordpress/wp-content/uploads/2010/02/assessment-1.doc

Putwain, D. (2008). Examination stress and test anxiety. *The Psychologist, 21*, 1026–9.

Raphael, T.E., & Au, K.H. (2005). QAR: Enhancing comprehension and test taking across grades and content areas. *The Reading Teacher, 59* (3), 206–21.

Ratnam-Lim, C.T.L., & Tan, K.H.T. (2015). Large-scale implementation of formative assessment practices in an examination-oriented culture. *Assessment in Education: Principles, Policy and Practice, 22* (1), 61–78.

Roach, J. (1971). *Public examinations in England 1850–1900*. Cambridge: Cambridge University Press.

Rodriguez, M.C. (2005). Three options are optimal for multiple-choice items: a meta-analysis of 80 years of research. *Educational Measurement Issues and Practice, 24* (2), 3–13.

Rogers, C.M., Lazarus, S.S., & Thurlow, M.L. (2016). *A summary of the research on the effects of test accommodations: 2013–2014*. NCEO Report No. 402. Minneapolis, MN: University of Minnesota, National Center on Educational Outcomes.

Rose, R., Shevlin, M., Winter, E., & O'Raw, P. (2015). *Project IRIS: Inclusive research in Irish schools*. NCSE Research Report No. 20. Trim, Ireland: NCSE.

Ruiz-Primo, M.A., & Li, M. (2013). Examining formative feedback in the classroom context: new research perspectives. In J.H. McMillan (ed.) *Handbook of research on classroom assessment* (pp. 215–32). Thousand Oaks, CA: Sage.

Sadler, D.R. (1989). Formative assessment and the design of instructional systems. *Instructional Science, 18* (2), 119–44.

Sadler, D.R. (1998). Formative assessment: revisiting the territory. *Assessment in Education: Principles, Policy and Practice, 5* (1), 77–84.

Sahlberg, P. (2015). *Finnish Lessons 2.0: What can the world learn from educational change in Finland?* (2nd edition). New York: Teachers College Press.

Salvia, J., & Ysseldyke, J.E. (2001). *Assessment* (8th edition). Boston: Houghton Mifflin Co.

Sargent, C., Foot, E., Houghton, E., & O'Donnell, S. (2013). *INCA comparative tables*. Slough: National Foundation for Educational Research. Available at: www.nfer.ac.uk/what-we-do/information-and-reviews/inca/INCA comparativetablesMarch2012.pdf

Scalise, K., & Gifford, B. (2006). Computer-based assessment in e-learning: a framework for constructing 'intermediate constraint' questions and tasks for technology platforms. *Journal of Technology, Learning and Assessment, 4* (6).

Schleicher, A. (2006). *The economics of knowledge: Why education is key for Europe's success*. Brussels: The Lisbon Council. Available at: www.lisboncouncil.net/component/downloads/?id=219

Schleicher, A. (2016). *Teaching excellence through professional learning and policy reform: Lessons from around the world*. Paris: OECD Publishing. Available at: www.oecd.org/publications/teaching-excellence-through-professional-learning-and-policy-reform-9789264252059-en.htm

Schumm, J.S., & Vaughn, S. (1995). Meaningful professional development in accommodating students with disabilities: lessons learned. *Remedial and Special Education, 16* (6), 344–53.

Schunk, D.H., & Zimmerman, B.J. (eds) (1994). *Self-regulation of learning and performance: Issues and educational applications.* Hillsdale, NJ: Lawrence Erlbaum Associates.

Scottish Government, The. (2008). *Curriculum for excellence: Building the curriculum 3 – A framework for learning and teaching.* Edinburgh: The Scottish Government.

Scottish Government, The. (2011). *Curriculum for excellence: Building the curriculum 5 – A framework for assessment: executive summary.* Edinburgh: The Scottish Government.

Scottish Government, The. (2012). *CfE briefing: Curriculum for excellence – Profiling and the S3 profile.* Available at: https://education.gov.scot/Documents/cfe-briefing-3.pdf

Scottish Qualifications Authority (SQA). (2015). *N5 national qualifications: Physical education portfolio – General assessment information.* Edinburgh: SQA. Available at: www.sqa.org.uk/files_ccc/GAInfoNational5PhysicalEducation Portfolio.pdf

Scriven, M. (1967). The methodology of evaluation. In R. Tyler, R. Gagné & M. Scriven (eds.). *Perspectives of curriculum evaluation* (American Educational Research Association monograph series on curriculum evaluation, Vol. 1, pp. 39–83). Chicago: Rand McNally

Sebba, J., Crick, R.D., Yu, G., Lawson, H., Harlen, W., & Durant, K. (2008). Systematic review of research evidence of the impact on students in secondary schools of self and peer assessment. Technical report. In: *Research Evidence in Education Library.* London: EPPI-Centre, Social Science Research Unit, Institute of Education, University of London.

Shepard, L.A. (2000). The role of assessment in a learning culture. *Educational Researcher, 29* (7), 4–14.

Shepard, L.A. (2006). Classroom assessment. In R.L. Brennan (ed.) *Educational Measurement* (4th edition, pp. 623–46). Westport, CT: Praeger Publishers.

Shiel, G., & Murchan, D. (2011). *Basic education program: Supporting teachers in implementing assessment for learning in schools and supporting the Ministry of Education in the development of principles, standards and ethical guidelines for assessment.* Unpublished consultants' report. Pristina: Academy for Educational Development & Kosovo Education Centre.

Shiel, G., Kavanagh, L., & Miller, D. (2014). *The 2014 national assessments of English reading and mathematics, volume 1: Performance report.* Dublin: Educational Research Centre. Available at: www.erc.ie/documents/na14report_vol1perf.pdf

Shiel, G., Kellaghan, T., & Moran, G. (2010). *Standardised testing in lower secondary education.* Research Paper No. 12. Dublin: National Council for Curriculum and Assessment. Available at: www.ncca.ie/en/publications/reports/standardised_testing_in_lowersecondary_education.pdf

Shiel, G., Kelleher, C., McKeown, C., & Denner, S. (2016). *Future ready? The performance of 15-year-olds in Ireland on science, reading literacy and mathematics in PISA 2015.* Dublin: Educational Research Centre.

Sireci, S.G., & Zenisky, A.L. (2006). Innovative item formats in computer-based testing: in pursuit of improved construct representation. In S.M. Downing & T.M. Haladyna (eds) *Handbook of test development* (pp. 329–47). New York: Routledge.

Smyth, E., & Banks, J. (2012). High stakes testing and student perspective on teaching and learning in the Republic of Ireland. *Educational Assessment Evaluation and Accountability, 24* (4), 283–306.

Standards and Testing Agency. (2016a). *Clarification: Key Stage 1 and 2 teacher assessment and moderation guidance.* London: Crown. Available at: www.gov.uk/government/uploads/system/uploads/attachment_data/file/506177/Clarification_key_stage_1_and_2__teacher_assessment_and_moderation_guidance.pdf

Standards and Testing Agency. (2016b). *Key Stage 1 English grammar, punctuation and spelling test framework.* Available at: www.gov.uk/government/uploads/system/uploads/attachment_data/file/510943/2016_KS1_EnglishGPS_framework_PDFA.pdf

State Examinations Commission. (SEC). (2008a). *Junior Certificate ordinary level geography*. Athlone, Ireland: Author. Available at: https://www.examinations.ie/tmp/1486398113_2717970.pdf

State Examinations Commission. (SEC). (2008b). *Junior Certificate ordinary level science*. Athlone, Ireland: Author. Available at: https://www.examinations.ie/tmp/1486398448_2849951.pdf

State Examinations Commission. (SEC). (2015). *Junior Certificate ordinary level science*. Athlone, Ireland: Author. Available at: https://www.examinations.ie/tmp/1485961029_6941277.pdf

State Examinations Commission (SEC). (2016). *Reasonable accommodations at the 2017 certificate examinations. Instructions for schools*. Athlone: Author. Available at: www.examinations.ie/schools/cs_view.php?q=746932c1559a1f720973fca784ec3417af46b516

Stiggins, R.J. (1992). High quality classroom assessment: What does it really mean? *Educational Measurement Issues and Practice, 11* (2), 35–9.

Stiggins, R.J., Griswold, M.M., & Wikelund, K.R. (1989). Measuring thinking skills through classroom assessment. *Journal of Educational Measurement, 26* (3), 233–246.

Stobart, G. (2008). *Testing times: The uses and abuses of assessment*. Abingdon, Oxon: Routledge.

Stobart, G., & Eggen, T. (2012). High-stakes testing: value, fairness and consequences. *Assessment in Education: Principles, Policy and Practice, 19* (1), 1–6.

Stone, C.L. (1983). A meta-analysis of advance organizer studies. *The Journal of Experimental Education, 51* (4), 194–9.

Sunday Times, The. (2016, 6 November). *Standardised achievement tests queried as pupils' results improve* (by Seán McCárthaigh). Available at: www.thetimes.co.uk/edition/ireland/standardised-achievement-tests-queried-as- pupils-results-improve-fpjj32x6r

Taylor, R.L. (2008). *Assessment of exceptional students: Educational and psychological procedures* (8th edition). Boston: Pearson.

Teaching Council, The. (2016). *Code of professional conduct for teachers* (2nd edition). Updated July 2016. Available at: www.teachingcouncil.ie/en/Fitness-to-Teach/Code-of-Professional-Conduct/

Telegraph, The. (2012, 31 October). *Ofqual: 340,000 GCSE and A-level exams 'marked up'*. Available at: www.telegraph.co.uk/education/educationnews/9645848/Ofqual-340000-GCSE-and-A-level-exams-marked-up.html

Thompson, M., & Wiliam, D. (2008). Tight but loose: a conceptual framework for scaling up school reforms. In E.C. Wylie (ed.) *Tight but loose: Scaling up teacher professional development in diverse contexts*. ETS Research Report No. RR-08-29 (pp. 1–43). Wiley Online Library.

Thurlow, M.L. (2014). Instructional and assessment accommodations in the 21st century. In L. Florian (ed.) *The Sage handbook of special education*, Vol. 2 (2nd edition, pp. 597–612). Los Angeles, CA: Sage.

Tomlinson, C. (1999). *The differentiated classroom: Responding to the needs of all learners*. Alexandria, VA: Association for Supervision and Curriculum Development.

Tomlinson, C.A. (2000). *Differentiation of instruction in the elementary grades*. Champaign, IL: ERIC Clearinghouse on Elementary and Early Childhood Education, University of Illinois.

Topping, K.J. (2013). Peers as a source of formative and summative assessment. In J.H. McMillan (ed.) *Sage handbook of research on classroom assessment* (pp. 395–412). Thousand Oaks, CA: Sage.

Torrance, H. (2007). Assessment as learning? How the use of explicit learning objectives, assessment criteria and feedback in post-secondary education and training can come to dominate learning. *Assessment in Education: Principles, Policy and Practice, 14* (3), 281–94.

United Nations. (1989). *UN convention on the rights of the child*. Available at: www.unicef.org/crc/

United Nations. (2006). *UN convention on the rights of persons with disabilities*. Available at: www.un.org/development/desa/disabilities/

United Nations High Commissioner for Refugees (UNHCR). (2016). *Global trends: Forced displacement in 2015.* Geneva: UNHCR. Available at: www.unhcr.org

Van Bramer, J. (2011). Teacher talk and assistance and self-regulated learning within the context of RtI and explicit and systematic teaching. *The New England Reading Association Journal, 46* (2), 40–4.

Von Davier, A.A., & Halpin, P. (2013). *Collaborative problem solving and assessment of cognitive skills: Psychometric considerations.* Research Report No. ETS RR-13-41. Princeton, NJ: Education Testing Service.

Wall, E. (2004). *MICRA-T level 4 test manual.* Dublin: CJ Fallon.

Walsh, B., & Dolan, R. (2009). *A guide to teaching practice in Ireland.* Dublin: Gill & Macmillan.

Weiner, B. (2000). Intrapersonal and interpersonal theories of motivation from an attributional perspective. *Educational Psychology Review, 12* (1), 1–14.

Wiliam, D. (2011). What is assessment for learning? *Studies in Educational Evaluation, 37,* 3–14.

WJEC/CBAC. (2016). *WJEC Eduqas GCSE in French. Specification. Teaching from 2016. For award from 2018.* Cardiff: Author. Available at: http://www.eduqas.co.uk/qualifications/french/gcse/eduqas-gcse-french-spec-from-2016.pdf?language_id=1&dotcache=no&dotcache=refresh

World Health Organization (WHO). (2016). *Over a billion people live with some form of disability.* Available at: www.who.int/features/factfiles/disability/facts/en/

Wragg, E.C. (1997). *Assessment and learning.* London: Routledge.

Zimmerman, B.J. (2002). Becoming a self-regulated learner: an overview. *Theory into Practice, 41* (2), 64–70.

Index

Added to a page number 'f' denotes a figure and 't' denotes a table.